1992

# Reading and the Middle School Student

# Reading and the Middle School Student

## Strategies to Enhance Literacy

JUDITH L. IRVIN
FLORIDA STATE UNIVERSITY

**ALLYN AND BACON**
Boston   London   Sydney   Toronto

**Library of Congress Cataloging-in-Publication Data**

Irvin, Judith L., 1947–
    Reading and the middle school student : strategies to enhance
literacy / Judith L. Irvin.
        p.   cm.
    Bibliography: p.
    Includes index.
    ISBN 0-205-11958-1
    1. Reading (Elementary)—United States.   2. Reading (Secondary)—
United States.   3. Content area reading—United States.   I. Title.
LB1573.I73        1989
372.4′0973—dc20                                                    89-6797
                                                                        CIP

Printed in the United States of America
10 9 8 7 6 5 4 3 2   93 92 91 90

# Contents

## What Educators Need to Know to Make Programmatic Decisions

# Foreword

*Reading and the Middle School Student: Strategies to Enhance Literacy* speaks directly to all middle level educators who are responsible for the instructional and organizational aspects of middle school reading programs. Significant advances in the fields of reading and writing emerge in every chapter. These trends in literacy teaching and learning form the backdrop for a lively and engaging discussion of what middle level educators need to know in order to make informed instructional and programmatic decisions.

Practical suggestions abound. Teaching and learning strategies that motivate reluctant readers and encourage student sharing are juxtaposed with those that challenge the more willing and independent readers. Guidelines for conducting full and rich discussions are complemented by strategies that involve students in quiet reflection and self-monitoring behavior.

This book is a unique blend of theory, research, and practice. Analogies, metaphors, anecdotes, and student products from actual middle school classrooms figure into this blend and make the book one of the most readable texts that I have encountered. A special highlight is the inclusion of four middle school reading programs that have exemplary status. Within each program there is an emphasis on integrating reading, writing, speaking, listening, and thinking across the curriculum. District personnel from these four reading programs have written their own accounts of the programs they helped to develop. Besides lending credibility to the ideas espoused in this book, the exemplary programs make it possible for a reader to envision how a similar program might work in his or her own school district.

At one point in this book the author states, "Change is difficult and challenging. But change can also be fun and invigorating, and when teachers feel revitalized they cannot help but pass this enthusiasm for learning on to their students." I predict that *Reading and the Middle School Student: Strategies to*

*Enhance Literacy* will challenge and invigorate other middle level reading educators as much as it has me. The enthusiasm this book engenders deserves to be passed on to others.

Donna Alvermann
Reading Education Department
University of Georgia

# Foreword

The title of this book, *Reading and the Middle School Student: Strategies to Enhance Literacy* points to the heart of middle level education. How appropriate to focus on the reader, the young adolescent—*the* central focus of the entire middle school concept. And how sound to point to reading as the central skill in all formal education. An educational program that is appropriately student-centered and properly teaches the reading process is bound to be a success.

Formal education, or schooling as it more commonly known, is heavily dependent upon the ability to read—and middle level education is no exception. There are textbooks to be read in nearly every class, written reports to be prepared from library resources, assigned "speeches" requiring the gathering and organizing of data, questions whose answers are contained in written materials, math problems that have to be understood, and, of course, notes from a first or hoped-for love to be read and reread. The centrality of language, especially reading, in the middle level school simply is undeniable.

Yet most middle level teachers have not been prepared to teach reading. The majority were trained as high school teachers under the older erroneous notion that by the secondary level the students would know how to read sufficiently so that they could master the content that teachers presented. It is imperative in a modern middle school that *all* teachers be familiar with and comfortable in the processes involved in helping youth improve their competence in reading.

This book will make that objective possible. It is comprehensive and reflects current research and thinking. The thirteen chapters provide the information needed by all middle school teachers both to understand and, more importantly, to actually carry out appropriate activities in reading. Each chapter also includes ample elaboration of middle school issues and concepts.

John Lounsbury
Editor, *Middle School Journal*
National Middle School Association

# Preface

Reading and the Middle School Student: Strategies to Enhance Literacy is a book for prospective and practicing teachers, administrators, program specialists, and resource specialists concerned with improving literacy for middle level students. The last two decades have been a time of renewed interest in middle level education. Also, current research and theory in reading education/learning have contributed to what educators know about the most effective ways for students to improve their literacy abilities. The powerful and exciting implications for instruction that result from this renewed interest and this fine research motivated me to write this book. It seemed to me that teachers deserve to receive the benefits of research and theory in a readable, usable form. Additionally, middle level students deserve instruction chosen because it is research-based and known to facilitate improved literacy learning.

Those working with early adolescents are aware of the importance of knowledge about the physical, social, emotional, and intellectual characteristics of this age group. It is hoped that prospective as well as experienced teachers, administrators, and resource and reading specialists will find ways of using the information in this book to improve instruction and programs for middle level students.

Prospective middle level teachers will find a discussion of the basic processes of literacy instruction, the role of the teacher, grouping, and motivation techniques. Strategies are recommended for the instruction of vocabulary, comprehension, study skills, and the use of literature. Veteran teachers will find the discussion of research data readable and the strategies for use in content area instruction easy to apply.

The book is divided into two parts: what educators need to know to make *instructional* decisions and what they need to know to make *programmatic* decisions. The chapters in the first section include new views of learning and instruction, and strategies that enhance learning. The chapters included in the second part of the book give information on the history and philosophy of the middle school movement, detail components of successful reading programs, and describe exemplary programs.

Personally, I have long-standing interest and considerable experience at the middle level. Writing this book has strengthened my commitment to improved literacy learning for middle level students. I sincerely hope that the information contained in these pages is helpful to those educators who share my commitment.

## ACKNOWLEDGMENTS

Many friends and colleagues shared in the writing of this book. I would like to acknowledge my colleagues who patiently read and reacted to many revisions of each chapter: Julia Dorminey, Fran Kochan, Elaine Rose, and Neila Connors. From Richard Tortoriello I learned about closed punctuation style and the necessity of concise language; his copy-editing contributions were significant. I wish to thank all of the teachers who reacted to my ideas and tried out my lessons: Bob Spear and his teachers at Powder Mill Middle School, Southwick, Massachusetts; Bess Hinson and the teachers in the Orange County Public Schools, Orlando, Florida; and the teachers on Team 7-3 at Bellevue Middle School in Tallahassee, Florida.

I appreciate the contributions of Carol Lynch-Brown, Joy Monahan, Audrey Fielding, Elizabeth Rumohr, and Kay Sandweiss. I am also grateful to those individuals who reviewed the manuscript: Joy Monahan, Program Consultant, Orange County Public Schools, Orlando, Florida; Dr. Margery Sauer, Language Arts/Reading Coordinator, School District U-46, Elgin, Illinois; Dr. Donna Ogle, National College of Education; and Dr. Timothy Shanahan, University of Illinois at Chicago.

Finally, I wish to thank those who provided me with personal support: Bob Lathrop, my Dean; Paul Solaqua who first encouraged me to pursue this project; my indispensable secretary and student assistant, Theresa Matthews and Kim Waters; and Jalma Baker who endured reports of progress over numerous lunches. Last, but hardly least, I appreciate the patience of my family, Bruce, Brandon, and Alesha.

# Reading and the
# Middle School Student

# Chapter 1

# Literacy in the Middle Level School

Middle schools teem with language. Students eagerly relate stories of last night's events or triumphs on succeeding levels of a video game. Mounds of notes are passed, read, answered, and sometimes intercepted throughout a normal day. Early adolescents read, write, speak, and listen enthusiastically and for appropriate reasons; they wish to communicate.

Vygotsky (1962) maintained that the nature of learning language shifts in early adolescence to encompass a more social context. That is, language proficiency parallels the growth in the overall psychological and social development of students at this age. As students become more psychologically astute and socially aware, their language accommodates these new interests and abilities. *Ideally* their new social interests should also be reflected in their academic pursuits as well. Early adolescents actually strive to make sense of their learning by relating it to their new social interests and psychological awareness.

In fact, it is impossible to get middle level students to *stop* communicating. But how is it that Tammy's 6th period teacher cannot seem to get her to write a full page on Mesopotamia when she can write abundantly on the love life of Andy, Amy (who really is nobody important), Erika, and Alex? (See Figure 1.1.)

FIGURE 1.1 _____

Amanda —

   Guess What. Andy broke-up with me.
I'm really mad !!! But Amy (this girl,
nobody important). told me that Andy
said he still <u>really</u> liked me but
he never sees me so he wanted to break
up but also he said that he was
not going to go with anybody else
because he still likes me. I don't
understand why he won't go with me
if he likes me (oh well) see,
now I like Andy now that he
broke-up with me. (what a bummer!)
Erika is going with Alex.
Well, not yet but in a few minutes
as soon as Alex asks her, but
he got sent to the office so it
might take a while longer. I kind
of like Alex too but I like
Andy and Alex is going with
Erika and doesn't like me.
(Oh yeah I'm writing this in
6th period Its 1:55pm. gotta
go)

                              Tammy

_____

   Teachers really *know* how students feel about reading the assigned
"stuff," but they continue to teach day after day hoping that students will
share their love for learning. Although early adolescents rarely admit to
finding a subject of study interesting, if the material is presented in a way that
connects to their personal experience, students may become absorbed in a
topic. But sometimes their absorption revolves only around their social life
(see Figure 1.2).

FIGURE 1.2 _____

> Kate –
>
> I can't believe this woman actually expects us to read this stuff! She should know us better than that by now. God I hate where I sit Are you doing anything Saturday? Do you want to go to the Dance? Will your mom let you if your answers are No, Yes, Yes, Read the next question. Do you think I could spend the night with you and your mom could take us. But, if you don't want to thats OK. It was just an idea. Mrs. Hillert just started talking again. Why can't she leave us be. I don't wanna listen to her lectures. If you do want to go I would ask my mom to take us but I'm not allowed to go. What a bunch of rejects?! Call me when you get home and tell me.
>
> Gotta go.
>
> Love,
> Anna

"The Secret Admirer" (Figure 1.3) can, at a later date, use his romantic feelings for Pammy to understand literature or events in history, just as Paula (Figure 1.4) will be able to use her experience with friendship to understand much of what she reads later in life. For example, when Paula reads a story about divided loyalties between two friends, she will relate the story to her previous experience with friendship. Reading the story will then add to her store of experience and will equip her to resolve difficulties in her own relationships.

FIGURE 1.3 _____

Pammy,
Hi, How ya doin
 I'm okay. I've hadn't written
to you in awhile but do you
remember me? I've written you
two letters Before.
 I still like you a lot, lot, lot.
 I want you to go with me
to the movies Friday but I'm
afraid you wont like me.

 I love .
   you

expect                              love your
more
letters                          Secret
from                                 Admirer
  me        I love
later          you

FIGURE 1.4

Lynne,

I am writing you because you keep begging me so much. I asked Ms. Harris about our tests she said she have <u>everything</u> graded. I can't wait to join your Girl Scout troop. I bet you, me, and Karen have lots of fun.

(Best Friend Always)
<u>Paula</u>

P.S. Tell me the funny thing you said you had to tell me in your letter. Oh yeah, I forgot I am going to pay you your cookie money FRIDAY! tomorrow!

<u>Paula</u>

Sorry
o
Sloppy

Long
Letter
Later

Friends
Forever

So, how do we get the heartbeat of the hallway into the classroom and maximize its potential for language learning? Early adolescence is one of our last chances to help students become independent, confident producers and comprehenders of language. Students who do not develop the ability to use language in an academic setting by the time they leave middle school often drop out or experience failure in high school. If teachers could somehow capture the excitement and necessity of student communication and relate it to the content they want students to learn, perhaps educators would find the key to motivation and success for middle grades students.

## LITERACY AS A SOCIAL EVENT

In the past, the psychological and linguistic aspects of literacy have been considered by learning theorists, but only recently has attention been turned to the social aspects of reading and writing. No one would dispute the fact that the dialogue in the classroom doorway is a social event. But reading a play, discussing a chapter in a social studies book, and writing a story can be social events as well. Just as speakers and listeners interact in social situations, readers and writers can interact through text. "When readers understand a text, an exchange of meaning has taken place. Writers have succeeded in speaking to readers" (Nystrand and Himley, 1984, p. 198).

To understand a social studies chapter about another culture, students must possess and activate information about how people behave politically, economically, spiritually, and socially. After reading and understanding the text, students can add this information to their store of social knowledge and apply it to a new learning situation. To understand a piece of literature, students must activate what they know about people and their relationships (Bruce, 1981). For example, Paula (Figure 1.4) may use what she knows about friendship to empathize with a character who felt cheated by her best friend. In turn, the new insights gained from vicariously experiencing the story will add to her understanding of friendship.

Middle grades students are in a time of transition physically, socially, emotionally, and intellectually. Their intense interest in themselves, their social interactions, their emotional ups and downs, and their new capacity for analytical thought can be used to help them become more literate. Unfortunately, there are many teachers who view these manifestations as interruptions to instruction. There are other teachers, however, who recognize them as opportunities to capitalize on student strengths and interests to facilitate learning.

## PURPOSE AND OVERVIEW OF THE BOOK

Reading this book will assist educators in applying current research and theory in the field of literacy to teaching and learning in the middle grades. (*Literacy,* as used throughout this text, refers to any reading and writing event.) The focus of this book is primarily on reading. However, reading is only one of the four language systems and should be learned within the context of writing, speaking, listening, and thinking. Although topics such as the writing process and higher-order thinking are not specifically addressed in this book, most educators certainly recognize the necessity for integrating the instruction of all language systems with the development of thinking abilities.

The book is divided into two parts: what educators need to know to make *instructional decisions* and what educators need to know to make *programmatic decisions.* The graphic organizer shown in Figure 1.5 is intended as an outline of the relationships among chapters and subjects in this text.

FIGURE 1.5
Graphic Organizer

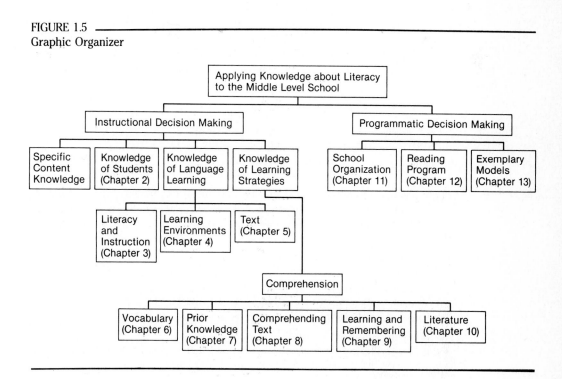

## What Educators Need to Know to Make Instructional Decisions

To make the best decisions about instruction, teachers need (1) a thorough knowledge of their content area(s); (2) an intimate understanding of students— how they feel, think, and react; (3) an understanding of the nature of the language and literacy learning process; and (4) a knowledge of how and when to apply instructional learning strategies to teach both process and content. By possessing an understanding of content, students, the learning process, and strategies that facilitate growth, educators can draw on students' natural desire to communicate and thereby improve their ability to read, write, speak, listen, and think.

1. *Content.* Since teachers at the middle level have presumably mastered knowledge of the content they teach (social studies, science, literature), knowledge of content will be not addressed in this book.

2. *Students.* Recent advances in medicine and education have yielded new knowledge about the physiology and psychology of early adolescents (ages ten through fourteen). Since this period is a unique time of life, it is imperative that middle level educators understand the special characteristics of early adolescents. Chapter 2 describes the characteristics of early adolescents so that teachers can plan instruction that meets students' needs. The implications for instruction, described at the end of Chapter 2, provide a basis for the strategies suggested throughout the remainder of the book.

3. *Nature of the learning process.* During the last decade, educators have witnessed unprecedented advances in knowledge of the basic processes involved in reading, teaching, and learning. A study by the National Association of Educational Progress (1985, p. 8) revealed:

> There has been a conceptual shift in the way many researchers and teachers think about reading, which gives students a much more active role in the learning and reading comprehension process. This shift is reflected in changes from packaged reading programs to experience with books and from concentration on isolated skills to practical reading and writing activities.

Part of this conceptual shift is a result of the work at the Center for the Study of Reading, funded since 1976 by the National Institute of Education. This group of researchers combined research from education and linguistics as well as other disciplines, such as cognitive psychology, to provide a more complete perspective on the process of reading. The Center published *Becoming a Nation of Readers* (Anderson, Heibert, Scott, and Wilkinson, 1985) "to summarize the knowledge acquired from research and to draw implications for reading instruction" (p. 3).

The more teachers understand the learning process, the better they will be able to evaluate and to improve the learning environments they create. The following statement from *Becoming a Nation of Readers* (p. 3) helps educators understand that we now have the tools to improve learning for students.

> The knowledge is now available to make worthwhile improvements in reading throughout the United States. If the practices seen in the classrooms of the best teachers in the best schools could be introduced everywhere, improvements in reading would be dramatic.

In Chapter 3, the nature of the learning process and suggested instructional methods are discussed. In Chapter 4, two teaching methods (cooperative learning and discussion) are described and methods for motivating reluctant learners are identified. In Chapter 5, factors relating to student interest and to the demands of text are discussed.

4. *Effective learning strategies.* Literacy instruction is designed to help students become more independent learners. The role of the teacher in this process is to model, guide, and provide for practice. Learning strategies help students to make sense of their reading and writing. In Chapters 6 through 10, many strategies are presented on developing vocabulary, improving reading comprehension, and using literature to teach content.

## What Educators Need to Know to Make Programmatic Decisions

The way a school is organized can help or hinder literacy instruction. Aspects of middle school organization lend themselves well to improved reading and writing instruction. A historical perspective of the middle school movement serves as a background for a description of current practices in middle level reading programs and the description of exemplary practices found in four middle level schools.

1. *Middle level schools.* In addition to advances in knowledge of reading and learning, the past two decades have also brought a transformation within the middle school movement. The middle school concept has matured and become more focused. The direction of this movement is to attain a better balance between a content-centered curriculum and a child-centered curriculum. Middle level educators are now more sensitive to their students' sometimes tumultuous

struggle to leave childhood behind as they enter young adulthood. The components of a "true" middle school and how these components, such as interdisciplinary team organization, can facilitate reading and writing instruction are discussed in Chapter 11.

2. *The reading program.*   Traditionally, reading instruction in the middle level school has been delivered in a separate class labeled "reading" and writing has been the exclusive domain of the language arts teacher. In Chapter 12, a discussion of traditional practices in reading instruction is presented as well as results from a national survey that sought information about the extent to which reading is taught in middle level schools and the nature of that teaching. Recommended components of a successful reading program at the middle level are presented.

3. *Exemplary practices.*   The gap between current research and theory and current practice disturbs most educators. One step toward bridging that gap is to take a look at schools that are actually implementing a program that is consistent with current research and theory. Four programs are described in detail in Chapter 13. Programs were selected because the schools were organized as "true" middle schools and their reading programs stressed content area reading. Descriptions illustrate how school organization can facilitate improved reading and writing instruction.

Any experienced teacher will tell you that teaching at the middle level is not boring—often frustrating—but never boring. Early adolescents are alive with language. Somehow that excitement seems to evaporate when they enter a classroom. As teachers, we must find the connection between the students' need to communicate and our need to educate.

## SUMMARY

The middle level school is the last chance for educators to help students become proficient readers and writers. Students who are confident in their ability to read and write hold the key to independent learning. What is necessary to enable students to achieve this goal? Teachers must understand their content, understand the physical, emotional, social, and intellectual needs of students, and understand the nature of learning and the teaching of language. Beyond this, those making administrative decisions must understand how to organize the learning environment for the teaching of reading and writing at the middle level. Finally, educators must find ways to capitalize on early adolescents' natural desire to use language in the way in which it was intended—as a means of communication.

# REFERENCES

Anderson, R. C., Hiebert, E. H., Scott, J. A., and Wilkinson, I. A. G. (1985). *Becoming a nation of readers: The report of the commission on reading.* Champaign, IL: Center for the Study of Reading.

Bruce, B. C. (1981). A social interaction model of reading. *Discourse Processes, 4,* 273–311.

National Assessment of Educational Progress (1985). *The reading report card.* Princeton, NJ: Educational Testing Service.

Nystrand, M., and Himley, M. (1984). Written text as social interaction. *Theory into Practice, 23,* 198–207.

Vygotsky, L. S. (1962). *Thought and language.* Cambridge, MA: MIT Press.

# Chapter 2

# Characteristics of Middle Grades Students

Anyone who has walked the halls of a middle level school has probably encountered flying arms and legs, changing voices, and behavior that ranges from childish to mature. Within any middle grades classroom, it is common to find students varying in height from six to eight inches and in weight as much as forty to sixty pounds. More extreme differences are not uncommon. This variety in physical growth is further compounded by a wide range of emotional maturity, intellectual ability, attentiveness, and interest. To make life still more interesting, individual students, reacting to changes in their bodies, may not display the same behavior from day to day. All of these factors make the middle level school a fascinating place in which to teach.

Knowledge of the rapid and profound changes that early adolescents experience can help teachers understand, if not fully endorse, the behavior they display. With the onset of puberty, students undergo a series of swift and dramatic physical changes. Along with these physical transformations are changes in intellectual capacity and in emotional stability. Many students begin to develop the ability to think abstractly. Well known to most middle level teachers is the fact that students' emotions tend to run high at this age and are often unpredictable. This period of life is also characterized by a new sense of social awareness in which students move from the security of the family to an added dependence on relationships with their peers. Coping with and adapting to all these new experiences is difficult for early adolescents.

In this chapter, the physical, social, emotional, and intellectual characteristics of middle grades students are examined as well as the way in which our culture influences children's development to maturity. Finally, implications for instruction are drawn from all of these factors for the teacher of these interesting students.

# PHYSICAL CHARACTERISTICS

With the exception of the period from birth to age three, more changes occur during early adolescence (approximately 10 to 14 years of age) than at any other time in a person's life. Consider how most adults would react if they were to undergo three years of radical changes in stature, sexual development and interest, and other bodily changes. Add to this list the fact that they will tend to be moody, physically awkward, and have numerous skin blemishes. Under such circumstances, most adults would likely become egocentric and self-conscious, just as most early adolescents do.

The most dramatic and obvious changes are those associated with rapid physical growth and development. Puberty is preceded by a growth spurt in which there is a marked increase in height, weight, heart rate, lung capacity, and muscular strength. Bone grows faster than muscle, which may leave bones unprotected by muscles and tendons. Middle level students often have problems with coordination as a result of this rapid growth; thus, they are often characterized as awkward. Although all early adolescents experience this growth spurt, girls tend to undergo these changes approximately two years earlier than boys.

Sexual maturation is another obvious physical change to which early adolescents must adjust. The appearance of secondary sex characteristics often makes them self-conscious about their bodies. Eichhorn (1966) reported that some behavioral patterns resulting from physical inadequacy, such as shyness, exhibited by a group of late-maturing boys at age seventeen were not found to alter by age thirty-three. Children seem to be affected in different ways. Boys who mature early are usually regarded as leaders and treated as adults, whether or not they behave as adults (Wiles and Bondi, 1986). Early-maturing girls tend to be more independent and have less internal conflict, whereas later-maturing girls sometimes feel unloved and misunderstood.

Experts agree that, at this age, physical differences between students should be minimized by adults and in the school setting. Group showers and competitive sports, for example, merely accentuate the differences in physical ability and development.

Information about the variability of growth spurts can be used to provide some reassurance for these students. It is helpful for students to realize that their development, whether early or late, is normal. Many teachers have found that books about adolescent development are helpful to students. Making an entry in a journal after each reading gives students an opportunity to identify with characters and to realize that "they are not the only ones."

A less obvious but fundamental physical change is the rate of basal metabolism. Early adolescents may be restless and active one minute and listless the next. Students at this age alternate between periods of great physical energy and fatigue. Understanding these different levels of activity can help teachers deal appropriately with the student who falls asleep every afternoon as well as the one who can never sit still. Activities in the classroom should be changed periodically; students simply cannot be expected to maintain quiet attention for forty to fifty minutes.

While students are attempting to adjust to these profound physical changes, changes in their relationships with parents and peers may compound the problem. If teachers understand the nature of these relationships, they can, perhaps, facilitate a smoother transition into new social situations.

## SOCIAL CHARACTERISTICS

Those who live and work with early adolescents know that peers and social relationships are of extreme importance. Friendships are vital at this age, especially same-sex relationships. Feeling comfortable and secure with peers of the same sex at ages ten to twelve helps adolescents progress toward opposite sex relationships that come later. Because rejection by peers represents a major crisis, students at this age spend much of their time trying to figure out ways to win acceptance by their peers. A few examples are presented in Figures 2.1 through 2.4.

Notes like these are, of course, common. Trying out different social situations is all a part of social learning. Some experiences are fleeting, some agonizing, and some thoughtful.

Many parents feel rejected by their children's heightened interest in and growing dependence on their peers. However, this new attachment does not occur at the expense of, but rather in addition to, parental affection. Hill (1980) asserts that research findings suggest that "authoritative parenting with its blend of nonsuffocating affection and moderate control provides a secure familial base for developing social competence in relation to peers and a degree of independence prior to adolescence" (p. 45).

In a 1977 study of over 5000 early adolescents across the country, Wiles and Bondi (1986) reported that in a choice among family, peers, self-acceptance, and the like, family cohesion ranked as the factor most valued. Although new peer associations are vital to the early adolescents' social and emotional maturity,

FIGURE 2.1 _____

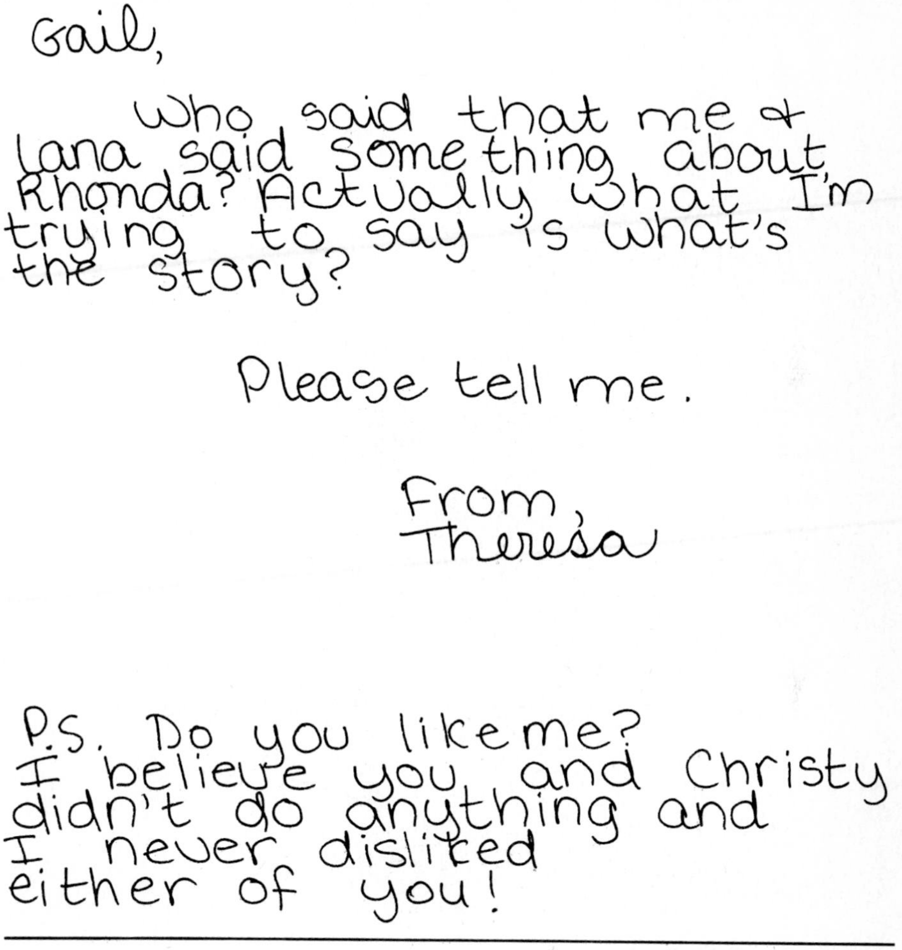

Gail,

    Who said that me &
Lana said some thing about
Rhonda? Actually what I'm
trying to say is what's
the story?

Please tell me.

    From,
    Theresa

P.S. Do you like me?
I believe you and Christy
didn't do anything and
I never disliked
either of you!

_____

the family remains important to them. Students' relationships with both family and peers at this time can either augment or diminish a positive self-concept.

## EMOTIONAL CHARACTERISTICS

As noted earlier in this chapter, some experts view early adolescence as a time of turbulence and disruption (Hill, 1980). The small percentage of students who exhibit signs of serious disturbance cause some adults to conclude that this period is one of turmoil and stress. Although the changes experienced are

FIGURE 2.2

Dear Bruce,

I like you but I am going with someone Already. When we break up I will go with you. Because I like you better. We will break up somehow. I might break up with him. Or tell him how I feel about you. And how you feel about me. Me and you have been together for a long time. And we will stay together.

Love,
Trish

FIGURE 2.3 _____

Catch me I'm fallen
fallen in Love

I was singing that
song wright befor you
told me you could
see <u>him</u> ♡ ♡

FIGURE 2.4 _____

Dear Allen,
I like you alot and
I think that this relationship could
work if me and you could just ignore
every thing that other people say, because
if we keep on listening to other people
both of us will end up hurt (emotional)
that is.

Love,
Tipphanee

stressful for most young people, Dorman and Lipsitz (1981) argue that early adolescence is a time of more emotional stability for most students than Hill would propose. Dorman and Lipsitz contend that adults should "distinguish between behavior that is distressing (annoying to others) and behavior that is disturbed (harmful to the young person exhibiting the behavior)" (p. 4). When adults expect irresponsible behavior, they may, indeed, exacerbate the occurrence.

Emotions, both happy and sad, run high at this age. A teacher of middle grades students may observe the same girl happy and giggling at one minute, and sad and tearful the next minute. These extremes in emotion, probably caused by hormonal activity, are normal experiences and are heightened by the early adolescents' feelings of confusion about the changes within themselves and about their place within the social group.

David Elkind (1967) reported that changes in intellectual functioning may be a partial cause of emotional changes. Sometime during the middle years, early adolescents develop the ability to think about their own thinking. Coupled with the extreme egocentrism exhibited by most early adolescents, this factor gives rise to two emotional responses: the imaginary audience and the personal fable.

Middle grades students presume that other people are as concerned with their thoughts and feelings as they are. For example, early adolescents believe that everyone else notices the blemishes that cause them so much concern. This "imaginary audience" accounts for much of the self-consciousness of middle level students.

At the same time, students create the "personal fable" that their feelings are unique and that no one else understands them. Some students carry this belief to the extreme and adopt the idea that "it can't happen to me—I'm different" (Elkind, 1967). This attitude of invincibility may result in reckless behavior. Although these behaviors are normal, they can be irritating and worrisome to those who live and work with these students.

As early adolescents attempt to accommodate mood swings and adjust to change, their self-concepts are naturally altered. Twelve- to fourteen-year-olds think less positively about themselves than they did in the previous three years (Dorman and Lipsitz, 1981). Teachers and other adults can help students understand and adjust to changes by remaining positive, tolerant, and understanding in order to preserve the students' positive self-concept during this time of transition.

## INTELLECTUAL CHARACTERISTICS

Understanding the cognitive changes that take place in students is of paramount importance in planning a meaningful curriculum and establishing appropriate classroom practices. This age is characterized by a new capacity for thought.

Students are moving from the concrete stage (able to think logically about real experiences) to the formal stage (able to consider "what if's," think reflectively, and reason abstractly). This intellectual change is gradual and may occur at different times for different students. Students may even shift back and forth from the concrete to the abstract, although it is important to remember that not all early adolescents, not even all adults, achieve this capacity. Research on intellectual functioning may serve as a guide to middle level educators in making decisions.

For example, some theorists suggest that 80 to 88 percent of middle grades students cannot handle material presented at the formal level of reasoning (Epstein and Toepfer, 1978). Girls, however, may reach this level of formal reasoning one year or more before boys. Table 2.1 shows the percentage of students reported to be operating at the various Piagetian stages of development.

Epstein further asserts that much of the formal curriculum material presented in the middle level classroom requires a somewhat sophisticated level of formal reasoning. Many middle level educators advise that learning in these grades should consist of as many real-life, concrete situations as possible.

TABLE 2.1 ———————————————————————————————————
Percentage of Individuals Age 5–18 Attaining Various Cognitive Levels

| Age | Preoperational | Concrete Onset | Concrete Mature | Formal Onset | Formal Mature |
|---|---|---|---|---|---|
| 5 | 85% | 15% | | | |
| 6 | 60% | 35% | 5% | | |
| 7 | 35% | 55% | 10% | | |
| 8 | 25% | 55% | 20% | | |
| 9 | 15% | 55% | 30% | | |
| 10 | 12% | 52% | 35% | 1% | |
| 11 | 6% | 49% | 40% | 5% | |
| 12 | 5% | 32% | 51% | 12% | |
| 13 | 2% | 34% | 44% | 14% | 6% |
| 14 | 1% | 32% | 43% | 15% | 9% |
| 15 | 1% | 14% | 53% | 19% | 13% |
| 16 | 1% | 15% | 54% | 17% | 13% |
| 17 | 3% | 19% | 47% | 19% | 12% |
| 18 | 1% | 15% | 50% | 15% | 19% |

*Source:* H. T. Epstein, "Brain growth and cognitive functioning," in *The Emerging Adolescent Characteristics and Educational Implications,* ed. D. Steer (Columbus, OH: National Middle School Association, 1980), p. 39. Reprinted with permission.

Students at this age need to personalize the abstract. Inferential leaps should be small, sometimes miniscule.

For example, one middle grades teacher knew from past experience that *Johnny Tremain* (Forbes, 1943), although a classic and a favorite of hers, caused students difficulty because it introduced such concepts as apprenticeship and revolution (Simpson, 1986). After deciding to try to personalize the story more, she read the book aloud to her class. After discussing a chapter, students made entries in their Response Journals for five to ten minutes. She received comments like: "I liked writing in journals because I can tell you how I feel about the story even if I don't share it out loud" (p. 49). Johnny's historical and personal perspectives came to be appreciated by these students. Through the discussion and the journal writing, Johnny's time, place, and struggle became real. Some teachers report that journal writing is a way to help students make small inferential leaps to more abstract thought.

Strahan and Toepfer (1984) hypothesized that "latent formal thinkers" can solve problems if given a second try and a moderate amount of prompting. Perhaps Simpson's strategy of having students listen to, discuss, and write about *Johnny Tremain* allowed the potential "latent formal thinkers" a chance to explore abstract thought in a success-oriented way.

The early adolescent is egocentric. But, for the first time, the emerging formal thinker is able to consider the thoughts of others. Eichhorn (1966) states that the medium that helps to dampen this egocentrism is social interaction with peers. As students discuss issues that are important to them and resolve conflicting viewpoints, they are forced to reexamine their own views in light of the views of others. This process of social interaction enables early adolescents to mature socially and intellectually.

## CULTURAL INFLUENCES ON EARLY ADOLESCENT DEVELOPMENT

Eichhorn (1966) coined the term *transescence* to designate the time of life just before puberty through the early stages of adolescence. Transescence is an important stage in life—the events experienced at this time largely shape a person's self-concept and go a long way toward determining his or her future success in school.

Every adult has experienced the biological changes that characterize transescence. Beyond these physical changes, however, "adolescence is culturally determined and defined" (Lipsitz, 1983, p. 9). That is, we all experienced similar biological changes, but families, neighborhoods, economic conditions, and our historical era were also factors that influenced our gracious or awkward transition into adulthood.

Parents are often heard making comments such as, "I wasn't doing that when I was in junior high school," "My mother would have never allowed such behavior," "These kids are eleven going on eighteen!" or "Kids these days just aren't what they used to be." These kinds of comments may reflect a sentiment of annoyance, and, in part, they are accurate. Boys are 6 to 8 percent taller and 12 to 15 percent heavier than they were half a century ago (Eichhorn, 1966). The average onset of puberty has occurred four months earlier every decade since 1840. Children *are* growing up faster than they used to. Whether a more rapid social and emotional adjustment accompanies the physical growth, however, is questionable and is still under investigation (Lounsbury and Vars, 1978).

One important factor in the social and emotional adjustment of the early adolescent has changed dramatically in the past few decades—the family. Although peers become more influential during this time, "in no grade does the influence of peers outweigh the influence of parents" (Benson, 1985, p. 3). Current trends indicate that parents are less available to play this role than they were in the past. By 1990, approximately three-quarters of all black children and one-third of all white children will spend some time in a single-parent family (Testa and Wulczyn, 1980). The greatest increase in single-parent families has occurred for children who are ten years and older. These children, whose mothers are likely to be working, will spend many hours alone after school. Most of this time will be spent watching television. It appears that as the parental presence diminishes, the influence of television increases.

The transmission of traditional values is an important component of education at home and in school, but neither parents nor teachers can predict the future needs of young people. Our society is changing rapidly both in terms of technology and in terms of cultural values. We cannot predict the future but we can understand the problems faced by adolescents growing up in our present society. By helping students to negotiate these problems, we will enable them to encounter the problems of the future with courage and determination.

## IMPLICATIONS FOR INSTRUCTION

Experiences during early adolescence have lasting effects in terms of the early adolescent's emerging personality characteristics and self-concept (Drash, 1980). To educate this unique group of children effectively, teachers must use learning strategies that accommodate their special and varied needs. Curriculum designers and instructional personnel must understand the intellectual changes of middle school students as well as their physical, social, and emotional needs.

Physically, middle school students need to move and change activities frequently. Socially, learning must include positive social interaction with peers. Students must realize that others may think differently or hold differing points of view. A positive learning environment, one of acceptance on the part of the teacher and other students, is essential. Emotionally, students need to feel competent and they need to achieve. They need to participate in school and classroom decisions, but they also require structure and clear limits.

Instruction in middle level schools must be different from that of the elementary and high schools. The middle level years are a time when students need to learn and experiment with "learning how to learn" and "learning how to think" (Popejoy, 1980). During this time of transition, material should be presented concretely, yet opportunities should be provided for progression to more abstract thought. Students need an opportunity to experiment with formal reasoning in a gradual and success-oriented way.

The strategies suggested in this book have two elements in common: they accommodate the needs of the early adolescent and they facilitate the development of reading and writing ability. These strategies are helpful for students at any state of their educational experience; however, middle level students have pronounced needs in this time of transition. These strategies develop learning processes that are needed by students to make a smooth transition into the high school. The strategies suggested in this book provide students with

1. The opportunity to work in groups (social needs)

2. A vehicle for connecting new information to what is already known, thus helping students to feel more confident about learning new material (intellectual and emotional needs)

3. Experiences in abstract thinking that may help students move gradually from the concrete to the abstract levels of reasoning (intellectual needs)

4. An opportunity to move and change activities (physical needs)

5. Successful experiences, which help students feel better about themselves as learners (emotional needs)

6. Motivation to learn since these strategies involve elements designed to heighten students' curiosity about the subject (emotional and intellectual needs)

Understanding the characteristics of the middle grades student is prerequisite to making informed decisions about a reading program or instructional practices. In the next chapter, reasons why students have difficulty with reading when they enter the middle grades will be discussed. Instructional methods based on current research and theory that can help students to become independent learners in preparation for the high school years will be suggested.

## SUMMARY

The onset of adolescence brings with it a profound set of physical, social, emotional, and intellectual changes. More than at any other stage of life, the early adolescent is in a state of flux. Rapid physical growth is accompanied by sexual maturation and changes in basal metabolism. An increased social awareness gives rise to an increased emphasis on peer relations. Emotions, stirred by hormonal and psychological changes, run high and many early adolescents begin to experiment with abstract thinking.

Middle level teachers must understand and accommodate the physical and psychological needs of their students. These students need to move and change activities frequently, to engage in positive social interaction with peers, to move slowly from the concrete to the abstract, and to gain confidence and emotional stability through success and the development of self-worth.

## REFERENCES

Benson, P. L. (1985). New picture of families emerges from research. *Common Focus, 6,* 3.

Dorman, G., and Lipsitz, J. (1981). Early adolescent development. In G. Dorman (Ed.), *Middle grades assessment program.* Carrboro, NC: Center for Early Adolescence.

Drash, A. (1980). Variations in pubertal development and the school system: A problem and a challenge. In D. Steer (Ed.), *The emerging adolescent characteristics and educational implications.* Columbus, OH: National Middle School Association.

Eichhorn, D. (1966). *The middle school.* New York: The Center for Applied Research in Education.

Elkind, D. (1967). Egocentrism in adolescence. *Child Development, 38,* 1025–1034.

Epstein, H. T. (1980). Brain growth and cognitive functioning. In D. Steer (Ed.), *The emerging adolescent characteristics and educational implications.* Columbus, OH: National Middle School Association.

Epstein, H. T., and Toepfer, C. F., Jr. (1978). A neuroscience basis for reorganizing middle school education. *Educational Leadership, 36,* 656–660.

Forbes, E. (1943). *Johnny Tremain.* New York: Dell Publishing Company.

Hill, J. P. (1980). *Understanding early adolescence: A framework.* Carrboro, NC: Center for Early Adolescence.

Lipsitz, J. (1983). *Making it the hard way: Adolescences in the 1980s.* Testimony prepared for the Crisis Intervention Task Force, House Select Committee on Children, Youth, and Families.

Lounsbury, J. H., and Vars, G. F. (1978). *A curriculum for the middle school grades.* New York: Harper and Row Publishers.

Popejoy, W. D. (1980). Piaget and middle school teaching. In D. Steer (Ed.), *The emerging adolescent characteristics and educational implications.* Columbus, OH: National Middle School Association.

Simpson, M. K. (1986). A teacher's gift: Oral reading and the reading response journal. *Journal of Reading, 30,* 45–51.

Strahan, D., and Toepfer, C. J. (1984). The impact of brain research on education: Agents of change. In M. Frank (Ed.), *A child's brain.* New York: Haworth Press.

Testa, M., and Wulczyn, F. (1980) *The state of the child.* Chicago, IL: University of Chicago.

Wiles, J., and Bondi, J. (1986). *The essential middle school.* Tampa, FL: Wiles, Bondi & Associates.

# Chapter 3

# Literacy and Instruction

As a group, middle grades students have problems with reading and writing. Recent national studies (NAEP, 1985) furnish evidence that students of various ages read better in 1984 than students at the same ages in 1971; however, 40 percent of thirteen-year-olds and 16 percent of seventeen-year-olds attending high school still have not acquired intermediate reading skills. This means that a large portion of adolescent and mature students are unable to search for information, determine relationships between ideas, or derive generalizations from literature, science, and social studies materials—tasks widely recognized as essential to success in school. Students unable to perform these tasks will be unable to read the range of academic material encountered in school. The important question is, What have we learned from current reading research that can help middle school students improve their ability to read and write?

The acquisition of new knowledge culled from reputable research has helped educators understand how students learn. This chapter addresses the problem of academic adjustment for middle grades students. New views of learning are explored, including schema theory, strategic learning, and integrating instruction. Finally, the reading/writing connection, the changing role of the teacher, and guidelines for instruction are presented.

# THE PROBLEM OF ADJUSTMENT

Profound changes occur within students during the middle school years. Growth spurts, social awareness, mood swings, and a new capacity for thought are all changes to which the early adolescent must adjust. While struggling with internal changes, they must also learn to cope with externally imposed changes as well. When students move from an elementary to a middle level school, they must adjust to a myriad of new situations. The nature of the school structure, the mode of instruction, the number of independent activities, and the nature of reading materials change as students move into this new environment.

## Changes in School Structure

Elementary schools are generally self-contained through grade 5, whereas middle level schools are departmentalized to some degree. Gone is the security of one teacher looking out for students. Also noticeably absent in many middle level schools is any systematic instruction in reading.

## Changes in Instruction

Most middle level teachers were trained in secondary education with an emphasis in a content area with little preparation in the strategies necessary to teach the content. Each content requires its own specialized vocabulary and organizational skills: map reading in social studies, scientific inquiry in science, literary criticism in language arts. Most secondary-trained teachers, however, have little or no formal training in reading and writing instruction. These teachers acknowledge that reading competence is important, but simply do not feel comfortable teaching the strategies students need to read and write successfully, even when these literacy abilities are necessary to learn content.

## Changes in Expectations of Independent Learning

The leap between elementary and middle school in terms of teachers' expectations of student independence is too wide for some students. Thus, students who appear to be unmotivated or disinterested may simply lack the ability to approach a task independently. Learning strategies that students can use to solve problems independently must be taught and reinforced frequently.

## Changes in Reading Material

Textbooks are more difficult in the middle grades. There are also more of them and students are expected to understand them with less assistance from the teacher. Studies by Armbruster and Anderson (1984) have shown that many of the texts students are given to read are poorly written and "inconsiderate." That is, they are written in such a way that the content is not easily understood or remembered, even by a proficient reader.

In contrast, elementary students most often read from basal readers, which are generally written in narrative style. Narrative text is usually recognized by an identifiable plot, setting, group of characters, and sequence. The vocabulary in these texts is carefully controlled. The sentence structure is usually short and somewhat choppy.

Expository text, which is most often found in content area texts, is more factual and usually contains a hierarchical pattern of main ideas and details; however, teachers do not spend much time teaching students to read from this kind of a book. In fact, after almost 300 hours of classroom observation, Durkin (1978–79) found that *no* time was spent in social studies lessons teaching students to comprehend expository text. Teachers taught only content and facts. With the exception of literature class, middle grades students are expected to read almost exclusively expository text as found in their science and social studies textbooks. But who takes the responsibility to teach students to read these texts?

Most often the responsibility for teaching reading in the middle grades falls upon the English teacher. After a review of practices and perceptions among content area teachers, Witte and Otto (1981) concluded that few English educators "express any concern for . . . [having students read] the expository materials of social studies, sciences, and other content areas" (p. 154). Also, Muth (1987) points out that "the pictures of story scenes typically found in narrative text are replaced by tables, graphs, diagrams, and flowcharts" (p. 6). Therefore, while middle level students are expected to read more expository text, no one, it seems, teaches them how to understand this type of text.

Attaining independence in reading the basal reader in elementary grades does not prepare students to read the expository material in their "science or social studies or arithmetic texts independently" (Herber and Nelson-Herber, 1987, p. 586). Students need to learn to adapt their reading ability to a variety of reading material. Ideally, students should receive a gradual introduction to reading expository text, beginning in the elementary grades. "At each grade level, in each subject area, teachers must help students learn to read to learn at a level of sophistication consistent with the concepts and resources being studied" (Herber and Nelson-Herber, 1987, p. 586). Becoming an independent learner is a lifelong process. For this reason, continued and systematic reading at the middle level is imperative.

# CONTRASTING GOOD AND POOR READERS

Much of the research conducted in the last ten years has focused on how the behavior and experiences of good readers differ from that of poor readers. This work has direct implications not only for the instruction of poor readers but for the instruction of *all* students. For example, poor readers report doing less independent reading than good readers. In fact, "poor readers report that their teachers use a narrower range of approaches than are used with better readers. The approaches that are used with poor readers are less likely to emphasize comprehension and critical thinking, and more likely to focus on decoding strategies" (Applebee, Langer, and Mullis, 1988, p. 6). Figure 3.1 presents a listing of what good and poor readers do before, during, and after reading.

The research on good and poor readers has implications for instruction. If teachers understand what strategies good readers use while reading, perhaps those students identified as poor readers can be taught to use those strategies. An understanding of schema theory, strategic learning, and integrating instruction with all the language systems can also be helpful to teachers in trying to help all readers improve.

## Schema Theory

Meaningful learning occurs when a student relates new information to what is already known. That is, it is nearly impossible to learn new information that has no connection to what is already known. *Schemata* comprise all of the information and all of the experience that the reader has stored in memory. A particular schema, then, represents all of the associations that come to mind when a person reads about a certain subject.

For example, you probably have a schema for computers. You have a mental picture of what does or does not characterize a computer. You also bring to that basic picture many other associations. If you are a "user," your schema of computers may be merged with positive feelings of limitless possibilities. If the computer revolution has left you behind with your yellow legal pads and typewriter, you may have feelings of anxiety or frustration as you approach a computer. Our schema determines the sum total of all our thoughts about and reactions toward a certain subject. A reader cannot separate his or her schema from what is read; thus, schema influences the interpretation of what is read.

Thelen (1986) likened schema to a file folder. Everyone has a unique and personal way of organizing cognitive structures (the cabinet). The schemata are the ideas contained within the file folders. Learners must be shown where and

FIGURE 3.1 ————————————————————————
Contrasting Good and Poor Readers

| **Good Readers** | **Poor Readers** |
| --- | --- |
| *Before Reading* | |
| Build up their background knowledge on the subject before they begin to read. | Start reading without thinking about the subject. |
| Know their purpose for reading. | Do not know why they are reading. |
| Focus their complete attention on reading. | |
| *During Reading* | |
| Give their complete attention to the reading task. | Do not know whether they understand or do not understand. |
| Keep a constant check on their own understanding. | Do not monitor their own comprehension. |
| Monitor their reading comprehension and do it so often it becomes automatic. | Seldom use any of the fix-up strategies. |
| Stop only to use a fix-up strategy when they do not understand. | |
| *After Reading* | |
| Decide if they have achieved their goal for reading. | Do not know what they have read. |
| Evaluate comprehension of what was read. | Do not follow reading with comprehension self-check. |
| Summarize the major ideas. | |
| Seek additional information from outside sources. | |

*Source:* Orange County Public Schools Department of Secondary Reading, Orlando, Florida. Reprinted with permission.

how new material fits into the existing structures. Because each reader has his or her own organization, it is important that teachers help students engage their schema to connect new information to what is already known. For this process to occur, students must be able to determine what is known and what is *not* known.

## Strategic Learning

Suppose that during a racquetball game you hit a straight shot down the right side of the court and your opponent misses the ball. The point is yours. This well-placed shot may have been a lucky one, but let's suppose it was the result of a strategy. Before you hit the ball, you noted that your opponent was standing in the middle of the court and you remembered that she is left-handed with a weak backhand. You hit the ball deliberately and strategically.

This analogy can be applied to reading. Strategic reading involves analyzing the reading task, establishing a purpose for reading, and then selecting strategies for this purpose (Paris, Lipson, and Wixson, 1983). A strategy is a conscious effort on the part of the reader to attend to comprehension while reading. Strategic readers know whether or not they are understanding what they are reading and are willing to use any of a number of available strategies to help them understand better. Over a period of years (and, it is hoped, beginning with early reading experiences) efficient readers develop a "repertoire of cognitive and metacognitive strategies" (Jones, Tinzmann, Friedman, and Walker, 1987, p. 38) to help construct meaning from text.

Reading is often referred to as a cognitive event. It is that, but it is also a metacognitive event. Cognition refers to using the knowledge possessed; metacognition refers to a person's awareness and understanding of that knowledge. "Cognition refers to having the skills; metacognition refers to awareness of and conscious control over those skills" (Stewart and Tei, 1983, p. 36).

Metacognition, then, is knowing how and when to use one's skills to solve problems in understanding. Proficient readers monitor their own comprehension and are able to apply strategies to help them understand, such as rereading, reading ahead, or searching one's prior knowledge to make sense of text. That is, they know when what they are reading is making sense, and they know what to do when it isn't. "Thinking about one's thinking is at the core of strategic behavior" (Paris, Lipson, and Wixson, 1983, p. 295). Metacognition develops as a student matures, usually during adolescence, but it can be taught and strengthened by explicit instruction and practice (Palincsar and Brown, 1983). As stated in Chapter 2, early adolescents are just beginning to be able to consider their own thinking in relation to the thoughts of others. The middle level years are an ideal time to develop metacognitive abilities in students.

## Integrating Instruction

As I reflect on my earlier teaching career, I visualize students climbing a series of ladders. I perceived that my job was to encourage students to attain new heights on the "social studies ladder." Of course, I integrated history, economics, psychology, political science, and sociology so that students could climb one ladder instead of five. I knew that as students gained knowledge, facts, concepts, and generalizations, they climbed higher and higher on the social studies ladder.

But after leaving my class, students climbed an English ladder, a math ladder, or a science ladder. They also had reading ladders, writing ladders, listening ladders, speaking ladders, and thinking ladders that they carried from class to class. I was not alone; other teachers in the building saw their job as a matter of adding rungs and encouraging students to climb higher.

Some students were able to build connections among the ladders, but some were not. As teachers we did little to help students make connections between their knowledge and their ability to process language. That is, we did little to help them use what they knew about reading and writing to learn content. Conversely, we did little to help them use their content knowledge to read and write. Most educators a decade ago (and many today) saw learning as a linear and nonrecursive process, a sort of piling up of isolated skills.

As a result of research, theory, and model building, educators now view instruction as a process of making cognitive connections. Imagine, if you will, students laying down their ladders of understanding as spokes in a wheel formation. The center of the wheel is content—a learning event. Students can scurry up and down their ladders using information about reading and writing process or knowledge about a historical event to understand the content. As they learn the content, they add it to their ladder. Ladders may even be built between ladders—bridges of sorts.

Learning is nonlinear and recursive. "The learner continually returns to earlier thoughts for revision as new information is understood and assimilated" (Jones, Tinzmann, Friedman, and Walker, 1987, p. 10). Our job, as educators, is to help students with this process—to help them learn content and develop their ability to process information at the same time. It is a challenging task for educators to help students understand that the learning processes—reading, writing, speaking, listening, and thinking—can be related to each other just as bits of knowledge can be related. This type of instruction involves the teacher helping students process information in meaningful ways so that they can become independent learners.

One way to make instruction more meaningful to students is to integrate reading instruction with instruction in other language areas. It may seem obvious that all four language systems—reading, writing, speaking, and listening—share the same cognitive and experiential base. But teachers do not generally take advantage of these relationships during instruction. It seems only sensible, then, to teach the language systems together and use as many of the language systems as possible to teach content.

## READING/WRITING CONNECTIONS

In the majority of our schools, reading and writing have traditionally been taught separately. Although teachers have observed the many similarities between the two processes, few have capitalized on these similarities by regularly integrating writing and reading instruction in the classroom. Research has indicated that good writers are often (but not always) good readers. Similarly, good readers are often good writers (Stotsky, 1983). Knowledge of one process appears to reinforce knowledge of the other.

Understanding these relationships is especially important to the middle level educator since the language development of the early adolescent, much like physical and social development, is in a transitional stage. During the early adolescent years, educators have an opportunity to help students improve their language abilities by integrating the instruction of all language areas.

Successful readers and writers must possess considerable knowledge, some of it specific to the medium of print and some of it related to language ability and experience in general. Specifically, readers and writers must acquire a wide base of experiences (prior knowledge); a knowledge of the conventional forms of written language (conventions of print); a knowledge of the words, concepts, and structure of language (linguistic competence); and a knowledge of and facility with ways to solve problems of meaning (thinking strategies). This section will examine the contributions of reading to writing and of writing to reading within each of these areas of knowledge.

### Prior Knowledge

Reading is more than a simple decoding of words; it involves an interaction between the author's words and all that the reader has experienced and thought. It is the reader, then, who brings meaning to the printed page by relating his or her prior knowledge to the author's written symbols.

It is usually taken for granted that reading books of quality can add to a person's range of experience (i.e., prior knowledge). Reading enables a person to learn about the world through the eyes of another. Reading can supply a person with information about the workings of the solar system or simply open the doors to the workings of the human mind. However, writing can also develop and give direction to this body of information. Writing serves less to add to these experiences than to clarify and deepen them. In order to present one's ideas to another through writing, one must reflect on personal experiences and clarify and evaluate them. It is one thing to have experienced the funeral of a relative; it is another to bring this experience together into a coherent and meaningful piece of writing that will add to the experiences of a reader. Thus, reading serves to build a person's prior knowledge, whereas writing serves to organize and personalize it.

## Conventions of Print

One of the major contributions of writing to reading and of reading to writing is that experience with each process helps to develop a person's awareness of the forms and conventions of written language. Through experience in reading and practice in writing, students learn spelling, punctuation, paragraph and text structure, the relationship of words to pictures, and other such conventions. As they endeavor to understand or to communicate a meaning, students also learn strategies to help them decipher the set of printed symbols we use to represent spoken words. These mechanical features (spelling, punctuation, text structure, letter/sound correspondences) are often taught to students, either formally or informally, but skill in applying these conventions is only acquired through practice.

Moreover, students seem to absorb and imitate conventions found in their reading, whether or not these reading materials are worthy of imitation. For example, Eckhoff (1983) found that young children who used a basal text in which all sentences were one line in length tended to use a capital letter at the beginning and a period at the end of each line in their own writing regardless of the actual length of their sentences. In fact, in many cases, children who had used this simplified text continued to punctuate in this manner even after they had progressed to a more sophisticated basal reader. Children also imitated in their writing many of the stylized conventions (e.g., "Once upon a time . . .") found in their reading. Thus, the quality of the text may well influence the quality of the writing.

## Linguistic Competence

Success in reading and writing is also dependent on knowledge of the forms, structures, and uses of the language. Experience with print, especially while reading, can build on students' internalized knowledge of language. Extensive reading has been linked to an increase in knowledge of vocabulary, idiom, stylistic devices, and the like. As with conventions of print, much of this linguistic knowledge appears to be acquired without a conscious effort on the part of the reader.

Another facet of linguistic competence related to reading and writing is the understanding that print, like speech, is used to communicate meaning. To a competent reader this may seem obvious. But too often, students learn to write and read in bits and pieces and in so doing lose touch with the meaning of the whole. Students may have difficulty connecting the words they encounter in texts with the language they use in their everyday lives. Providing experiences with expressive writing that focuses on meaning and not just mechanics is one way to help students make this connection.

## Thinking Strategies

Underlying all linguistic processes is the more basic process of thought. To deal successfully with print, readers and writers must command a set of thinking skills. Readers and writers engage in a process of constructing meaning: writers construct a symbolic representation of their own meaning on paper, and readers construct a "model" of the author's meaning in their head (Tierney and Pearson, 1983). Proficient readers and writers are strategic; they possess a variety of strategies for solving problems of meaning.

Boutwell (1983) asked eight-year-old Marta to tape record her thoughts and procedures as she wrote and read in the classroom. Boutwell found that her writing experience enhanced her ability to read strategically: "When Marta encountered confusing parts, she reread them. This strategy sprang from the same question she asked in her own writing: 'Does this make sense?' " (p. 725).

It seems that the ability to synthesize information, to see a text as an integrated whole rather than a series of unrelated parts, can improve comprehension of expository material. Taylor and Berkowitz (1980) found that sixth-graders who wrote one-sentence summaries of paragraphs from a content-area text scored higher on measures of comprehension and memory than those who used study guides or those who simply read the text. One-sentence summaries, abstracts, and the like can be used to help students understand the structure of reading assignments and plan the structure of writing assignments. In short, good readers and writers are more in control of their purposes and strategies for dealing with print and are able to view a text as a group of interrelated parts.

# THE ROLE OF THE TEACHER

Good readers do not spend a lot of time analyzing their reading behaviors, they just do it naturally. But what can teachers do to facilitate effective reading and writing behavior in their students? The first step is to be concerned about "improving children's comprehension ability rather than just their comprehension" (Johnston, 1985, p. 643). That is, the goal of instruction should be to produce strategic learners who are as concerned about the process of learning as the product.

An analogy developed by Moore, Moore, Cunningham, and Cunningham (1986) may be helpful in understanding the teacher's role in instruction. Suppose that a guest in your home walked through your garage and spotted a bicycle. She had never seen a bike before and asked what it was and how it worked. You explained then you demonstrated how to get on and ride the bike. Now, it is your guest's turn. You hold the bike while she gets on and gets the feel of the bike. Then you run along side until she maintains her balance. Finally, you let go and shout instructions from across the yard as she circles on the pavement. You then plan a longer trip but want to accompany her for support. At last, you are confident that she can ride the bike independently as she pedals off into the sunset.

Instruction is similar to the guidance you might give to the novice bicycle rider. The goal of reading instruction is to produce independent, strategic learners. The role of the teacher is to inform, model, guide, observe, correct, and encourage (Vygotsky, 1962). This type of instruction provides for the gradual release of responsibility from teacher to student.

The first component in instruction is *planning*. The teacher must take into consideration the background knowledge of the students relative to the content to be learned, the text complexity and structure, and the strategy or skill to be developed. During this phase of instruction, the teacher must decide on appropriate materials and an appropriate method of presentation.

During the *teaching* phase, the teacher presents, models, and conducts an informational session on the strategy or skills to be learned. The teacher explains to students when, how, and why to use the particular strategy. One important aspect of this "before" reading time is the activation of prior knowledge or the building of background. Some experts (Vaughn and Estes, 1986) contend that 60 percent of instructional time should be spent on prereading and prewriting activities. (Chapter 7 contains many such activities for use at this stage of instruction.)

The student then engages in *guided practice* and the teacher becomes a coach. The teacher needs to evaluate the students continuously and provide additional assistance to those students who are having difficulty with the assignment/strategy. The "during" reading activities should focus on helping students use their cognitive and metacognitive abilities to comprehend text. (Activities to facilitate active reading can be found in Chapter 8.) "After reading" activities include summarizing, synthesizing, and evaluating the reading. (Activities that promote these abilities can be found in Chapter 9.)

The student then needs *independent practice*. The teacher must determine how much additional practice the student needs and how much guidance is still needed from the teacher. After this stage, it is hoped that the student can add the strategy/skill to his or her repertoire of available strategies for later use.

# GUIDELINES FOR INSTRUCTION

Middle level educators can do much to help students become better readers and writers. Helping students to improve their language competence in reading will naturally improve their ability to write and vice versa. Students can learn much about writing from reading. Readers can expand their prior knowledge, encounter different conventions of print, extend their linguistic competence, and develop their thinking skills. All of these abilities can then be applied to the students' writing. The guidelines below may help middle level educators to incorporate reading/writing relationships in their instructional and curricular planning to help facilitate strategic learning.

1. *Teach students how to be "strategic" readers and writers.* Students must learn what to do when they encounter problems in reading and writing, and they must learn to deal with such problems strategically. Research has identified two general skills in thinking that characterize strategic readers and writers:
   a. They learn to evaluate whether something is making sense, and, when something does not make sense, they figure out why.
   b. They learn to be aware of what they are thinking and why they are doing what they are doing.

Teachers can facilitate the learning of these strategies by modeling their own thought processes as they read and write, by providing small group instruction that deals with specific strategies, and by holding conferences with students to help identify problems and discuss possible solutions.

2. *Provide instruction in a meaningful context.* Students must learn to see the usefulness of printed language. For students who see no practical utility in reading and writing, such activities are simply exercises to be completed and forgotten. If students are to view written language not mechanically but creatively, they must begin to see what they can do with it. This means that students must use reading and writing in as many practical and purposeful ways as possible. They may use written language to communicate directly with others through shared journals, message boxes, or "published" books by student authors. They may use texts and writing to find out and organize information, or they may write to express their own ideas and emotions or read to experience another's. Students must learn, through experience, that reading and writing are useful tools for communicating meaning.

3. *Encourage students to focus on the main idea of what they read and what they write.* Squire (1983) stated that "focusing instruction separately on the word, the sentence, the paragraph, and then the longer piece of discourse may seem logically right, but it is psychologically wrong. From the very beginning children seek to communicate within a total context" (p. 585). In order to facilitate comprehension in reading and coherence in writing, students must

learn to grasp larger and larger chunks of meaning. That is, they must learn to get at the *main idea* of what they read and what they write. Grasping a main idea involves synthesizing information and seeing a text as a set of interrelated parts.

4. *Provide numerous language opportunities for students.*   Just as children learning to speak must listen, imitate, and practice extensively, children learning to read and to write must be immersed in reading and writing. Much of what students learn about language is acquired without a conscious effort on their part. This means that students must read as much as possible and then practice what they learned in their reading through writing. Teachers who establish a successful reading-for-pleasure program in their classrooms are doing much to increase the linguistic and literary competence of their students.

5. *Provide quality reading experiences for students.*   Reading material, even on the most basic level, should be of high quality and worthy of imitation. Since students learn a great deal simply through involvement with print, the print they are involved with needs to be well written.

6. *Provide opportunities for students to discuss their reading and writing.*   Students need to discuss, evaluate, and organize the ideas they encounter in print. Feedback provided by others often helps students discover the importance of their ideas and how those ideas fit in with what the students already know. Discussion in a small or large group also helps students improve their listening and speaking abilities as well as enhance their reading and writing experiences.

7. *Provide students a choice whenever possible.*   To a certain extent, students should be given a choice over their reading selections or writing topics. Structure, of course, is essential to instruction, but freedom of choice also fosters motivation. Hence, a teacher may wish to assign reading and writing activities that are useful to developing particular skills, and allow students to choose others or select among a group of choices. Students seem to benefit from structure early in instruction and then move naturally into more open assignments later.

# SUMMARY

Students moving from the elementary to the middle school must adjust to an increasingly departmentalized and content-focused system. Many middle level teachers forsake reading and writing instruction for content. Yet, the early adolescent years represent a productive opportunity to help students make the transition from the narrative-based reading of the elementary school to the almost exclusively expository-based reading of the high school.

To make this transition, students must learn to become strategic and independent readers. They must learn the strategies that good readers use before, during, and after reading. An effective writing program contributes much to reading and vice versa. By integrating the language arts, teaching strategies for effecting reading, and providing an abundance of quality literary experiences for students, teachers can help students become flexible and effective readers.

# REFERENCES

Applebee, A., Langer, J., and Mullis, I. (1988). *Learning to be literate in America: Reading, writing, and reasoning.* Princeton, NJ: National Assessment of Educational Progress, Educational Testing Service.

Armbruster, B., and Anderson, T. (1984). Producing "considerate" expository text: Or easy reading is damned hard writing. (Reading Education Report No. 46). Champaign, IL: Center for the Study of Reading.

Boutwell, M. A. (1983). Reading and writing process: A reciprocal agreement. *Language Arts, 60,* 723–730.

Durkin, D. (1978–79). What classroom observations reveal about comprehension instruction. *Reading Research Quarterly, 14,* 481–533.

Eckhoff, B. (1983). How reading affects children's writing. *Language Arts, 60,* 607–616.

Herber, H. L., and Nelson-Herber, J. (1987). Developing independent learners. *Journal of Reading, 30,* 584–589.

Johnston, P. (1985). Teaching students to apply strategies that improve reading comprehension. *Elementary School Journal, 85,* 635–645.

Jones, B. F., Tinzmann, M. B., Friedman, L. B., and Walker, B. B. (1987). *Teaching thinking skills: English/Language arts.* Washington, DC: National Education Association.

Moore, D. W., Moore, S. A., Cunningham, P. M., and Cunningham, J. W. (1986). *Developing readers and writers in the content areas: K–12.* New York: Longman.

Muth, K. D. (1987). What every middle school teacher should know about the reading process. *Middle School Journal, 19,* 6–7.

National Assessment of Educational Progress (1985). *The reading report card: Progress toward excellence in our schools: Trends in reading over four national assessments, 1971–1984.* Princeton, NJ: Educational Testing Service.

Palincsar, A. S., and Brown, A. L. (1983). Reciprocal teaching of comprehension-monitoring activities. (Technical Report No. 269). Champaign, IL: Center for the Study of Reading.

Paris, S., Lipson, M. Y., and Wixson, K. K. (1983). Becoming a strategic reader. *Contemporary Educational Psychology, 8,* 293–316.

Squire, J. R. (1983). Composing and comprehending: Two sides of the same basic process. *Language Arts, 60,* 581–589.

Stewart, O., and Tei, O. (1983). Some implications of metacognition for reading instruction. *Journal of Reading, 26,* 36–43.

Stotsky, S. (1983). Research on reading/writing relationships: A synthesis and suggested directions. *Language Arts, 60,* 627–642.

Taylor, B., and Berkowitz, S. B. (1980). Facilitating children's comprehension of content material. In M. L. Kamil and A. J. Moe (Eds.), *Perspectives in reading research and instruction.* Clemson, SC: National Reading Conference.

Thelen, J. N. (1986). Vocabulary instruction and meaningful learning. *Journal of Reading, 29,* 603–609.

Tierney, R. J., and Pearson, P. D. (1983). Toward a composing model of reading. *Language Arts, 60,* 568–580.

Vaughn, J. L., and Estes, T. H. (1986). *Reading and reasoning beyond the primary grades.* Boston, MA: Allyn and Bacon.

Vygotsky, L. S. (1962). *Thought and language.* Cambridge, MA: MIT Press.

Witte, P. L., and Otto, W. (1981). Reading instruction at the postelementary level: Review and comments. *Journal of Educational Research, 74,* 148–158.

# Chapter 4

# Learning Environments That Motivate Students

Teachers at the middle level spend a lot of their time and energy trying to prevail upon students to do their own work. Students at this age have a natural inclination toward social interaction and they also have a strong desire to be accepted by their classmates. The most satisfying reward a teacher can give middle grades students is to give them time together. Most teachers and administrators, however, see this tendency toward social interaction as a factor that interrupts academic achievement.

But this social urge can be academically productive if properly channeled (Lounsbury, 1985). In fact, "evidence suggests that cooperative reward structures can promote positive self-esteem while also enhancing academic achievement" (Slavin, 1981; Johnson, Johnson, Holubec, and Roy, 1984). In other words, cooperative learning arrangements that allow for social interaction ought to pervade the middle school (Beane and Lipka, 1987). This approach stimulates discussion, enhances self-esteem, promotes academic achievement, lends itself to improved social skills, and motivates reluctant learners.

This chapter first presents the types of learning environments generally found in classrooms. Then research on the value of cooperative learning is discussed and methods for implementing and managing cooperative learning are explained. Next, the value of full and rich discussions is explored. The chapter concludes with some ideas for motivating reluctant learners.


## TYPES OF LEARNING ENVIRONMENTS

The competitive classroom environment can be characterized as one in which students are praised when they do better than other students. Such an environment seems to work against the early adolescents' desire to be accepted. Students who consistently perform well are set apart from the group, whereas students who do not perform well are labeled (explicitly or implicitly) as failures. Thus, a competitive environment may turn many students away from academic achievement. Such an environment, however, is not the only way in which a classroom can be structured. Instructional activities are usually structured in three different ways: competitively, individualistically, or cooperatively.

*Competition* among students can cause them to perceive that they can obtain their goal only if classmates fail.

*Individualistic* work requires that students work by themselves, with their own materials, and at their own pace. Interaction with other students is usually not accommodated or allowed.

*Cooperation* among students creates the perception that they can attain their goal only if the students they are working with attain their goals. Rewards come to students based on the quality of the group effort. Cooperative learning does not exist by merely placing students in close proximity and asking them to work together on an assignment. "Cooperative interdependence means that the students perceive their success to be dependent on the efforts of all the members of the group so that their efforts as a group are evaluated against present criteria of excellence and all members of the group must master the assigned material" (Johnson and Johnson, 1982, p. 27).

Proponents of cooperative learning, such as Slavin, and Johnson and Johnson, do not advocate using this method exclusive of other means of instruction. Rather, it should be used with competitive and individual experiences. This method of instruction has value at any age, but it is especially effective with middle grades students in that it fulfills their needs for social contact, physical motion and variety of activity, emotional acceptance, and experimentation with abstract thought. After presenting some of the research documenting the value of cooperative learning, ways to implement and manage this method of instruction will be described.

## COOPERATIVE LEARNING

### The Value of Cooperative Learning

Cooperation is one value that most adults would like to instill in their children. Cooperation cannot be taught by defining the concept, listing the attributes, and providing two examples and three non-examples. Cooperation must be experienced to be understood.

Beyond providing students with an object lesson in the value of cooperation, cooperative learning methods have many other benefits. "Cooperative learning methods can be used by teachers to achieve social and academic goals at the same time, without sacrificing one for the other" (Slavin, 1981, p. 658).

One of the *social values* of cooperative learning is in the development of interpersonal skills such as communication, leadership, and trust building. This method also stimulates the development of the processes of problem solving and inquiry ( Johnson and Johnson, 1982, p. 33), which are essential at the high school level.

Numerous studies have shown that cooperative learning methods improve "relationships between Black, White, and Hispanic students" (see Slavin, 1981, p. 657 for summary of research). Improved self-esteem has been found to be another benefit of cooperative learning methods. Students on teams seem to feel more liked by their peers and feel more academically successful. For the middle grades student, the most powerful way to build a positive self-concept is through peer acceptance and through successful academic experiences. Cooperative learning experiences encourage both acceptance and academic success.

Cooperative learning has been shown to improve *academic performance* as well as social skills and acceptance by peers. In a synthesis of research on cooperative learning, Slavin (1981) stated that "the positive effects of cooperative learning methods on student achievement appear with equal frequency in elementary and secondary schools, in urban, suburban, and rural schools, and in subjects as diverse as mathematics, language arts, social studies and reading" (p. 657).

Considering the viewpoints of other people, especially peers, is one way in which students move from the egocentrism that is characteristic of the early adolescent to a more balanced view of life. When students are given the opportunity to compare their value system with those of others, they can become more aware of others, they can see that their concerns are shared by others, and they can develop their emerging value systems.

As discussed earlier, connecting new information to what is already known is a key to learning. The very nature of cooperative learning methods is particularly conducive to activating prior knowledge through discussion with other students (Flood, 1986). This method of instruction "significantly decreases inattention, while increasing comprehension and active engagement in learning" (Uttero, 1988, p. 391).

Using cooperative learning methods, of course, will not solve all problems in the classroom or raise all students to great heights of academic performance. But, perhaps by including cooperative learning as a part of the regular instruction in content area classrooms, middle grades students can practice the interpersonal skills they need to develop, have an opportunity to consider the viewpoints of others, develop thinking and other problem-solving skills, and experience social acceptance and academic success.

## Implementing Cooperative Learning

Cooperative activities can be as simple as having students turn to their neighbor to verify an answer or as complex as the Jigsaw Method. According to Johnson, Johnson, Holubec, and Roy (1984, pp. 7–8), the key elements of Cooperative Learning (that distinguish it from activities in which students are merely placed in groups to work) are positive interdependence, face-to-face interaction, individual accountability, and interpersonal and small-group skills.

Three of the more complex and structured cooperative learning strategies are presented below. Student Team Learning is one result of many years of research at the Center for Social Organization of Schools, The Johns Hopkins University. The three processes of implementing cooperative learning are Teams-Games-Tournaments (TGT), Student Teams-Achievement Divisions (STAD), and Jigsaw. All of these methods involve having the teacher assign three to six students to learning groups, each group having a mixture of high-, average-, and low-achieving students (Slavin, 1981). These groups should be well-balanced in terms of sex and race. In each method, the teacher presents the initial information through the preferred mode of delivery, such as giving a lecture or showing a film.

In *Teams-Games-Tournament* (TGT), the teacher first presents information on a particular topic to students, using lecture, discussion, audio-visual, or any other method of instruction. After the initial information is presented, the teams work together to make sure that they understand the information. They can review notes together, work on a worksheet, write a summary, create a semantic map, or other activity.

After this practice phase, the team members compete in academic tournaments against members of other teams and earn points for their team. The teacher structures this activity so that high achievers compete with other higher achievers and so on. This activity is arranged so that all members can contribute points to their team if they study hard. After the tournament, team points are calculated, a winner is declared, and the results are publicized in some manner. The cycle of teacher presentation of information, team practice, tournament, and publicizing results is carried out about once a week for six to eight weeks. When a winning team is declared, new teams are formed by the teacher and another cycle begins.

In *Student Teams-Achievement Divisions* (STAD) the teacher again presents information to the entire class. The students then meet in teams to master the information. Finally, the students take individual quizzes on the material. The team accumulates points according to how well each student did in comparison with his or her own past average. The teams with the highest scores are recognized in some fashion. Any student who prepares well in this method can be successful and make a contribution to the team. Results are publicized, new teams are chosen, and the cycle begins again. Some teachers prefer to use TGT one week and STAD the next week.

In the *Jigsaw* method, students are again assigned to groups. Two different types of groups are used: the original team and the expert group. The "expert" group studies a topic that is under consideration for the whole group. After the "experts" have read and studied their information, they return to their original teams to share their information with their teammates. Finally, the students take a quiz on the material; the quiz scores are used as in the STAD to form individual and team scores.

For example, if a social studies class studies a particular culture, four different topics might be established: religious beliefs, economic life, history, and family organization. Students become "experts" on their particular topic. Then they move back to their teams to teach about the topic studied. The "expert" must teach the other three students about the topic. Together, the second group puts together a report on the culture under study. The jigsaw strategy assures a purpose for reading and motivation to understand the topic for study.

Cooperative learning is designed to be fair competition. That is, each student has an opportunity to contribute to the team and each team has an opportunity to win if it tries. Students are motivated to do well because the acceptance of their peers is dependent on their effort.

Some educators wonder if teams hinder the progress of high-achieving students. These students not only have an opportunity to help fellow students but the old adage that "teaching is learning twice" seems appropriate here. Low achievers have the opportunity to contribute to the team effort and be stimulated by the ideas of the high achievers.

Grades can continue to be a reflection of individual achievement. Students can be told that the team competition is a motivational system that helps students learn better. The grade given, however, is an evaluation that is based on individual performance, such as a report or a test.

Some teachers and administrators are cautious about using cooperative learning methods because it decreases teacher control and increases student responsibility. Classrooms become noisier and movement is permitted. But noise and movement do not necessarily indicate a lack of control. A few guidelines for getting started and managing cooperative learning are presented below.

## Managing Cooperative Learning

When first implementing cooperative learning methods, teachers should move slowly but persevere. This method will likely be as new to the students as it is to the teacher. It is important to explain the process to students and monitor progress at the beginning. After everyone settles into the routine, it will become easier for both. Johnson and Johnson (1987) offer the following advice for starting cooperative learning.

1. *Make up the groups yourself.* For optimum success, each group should have a high-, medium-, and low-achieving student in it, with a mix of sexes, cultural groups, and motivation levels. Do not put students with their friends unless you have a good reason. If students protest their group membership, explain that you will make new groups later on, so they will not always be with the same people.

2. *Seat students close to their group members.* This makes it quick and easy for you to get them into and out of their groups.

3. *Start out with small groups.* Groups of two or three are best until students become skillful in including everyone. Then proceed carefully to four members if you feel students are ready.

4. *Integrate group work into your curriculum.* Anything one can do, two can do better. Have students drill each other in pairs on material taught. Review for tests in trios. On some assignments, have them do the work individually first and then decide on the group answers. Students can check each other's papers for accuracy, then you can select one paper to grade. Three students can discuss chapter questions and turn in one paper for the group. The more oral discussion and summarizing of the material the students do, the more they will learn.

5. *Assign each student a job or role.* Possibilities include Reader, Recorder, Checker (makes certain everyone knows and can explain the answers by having group members summarize), Encourager (encourages full participation by asking silent members what they think or what they have to add), and Praiser (praises good ideas or helpful group members).

6. *Make your expectations of group behavior clear.* A teacher may wish to say something to the students before group work begins; for example, "I expect to see everyone staying with the group, contributing ideas, listening carefully to other group members, making certain everyone is included in the work, and making certain everyone understands and agrees."

7. *Observe and question while students are working.*    Ask anyone you do not think is helping to explain an answer. Make it clear to the group that it is responsible for making sure all group members participate and know the answers. Expect that some groups will finish before other groups; check over their work and have them correct any glaring errors, then let them review, talk quietly, study, or read until the other groups are finished.

8. *Evaluate each session.*    After each session, have each group answer these questions: What did we do well today in working together? What could we do better tomorrow? Let them know what you saw them do. Be positive and reward positive behavior.

In order to control noise and behavior, teachers can give extra points for the team's good behavior, cooperativeness, and effort. During the cooperative learning activity, teachers should move from team to team and comment on what each member is doing right. This is not the time to grade papers. After group work, teachers can comment on particular good things that they saw in groups.

Teachers should resist the temptation to rush in and solve problems for students. Instead, students should be allowed time to work out a solution cooperatively. One teacher who was especially concerned about being able to monitor each group's activities placed a tape recorder with each group. She listened to the tapes to and from work each day and made positive comments and suggestions to each group after listening to the tape. Cooperative learning allows the teacher to be a facilitator and the students to learn from each other and on their own.

Nickolai-Mays and Goetsch (1986, p. 29) suggest the following guidelines for conducting and evaluating cooperative learning groups.

1. Do not allow too much time for activity. Keep the students busy with no time to waste.

2. Have something concrete for the students to hand in each day. Spot check their work to keep students on task and help them monitor the quality of work throughout the process.

3. Begin and end each class period with brief, pertinent teacher comments that provide the students with a daily sense of organization.

4. Arrange work areas and designate a specific spot in which each group is to work before the activity begins. This saves time and avoids confusion.

5. Devise a signal to get the attention of the students while they are working. For example, flashing the lights works as an instant attention getter; it is easier than shouting and gets a much quicker response.

6. Have in the room all necessary materials and supplies. This will insure that students can use their time more efficiently.

7. Move around the room monitoring the process. Teachers can learn a great deal about their students from the perspective of an observer.

8. Allow sufficient time for clean-up and counting of materials. This helps in organizing the room and the materials for the next class.

# FULL AND RICH DISCUSSIONS

The positive benefits of conducting classroom discussions have been noted by researchers for years. Sternberg (1987) stated that "our ability to think originates outside ourselves, we must view class discussion as more than just a peripheral part of a think-skills program. Discussion is essential" (p. 459). As discussed earlier in this chapter, this interchange of ideas facilitates the maturation of early adolescents from total egocentricism to a more balanced world view.

In a monograph titled *Using Discussion to Promote Reading Comprehension,* Alvermann, Dillon, and O'Brien (1987), state that "discussion is an integral part of the comprehension process" (p. 13). The authors maintained that the use of "recitation and lecture . . . cannot compete with discussion in offering opportunities for students to communicate their views to other students with different views" (p. 9). Furthermore, reading is placed in a social context. That is, discussion reduces the isolation that students sometime feel when they are left alone to interact with text. A postreading discussion helps them to communicate, refine, and enrich their understandings of the assigned reading.

Alvermann, Dillon, and O'Brien maintained that discussion has the following three criteria:

1. Discussants should put forth multiple points of view and stand ready to change their minds about the matter under discussion;

2. Students should interact with one another as well as with the teacher; and,

3. The interaction should exceed the typical two or three word phrase units common to recitation lessons (p. 7).

Recitation might be visualized as a telephone switchboard operator—all lines run from the teacher to and from individual students; interaction *between* students is minimal. According to the preceding definition, recitation is not considered to be a "discussion."

Three types of classroom discussions are considered to be basic to the classroom environment: (1) *subject mastery discussions,* which extend student learning through talking about a topic. As will be discussed in Chapter 7, activating prior knowledge and building background information is necessary in facilitating comprehension of any new topic of study; (2) *issue-oriented discussions,* which may depend on student needs and interests; and (3) *problem-solving discussions,* which may grow out of a textbook assignment, lecture, or previous discussion or assignment.

In order to have a successful classroom discussion, it is necessary to have the proper setting and climate. Students must feel free to express their opinions and see that what they say will be accepted. A physical arrangement that is conducive to discussion is one in which the chairs are arranged in a circle or horseshoe shape. The teacher must be an effective listener who instills respect for the opinions of others. Teachers should clarify, reflect feelings, resolve different points of view, interpose summaries, and redirect questions to students.

Discussions should be limited. The teacher should announce the length of the discussion ahead of time, along with the purpose. The teacher should also maintain the focus of the discussion and should respect the privacy of individual students by not insisting on direct participation.

One way to get full participation from the entire class without putting any individual "on the spot" is through a strategy called Think-Pair-Share (McTighe and Lyman, 1988). A question, usually requiring some bit of abstract thought, is posed. Students *think* and jot down an answer. Then students *pair.* That is, they talk about their answer with a partner. Then, as a class, they *share* answers. This strategy allows every student an opportunity to answer, at lease to a partner. It also allows students time to think, respond, and try to make connections with the world they understand. In Chapter 2, it was suggested that "latent abstract thinkers" need time to consider their response and can then perhaps respond at a higher level of thinking. Think-Pair-Share allows such time for thought and reaction, as well as providing for a fuller, richer, and more thoughtful discussion.

Discussions can improve oral communication, allow students to verbalize their opinions, and consider the viewpoints of peers. Discussion can help students to build upon and to activate what they know about a particular topic of study, to clarify their thoughts during postreading, and thus to promote reading comprehension.

## MOTIVATING RELUCTANT LEARNERS

I recently had a conversation with Jason, a seventh-grade student who had a bit of a chip on his shoulder about school. The discussion centered around the kinds of books that he had read. Jason loved mysteries and adventure and had read the *Lord of the Rings* trilogy (Tolkien, 1937). After a lively dialogue about Frodo and his adventures, I asked him why his teachers complained that he did not and would not read at school. The twinkle left his eye and he replied, "I don't like to read the stuff they give us in school." Part of Jason's problem could, I suppose, be blamed on his age, but Jason's lack of motivation to read "school stuff" may be attributed to three factors: attitude, interest, and self-concept.

First, Jason did not have a good *attitude* about reading expository text and, perhaps generally, about anything that was assigned by a teacher. Men and women who spend hours in a weight room have an attitude about working out. This attitude motivates them to endure pain and continue working out. A positive attitude toward reading can motivate a student to keep going and to try different types of reading challenges.

Second, Jason's *interests* were in mystery and fantasy. Why is it, then, that he could not become interested in studying ancient civilizations? Why is it that he could not become interested in reading about the discovery of King Tut's tomb? I suspect that his teacher did not know about his interests and that the connection between his reading interests in mysteries and the mysteries of the real world was not made.

Jason is a happy, well-adjusted young man at home. He gets along well with his family and they discuss favorite books. His *self-concept* about himself as a learner at school, however, is poor. He does not see himself as one who can succeed in school work. This lack of confidence manifests itself in resistance to assignments and in an "I don't care" attitude.

Reading is a highly valued skill in our society; it is especially valued in school. Children who believe they are not competent at performing a task that society has determined as important often develop a negative self-concept (Quandt and Selznick, 1984). Quandt and Selznick suggest that, as well as building an accepting classroom environment, teachers can use student interests as a powerful way to help students who have a low self-concept. The teacher's challenge is to help the student achieve success by tapping the student's own interests and strengths.

What can be done to help those students who can read but won't and those students who have difficulty reading and don't like to read? Identifying and using student interests can help build self-esteem and motivate reluctant learners.

## Assessing and Using Student Interests

Students seem to understand high-interest material better than low-interest material. Wigfield and Asher (1984) give two possible explanations for this phenomenon: (1) high-interest material sustains the student's attention and/or (2) a large store of prior knowledge facilitates comprehension. Interest seems to play an important part in comprehension for both high-ability students (Stevens, 1979) and low-achieving students (Belloni and Jongsma, 1978).

In dealing with the problem of motivation, there is no substitute for firsthand knowledge about students' interests, attitudes, values, and aspirations based on informal observation and personal interaction. Valuable insights can be obtained from interest inventories, structured interviews, attitude scales, and even the circulation records of school libraries.

A typical question asked in an interest inventory is: Do you read a newspaper regularly? If so, what sections do you read? Other questions may be asked about preferences for school subjects, television programs, and hobbies. Some writers advocate the "incomplete-sentence" technique. The student is asked by the teacher to complete such statements as "When I read history (or political science or geography), I _____," or "If I could read what I want, I would _____." Teachers may use a more formal inventory, such as the one presented in Figure 4.1, or they may choose to use incomplete-sentence tests that they create on their own.

Using student interest to motivate readers can have a powerful effect. Not only are students motivated to read in their area of interest but they will probably be more successful in their reading because of their large store of prior knowledge about the topic.

FIGURE 4.1 ————————————————————————————————————
Reading Interest Inventory

Please answer the following questions to help us learn more about you and your reading interests.

1. What do you like to do most in your free time? (Check any that apply.)

   Listen to music _____
   Play games _____
   Draw/Paint _____
   Read newspapers or magazines _____
   Read books _____
   Do homework _____
   Play a musical instrument _____
   Watch television _____
   Cook _____
   Write letters, poems, stories _____
   Talk to friends _____
   Watch movies _____
   Other (Please list) _____
   _____
   _____

2. What kinds of books do you most like to read? (Check your three favorite types.)

   History _____
   Biography _____
   Sports _____
   Science _____

Religion _____
Fairy tales or folklore _____
Mystery and detective _____
Romance/love stories _____
Science fiction _____
Poetry _____
Other _____
_____
_____

3. Answer each question briefly. Use the back of the paper if necessary.
   a. Do you have pets? _____
   What kind? _____
   b. What things do you collect? _____
   _____
   c. Suppose you could have one wish come true, what would that be? _____
   _____
   d. What is the best book you have ever read? _____
   _____
   e. What other books have you really enjoyed reading? _____
   _____
   f. Do you have any books that belong to you? _____
   g. What are some of their titles? _____
   _____
   h. Does anyone read to you? _____
   i. Do you enjoy having someone read to you?_____
   j. How often do you go to the public library? _____
   _____
   k. What kind of work do you think you will do when you finish high school or college? _____
   _____
   l. What is your favorite school subject? _____
   _____
   m. If you could request your school media center to purchase two particular books, what would they be? _____
   _____

*Source:* Donna Calloway, Leon County Public Schools, Tallahassee, Florida. Reprinted with permission.

## Motivation Strategies

A few strategies have proven helpful in motivating early adolescents. Taylor, Harris, and Pearson (1988) have made recommendations for motivating reluctant learners. Part of that list follows:

1. *Read aloud.*  Students of all ages love having someone read to them. Often, they will become interested in reading a particular book because one by the

same author has been read to them. Also, students gain much in the way of vocabulary knowledge and thinking abilities by having others read to them. Chapter 10 offers suggestions in full detail about the best ways to read aloud to students.

2. *See the movie; read the book.*   Many of the popular movies, such as *Star Wars,* are available in written form. Already knowing the story line and characters helps students have more success with such books.

3. *Display evidence of book reading.*   Alvermann (1987) suggests using a systematic way for students to share their evaluations of the books they have read. As a student finishes reading a book, one assignment could be for him or her to fill out a simple card, listing the name and author of the book and one or two lines about why the student liked or disliked the book. These cards can then be made available to other students as they select their own reading material. Teachers can suggest books that are written by the same author or that are conceptually related. The power of using trade books to build motivation and enhance reading and writing ability has been affirmed by both research and teacher testimonial.

4. *Develop an advertising campaign.*   After students finished reading a book, one teacher sent two students to the library to be interviewed and videotaped. The interviewer had a teacher-prepared list of questions to ask, although deviation from the list was encouraged. Every few weeks, the video tapes were shown to the whole class. This teacher found that shortly after the viewing, many students wanted to check out the books read by those students who were interviewed. Also, students can make up commercials, dress up in costumes like the characters and explain the book, or make a poster about the book.

5. *Use comic books.*   Students will often read comic books when they will not read something else. Also, students can write new stories using the pictures. Comic strips from the newspaper can be used in much the same way.

6. *Read to younger children.*   Reading to younger children is an excellent way to have low-achieving students read materials that are below their grade level; it also provides an opportunity for older students to be in a position of authority and respect. Books should be selected with guidance from the teacher and rehearsed ahead of time.

7. *Employ language experience.*   Language experience is a way to use the vocabulary of a student to improve his or her reading ability. A student dictates a story or an event to someone else. The student then reads his or her story back to the transcriber. Language experience enables low-ability readers to experience success through the use and extension of the vocabulary they already possess as well as through involvement with topics of their own interests. Usually the listening vocabulary of these students is larger than their reading or writing vocabularies. That is, students know and can use more words orally than

they are able to read or write. Thus, language experience enables students to use their larger oral vocabularies to build upon their reading and writing vocabularies. Students are also likely to identify with their own writing or dictated ideas. The basic procedures in adapting the language experience approach to a content classroom follow:

a. The students are asked to interpret, explain, or describe, in their own words, an event, problem, or issue related to the content being studied. The subject should be something meaningful to the student. For example, if a social studies class is studying Indians, a student might look at several pictures of Indians, then tell a story about the life of a twelve-year-old Indian.

b. The teacher then tapes the unrehearsed accounts and types them out verbatim.

c. The students then read their stories or accounts orally.

d. The teacher discusses with the students the meaning of the story and how they might change the story to improve it. If students have difficulty reading some of the words they dictated, these words should be marked and activities developed to use these words in a different context. For example, if a student had trouble with *culture, elk,* and *tribal,* using these words in a new short story would help to reinforce learning these words.

The Language Experience Approach requires time on the part of the teacher, but it clearly can be a valuable tool in providing many disabled readers with successful reading experiences. Teachers may be able to secure some help in taping and transcribing stories from teacher's aides, volunteers, typing classes, and even older students. The teacher can use a word-processing program to type the story as it is dictated by the student, thus enabling taping and transcription. Some teachers have taught entire units using language experience activities. Collections of students' stories can be displayed and read by other students.

8. *Incorporate newspapers into classroom instruction.*   The newspaper is the most widely and consistently read piece of literature published (Cheyney, 1984). The International Reading Association and the American Newspaper Publishers Association Foundation have worked together over the last decade to make Newspaper in Education Week more popular in our country. Current events, sports, comics, and editorials can relate to the content being covered. Additionally, the controversial issues so commonly found in newspapers can be used to motivate students to read further (Lunstrum, 1981).

9. *Use music and art to build motivation.*   Contemporary music and lyrics can be used to motivate students and enable them to relate the content they are studying to their experiences. Smith (1981) suggests that "lyrics of many songs provide excellent sources for teaching vocabulary development at both literal and higher levels of comprehension" (p. 32).

The use of music to evoke emotion, instill nationalistic pride, and develop a feeling of unity can be an interesting subject of study, and one that is directly related to historical movements. For substantiation of this claim, one need only point to the impact of "We Shall Overcome" on the civil rights movement. More recently, "Hands Across America" was a song that literally "united," if only for a time, the nation from coast-to-coast, and "We Are the World" was sung with pride by children and adults. Music is a powerful force in our society and it is one in which students are intensely interested.

If students have an interest in drawing, art has also been used effectively in the content classroom to improve students' motivation to read. Students can be encouraged to create original cartoons of historical problems and events. Captions for these cartoons can be written and shared with others.

## Motivating Early Adolescents

Most educators would agree that students are most motivated to learn if they are placed in a positive atmosphere and supported by peers and teachers. A sense of achievement is necessary as well. Gnagney (1980) examined the needs of students aged thirteen to nineteen. He found that boys are most motivated by the need to know. They like experiments, novel approaches to material, and challenges to their ability to understand a particular event. Girls, on the other hand, are more motivated by needs related to esteem, love, and belonging. Girls respond most to group work with their friends and to comments from the teacher that enhance their self-concept.

Johnston and Markle (1982) established some guidelines for motivating the middle level student to achieve. They include: (1) instilling in students the belief that they can learn or that they will develop the ability to achieve, (2) giving students a clear idea of what must be done in order to achieve the instructional goal, and (3) helping students to recognize how the goals of instruction relate to their everyday lives.

Basically, if the needs of the early adolescent are kept in mind, it is not difficult to establish practices that will motivate middle level students. Creating success opportunities for students, relating to students as individuals, and building their feelings of self-worth are all necessary components of motivating early adolescents.

## SUMMARY

Most early adolescents, by nature, want to engage in an increasingly broad range of social relations. These social inclinations are often seen by educators to be an impediment to academic achievement; however, social interaction can be directed toward useful personal and academic ends. Cooperative learning allows students to work together to solve problems and to achieve academic goals. Cooperative learning also develops communication and leadership skills, and fosters understanding among students of different cultural backgrounds and ability levels. Full and rich discussions also provide opportunities for students to interact, share in the thought processes of others, and consider different viewpoints on a topic.

Student interests can also be used as a means of promoting academic achievement and cultivating a positive attitude toward learning. By tapping students' interests, teachers can create an environment conducive to success, thus enhancing confidence, a positive attitude, and self-esteem. Activities based on music, art, and real-life situations can all be used to capitalize on student interest. Success is also fostered in an environment where students are supported in their efforts to learn by both peers and teachers.

## REFERENCES

Alvermann, D. E. (1987). Developing lifetime readers. In D. E. Alvermann, D. W. Moore, and M. W. Conley, (Eds.), *Research within reach: Secondary school reading.* Newark, DE: International Reading Association.

Alvermann, D. E., Dillon, D. R., and O'Brien, D. G. (1987). *Using discussion to promote reading comprehension.* Newark, DE: International Reading Association.

Beane, J. A., and Lipka, R. P. (1987). *When the kids come first: Enhancing self esteem.* Columbus, OH: National Middle School Association.

Belloni, L. F., and Jongsma, E. A. (1978). The effects of interest on reading comprehension of low-achieving students. *Journal of Reading, 22,* 106–109.

Cheyney, A. B. (1984). *Teaching reading skills through the newspaper.* Newark, DE: International Reading Association.

Flood, J. (1986). The text, the student, and the teacher: Learning from exposition in middle schools. *The Reading Teacher, 39,* 784–791.

Gnagney, W. J. (1980). Changes in student motivational structure during adolescence. *Adolescence, 15,* 671–681.

Johnson, D. W., and Johnson, R. T. (1987). *Learning together and alone: Cooperative, competitive, and individualistic learning.* Englewood Cliffs, NJ: Prentice-Hall.

Johnson, D. W., Johnson, R. T., Holubec, E. J., and Roy, P. (1984) *Circles of learning: Cooperation in the classroom.* Alexandria, VA: Association of Supervision and Curriculum Development.

Johnson, R. T., and Johnson, D. W. (1982). What research says about student-student interaction in science classrooms. In A. Rowe and W. S. Higuchi

(Eds.), *Education in the 80's: Science.* Washington, DC: National Education Association.

Johnston, H. J., and Markle, G. C. (1982). What research says to the practitioner. *Middle School Journal, 13,* 22–24.

Lounsbury, J. (1985). Do your own work? *Middle School Journal, 17,* 2.

Lunstrum, J. P. (1981) Building motivation through the use of controversy. *Journal of Reading, 24,* 687–691.

McTighe, J., and Lyman, F. T., Jr. (1988). Cueing thinking in the classroom: The promise of theory-embedded tools. *Educational Leadership, 45,* 18–24.

Nickolai-Mays, S., and Goetsch, K. (1986). Cooperative learning in the middle school. *Middle School Journal, 18,* 28–29.

Quandt, I., and Selznick, R. (1984). *Self-concept and reading.* Newark, DE: International Reading Association.

Slavin, R. E. (1981). Synthesis of research on cooperative learning. *Educational Leadership, 38,* 655–659.

Smith, C. F., Jr. (1981). Motivating the reluctant reader through the top twenty. In A. J. Ciani (Ed.), *Motivating reluctant readers.* Newark, DE: International Reading Association.

Sternberg, R. J. (1987). Most vocabulary is learned from context. In M. G. McKeown and M. E. Curtis (Eds.), *The nature of vocabulary acquisition.* Hillsdale, NJ: Lawrence Erlbaum Associates.

Stevens, K. (1979). The effect of topic interest on the reading comprehension of higher ability students. *Journal of Educational Research, 73,* 365–368.

Taylor, B., Harris, L. A., and Pearson, P. D. (1988). *Reading difficulties: Instruction and assessment.* New York: Random House.

Tolkien, J. R. R. (1937). *The lord of the rings.* New York: Ballantine Books.

Uttero, D. A. (1988). Activating comprehension through cooperative learning. *The Reading Teacher, 41,* 390–395.

Wigfield, A., and Asher, S. R. (1984). Social and motivational influences on reading. In P. D. Pearson (Ed.), *Handbook of reading research.* New York: Longman.

# Chapter 5

# The Demands of Text

A young child once confided in me, "You've got to know lots to be a teacher." Out of the mouth of babes, it seems, comes truth. Teachers need to know their content, their students, the learning process, and instructional materials available to them. The most commonly used instructional material is the textbook. Sometimes teachers have a choice over the selection of the textbook and sometimes one is assigned—with varying degrees of pressure to use it. But every teacher must decide how and when to use a textbook.

When making instructional decisions about the use of the textbook, the teacher should do two things: assess how difficult the text is to read and assess how much the students already know about the topic under study. A textbook does not automatically convey meaning; rather, meaning is constructed in the mind of the student. The words of the text activate the student's prior knowledge and thus the student builds a meaning. In this chapter, two different types of text (narrative and expository) are explored and ways of helping students to become more sensitive to these text structures are suggested. Factors that make expository text "considerate" are then discussed, followed by ways for teachers to help students overcome the obstacles of "inconsiderate text." The chapter concludes with the readability issue and offers an alternative method of assessing the difficulty of a textbook.

# KINDS OF TEXT

When students are sensitive to text structure, they tend to remember what they read better and over a longer period of time (Taylor, 1982). However, teachers often fail to devote any time to helping students learn to be aware of text structure. Awareness of text structure is an important metacognitive skill that should be made a part of learning to read and write. Generally, two types of text are found in school settings: narrative and expository.

*Narrative* text is usually encountered in stories such as those commonly found in basal readers and literature anthologies. Narrative text usually has the following elements: setting, sequence, characterization, and plot. In general, middle level students have less trouble with this type of text because it usually has a clearly defined structure. A reader can expect to meet characters, a time period and a setting, a series of events, and some sort of resolution. Story grammars have been developed to heighten student awareness of the structure of stories. Story grammars facilitate the identification of the predictable aspects of a story. Cunningham and Foster (1978) used story grammars with sixth-grade students. They showed students a diagram of stories before the reading. Then, as stories were read aloud, students noted the structure and seemed better able to understand the story and the structure as a result of this exercise. Figure 5.1 is a diagram of a story's structure as developed by Cunningham and Foster.

This diagram may be modified to fit different purposes. Students can fill in the different parts of the diagram as a teacher reads a story to them. This diagram can then be used as a springboard for discussion. Another option is to ask the students to read the story first and then fill in the story structure.

*Expository* text, on the other hand, is the type of writing typically found in social studies or science textbooks. This type of writing provides an explanation of facts and concepts, and a reader can usually identify a hierarchy of ideas. Research in the area of expository text has helped us understand the ways in which these types of books are organized. The most common types of text organization are simple listing, cause and effect, time order, comparison/contrast, and problem/solution (Armbruster and Anderson, 1984).

## Text Structure Activity

Taylor (1982) found that students who are sensitive to text structure remember more of what they read. The text structure activity was designed by Readence, Bean, and Baldwin (1985) to help students recognize and use different types of textual organization. For these activities, teachers should choose a well-organized text that has a clearly defined structural type.

FIGURE 5.1

Diagram of a Story Structure

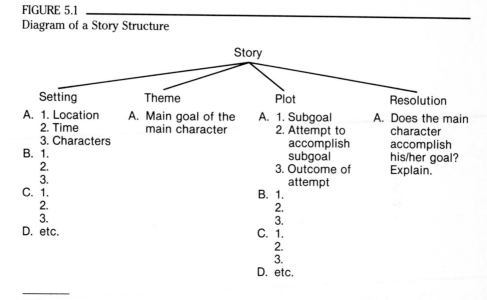

Source: J. Cunningham and E. O. Foster, "The Ivory Tower Connection: A Case Study," *The Reading Teacher,* 31 (January 1978): 367. Reprinted with permission of the International Reading Association.

▶ STEP 1:   **The teacher *models* the thinking process used in determining the text structure.**   Essentially, the teacher thinks aloud about how and why a text is organized the way it is. He or she should point out to the students any connectors or signal words that provide cues to the structure of the text. For example, a section in a social studies textbook may be organized around a cause-and-effect structure. The teacher would point out that signal words such as *because, since, therefore, consequently,* and *if. . . then* are generally found in the cause-and-effect organization.

▶ STEP 2:   **Students are asked to *recognize* certain text structures.**   If the text is difficult to read, this part of the activity can be done at the listening level. Passages need not be long. To continue with the social studies example, the teacher would provide students with paragraphs organized in a cause-and-effect structure. Students would be asked to identify the signal words that alert the reader to this type of organization.

▶ STEP 3:   **Students *produce* the same text structure recognized earlier.**   Through writing, students can reinforce their learning about how the text is organized. After discussing a cause-and-effect relationship in a social studies class, one student wrote the following paragraph:

> Americans rebelled against England *because* they wanted to be independent. They realized that *if* they fought, *then* they would pay a price in lives and resources. *Since* they felt strongly about their freedom, they joined hands and began the rebellion.

Taylor and Beach (1984) demonstrated that the comprehension of middle school students could be improved by teaching them to understand text structure. However, just as skill instruction in isolation is not recommended to teach comprehension, text structure instruction should not occur out of context. Students learn reading strategies best when such strategies are related to the content they are expected to learn. Students can be given many opportunities to learn text structure in relation to the texts they read. Students who are taught this skill in isolation and expected to apply it later may never take the next step.

## Considerate Text

Armbruster and Anderson (1984) analyzed middle school American history textbooks in terms of organization and the types of questions contained. They concluded their study by saying:

> We are struck by the complex world of middle grade social studies text structures, question types, the background knowledge required, and the sheer amount of information that students and teachers face . . . each of these factors come to bear on the complicated task of teaching students to read in the content areas (p. 65).

Textbooks are often difficult to understand because they are "inconsiderate." That is, the way they are written may lack structure, unity, and coherence. Yet we expect students to read, often independently, these poorly written textbooks. *Structure* refers to the plan for how the ideas are arranged and connected to each other. *Unity* of purpose helps readers understand main ideas since only relevant information is included. *Coherence* refers to the clarity of relationships between ideas.

## Helping Students Deal with Inconsiderate Text

Teachers must learn to recognize poorly written textbooks and try to avoid them. Questions to ask about a text's comprehensibility include (Clewell and Cliffton, 1983):

Does the book contain an ample amount of *textual aids*—illustrations, headings, and so forth—intended to serve as a guide to the reader?

Is the *content* appropriate to the target audience—in this case, your students? Is information accurate and explicit?

Is the text *coherent?* That is, are ideas clearly related and organized? Are transitions clearly indicated? Are all references clear?

Is the *style* of the text appropriate and interesting?

Is *language* clear? Is all terminology defined as it is used? Does sentence structure and length lend to clarity?

When inconsiderate texts cannot be avoided, teachers can assist students in dealing with difficult texts by helping them to create their own pattern of organization. A textbook I recently encountered was written specifically for low-level readers but contained no subheadings. While discussing this text with her class, one clever teacher talked with students about appropriate subtitles. The students then wrote these subtitles *in the book.* The lesson provided students with practice in organizing ideas and a better understanding of the content of the text. Moore, Moore, Cunningham, and Cunningham (1986, pp. 165–166) have developed a set of guidelines for teachers who are obliged to use inconsiderate texts.

1. *Hold students responsible for only part of a text.* Students do not need to read every page of every chapter in the textbook. Chances are that they will not remember most of it anyway. The teacher should make the decision as to what parts of the text are most important, most interesting, and most comprehensible.
2. *Help students to prepare for reading and to set a clear purpose for reading.* Activities that activate prior knowledge or build background information are necessary for students to get the maximum benefit from their reading. The more students understand the purpose for their reading, the more likely they are to understand what they read.
3. *Use difficult but important material in a listening comprehension lesson.* Listening comprehension involves the same process as reading comprehension except that students listen rather than read material. Since listening and speaking vocabularies are usually larger that reading and writing vocabularies, students can learn the information through this approach and improve their listening comprehension at the same time.
4. *Make extensive use of visual aids.* Pictures, charts, maps, diagrams, and other visual aids provide and clarify information. Often, students can guess what the text will say based on the visual information.

## Helping Students Understand Text Structure

Another way of helping students to comprehend text is to teach them to see the structural patterns in text. Searching for signal words is probably one of the most helpful ways to understand a text's organization. A list of common signal words (or structure words) is presented in Figure 5.2.

FIGURE 5.2 ———————————————————————————————————
Structure Words

| Paragraph Pattern | Structure Words |
| --- | --- |
| Simple listing | for example, for instance, specifically, another, besides, also, in addition, moreover, furthermore, in particular |
| Cause/effect | consequently, therefore, thus, as a result, however, hence |
| Contrast/compare | on the other hand, but, by contrast, yet |
| Time order | another, additionally, next, first, second (etc.), then, and, furthermore, also |

*Source:* M. W. Olson and B. Longnion, "Pattern Guides: A Workable Alternative for Content Teachers," *Journal of Reading,* 25 (May 1982). Reprinted with permission of M. W. Olson and the International Reading Association.

One way to encourage students to recognize signal words while reading and to use signal words in writing is through the use of the two activities: paragraph frames and pattern guides.

*Paragraph Frames.* A paragraph frame is a teacher-constructed form in which the students complete several sentences. It is an excellent way to teach students how to use signal words and text structure to understand content reading material. Figures 5.3 through 5.5 are examples of this activity.

*Pattern Guides.* Pattern guides are similar to many other study guides except that they are intended to focus on the organization of expository text. A few examples of pattern guides are shown in Figure 5.6.

## THE READABILITY QUESTION

Readability formulas have been used for many years to describe text difficulty. Word difficulty and sentence length are the two most common factors considered. These formulas have been so widely used that word-processing programs can now be purchased with readability formulas built in for instant

FIGURE 5.3 _____
Character Analysis

In the story _____ by _____ the
major character is _____ who is _____.
Another main character is _____ who
_____ is also important in the story.
The problem which the major character faces is that
_____.
The problem is finally resolved when _____.
The story ends with _____.
The lesson I learned from reading this story was that _____
_____.

_____

*Source:* J. N. Nichols, "Using Paragraph Frames to Help Remedial High School Students with Written Assignments," *Journal of Reading,* 23 (December 1980). Reprinted with permission of J. N. Nichols and the International Reading Association.

FIGURE 5.4 _____
Time Order

At the end of _____ what happened was that _____
_____ . Previous to this _____
_____.
Before this _____.
The entire chain of events had begun for a number of
reasons including _____
_____.
Some prominent incidents which helped to trigger the
conflict were _____
_____.

_____

*Source:* J. N. Nichols, "Using Paragraph Frames to Help Remedial High School Students with Written Assignments," *Journal of Reading,* 23 (December 1980). Reprinted with permission of J. N. Nichols and the International Reading Association.

analysis of reading level. However, current researchers have questioned the validity of readability formulas. Bruce, Rubin, and Starr (1981) cite three weaknesses in readability formulas: (1) they ignore or violate much of current knowledge about reading and the reading process, (2) the statistical bases are shaky and poorly supported, and (3) as a practical tool—either to match the student to material or to provide guidelines for writers—they are totally inappropriate. These authors go on to state that readability formulas do not

FIGURE 5.5 ─────────────────────────────────────
Comparison-Contrast

_____ are different from _____
_____ in several ways. First of all _____
_____ while _____
_____.
Secondly, _____
while _____.
In addition, _____
while _____.
Finally, _____
while _____.
So it should be evident that _____
_____.

────────

*Source:* J. N. Nichols, "Using Paragraph Frames to Help Remedial High School Students with Written Assignments," *Journal of Reading,* 23 (December 1980). Reprinted with permission of J. N. Nichols and the International Reading Association.

FIGURE 5.6 ─────────────────────────────────────
Sample Pattern Guides

"Kinetic Theory"—Chapter 12

Example 1: *Cause/Effect*

The kinetic theory explains the effects of heat and pressure on matter. Several ramifications of the theory are discussed in this chapter. Be alert to causal relationships as you read.

1. Gas exerts pressure on its container because
   A. *p. 261, par. 1*
   B. *p. 261, par. 1*

2. What causes pressure to be exerted in each arm of the manometer?
   A. *p. 261–2*
   B.

3. The effects of colliding molecules which have unequal kinetic energy is *p. 266.*

4. What causes the particles of a liquid to assume the shape of the container? *p. 269, par. 1*

(Pattern guide created from *Chemistry, A Modern Course,* Smoot and Price, 1975.)

"The United States Divided"—Chapter 14

Example 2: *Contrast/Compare*

Using pages 264–265, you will contrast and compare the repercussions in the South and the North to the Supreme Court's decision in the Dred Scott case.

| The South | The North |
|-----------|-----------|
| 1. | 1. |
| 2. | 2. |
| 3. | 3. |
| 4. | 4. |

(Pattern guide created from *The Adventures of the American People,* Craft and Drout, 1970.)

"Sleep, Fatigue, and Rest"—Chapter 4

Example 3: *Listing*

This section of your textbook lists many causes of fatigue (pp. 96–97). Some of the causes are physical and some are mental. Fill in the causes under the appropriate heading.

1. Physical causes of fatigue
   A. short burst of intense effort
   B. rapid growth
   C. Lack of important food
   D. p. 96, par. 3
   E.
   F.
   G.

2. Mental causes of fatigue
   A. p. 96, par. 1
   B.

(Pattern guide created from *Investigating Your Health,* Miller, Rosenberg, and Stackowski, 1971.)

"Religious Change in Western Europe"—Unit 4, Chapter 3

Example 4: *Time Order*

A time line is an excellent way to see the sequence of events. As you read about the religious leaders (pp. 229–236), fill in the events on the time line below. Write what happened under the date.

| 1517 | 1521 | 1526 | 1546 | 1555 | 1558 |
|------|------|------|------|------|------|
| p. 229 | | p. 230 | p. 231 | | p. 234 |

(Pattern guide created from *People and Our World: A Study of World History,* Kownslar, 1977.)

---

*Source:* M. W. Olson and B. Longnion, "Pattern Guides: A Workable Alternative for Content Teachers," *Journal of Reading,* 25 (May 1982). Reprinted with permission of M. W. Olson and the International Reading Association.

measure such things as the degree of discourse cohesion, the number of inferences required, the dialect and background knowledge required, as well as motivation, interest, and purpose for reading.

Klare (1984) describes those elements measured by readability formulas as "low level" text characteristics. Factors such as prior knowledge, motivation, interests, and the depth and number of concepts presented are referred to by Klare as "higher level" text characteristics. After a review of the literature on the readability question, one must conclude that people, their ideas, and their language are just too complex to reduce to formulas.

Important factors of reading comprehension such as concept load, organization, style, reader familiarity with the material, reader motivation, and purpose are simply not taken into account by readability formulas. An approach that has been helpful to content teachers in evaluating their textbooks is the *Readability Checklist* developed by Irwin and Davis (1980) (see Figure 5.7). The two major categories of *understandability* and *learnability* are presented as a framework for analyzing textbooks.

FIGURE 5.7 _____
Readability Checklist

This checklist is designed to help you evaluate the readability of classroom texts. It can best be used if the text is rated while thinking of a specific class. This checklist is not designed to compare one textbook with another. Your goal is to find out what aspects of the text are or are not less than ideal. Finally, consider supplementary workbooks as part of the textbook and rate them together.

Rate the questions below using the following rating system:

5—Excellent
4—Good
3—Adequate
2—Poor
1—Unacceptable
NA—Not applicable

Further comments may be written in the space provided.

Textbook Title:
_____

Publisher:
_____

Copyright date:
_____

*Understandability*
_____ A. Are the assumptions about students' vocabulary knowledge appropriate?
_____ B. Are the assumptions about students' prior knowledge of this content area appropriate?

_____ C. Are the assumptions about students' general experiental backgrounds appropriate?

_____ D. Does the teacher's manual provide the teacher with ways to develop and review the students' conceptual and experiential backgrounds?

_____ E. Are new concepts explicitly linked to the students' prior knowledge or to experiential backgrounds?

_____ F. Does the text introduce abstract concepts by accompanying them with concrete examples?

_____ G. Does the text introduce new concepts one at a time with sufficient numbers of examples for each one?

_____ H. Are definitions understandable and at a lower level of abstraction than the concept being defined?

_____ I. Is the level of sentence complexity appropriate for the students?

_____ J. Are the main ideas of paragraphs, chapters, and subsections clearly stated?

_____ K. Does the text avoid irrelevant details?

_____ L. Does the text explicitly state important complex relationships (e.g., causality, conditionality) rather than always expecting the reader to infer them from the context?

_____ M. Does the teacher's manual provide lists of accessible resources containing alternative readings for poor or advanced readers?

*Learnability*
Organization

_____ A. Is an introduction provided for each chapter?

_____ B. Is there a clear and simple organizational pattern relating the chapters to each other?

_____ C. Does each chapter have a clear, explicit, and simple organizational structure?

_____ D. Does the text include resources such as an index, glossary, and table of contents?

_____ E. Do questions and activities draw attention to the organizational pattern of the material (e.g., chronological, cause and effect, spatial, topical)?

_____ F. Do consumable materials interrelate well with the textbook?

Reinforcement

_____ A. Does the text provide opportunities for students to practice using new concepts?

_____ B. Are there summaries at appropriate intervals in the text?

_____ C. Does the text provide adequate iconic aids such as maps, graphs, illustrations, etc. to reinforce concepts?

_____ D. Are there adequate suggestions for usable supplementary activities?

_____ E. Do these activities provide for a broad range of ability levels?

_____ F. Are there literal recall questions provided for the students' self review?

_____ G. Do some of the questions encourage the students to draw inferences?

_____ H. Are there discussion questions which encourage creative thinking?

_____ I. Are questions clearly worded?

*Motivation*

_____ A. Does the teacher's manual provide introductory activities that will capture students' interest?

_____ B.  Are chapter titles and subheadings concrete, meaningful, or interesting?
_____ C.  Is the writing style of the text appealing to the students?
_____ D.  Are the activities motivating? Will they make the student want to pursue the topic further?
_____ E.  Does the book clearly show how the knowledge being learned might be used by the learner in the future?
_____ F.  Are the cover, format, print size, and pictures appealing to the students?
_____ G.  Does the text provide positive and motivating models for both sexes as well as for other racial, ethnic, and socioeconomic groups?

*Readability Analysis*
Weaknesses
1. On which items was the book rated the lowest?
2. Did these items tend to fall into certain categories?
3. Summarize the weaknesses of the text.
4. What can you do in class to compensate for the weaknesses of this text?

Assets
1. On which items was the book rated the highest?
2. Did these items fall in certain categories?
3. Summarize the assets of this text.
4. What can you do in class to take advantage of the assets of this text?

---

*Source:* J. W. Irwin and C. A. Davis, "Assessing Readability: The Checklist Approach," *Journal of Reading,* 24 (November 1980). Reprinted with permission of J. W. Irwin and the International Reading Association.

---

# SUMMARY

Textbooks are an integral part of our educational system. However, teachers who use them must proceed with knowledge and caution. It is important that teachers accurately assess both the difficulty of the text and the base of knowledge that students bring to the text. A *considerate* text is one that has a clear and unified structure, a coherent manner of presentation, and an interesting and readable language and style. By understanding the structure of such a text, students can increase their understanding of its important ideas and relationships. *Inconsiderate* texts, however, abound. One effective way to use such texts is to have students rewrite or reorganize selected portions of text.

Traditionally, readability formulas have been used to determine the difficulty level of individual texts. However, these formulas leave out such important factors as concept load, the interests and knowledge of the students, and organization of text. Thus, it is recommended that teachers employ one or more informal measures to assess the difficulties of a textbook.

# REFERENCES

Armbruster, B., and Anderson, T. (1984). Producing "considerate" expository text: Or easy reading is damned hard writing. (Reading Education Report No. 46). Champaign, IL: Center for the Study of Reading.

Bruce, B., Rubin, A., and Starr, K. (1981). Why readability formulas fail. (Reading Education Report No. 28). Champaign, IL: Center for the Study of Reading.

Clewell, S. F., and Cliffton, A. M. (1983). Examining your textbook for comprehensibility. *Journal of Reading, 27,* 219–224.

Cunningham, J., and Foster, E. O. (1978). The ivory tower connection: A case study. *The Reading Teacher, 31,* 365–369.

Irwin, J. W., and Davis, C. A. (1980). Assessing readability: The checklist approach. *Journal of Reading, 24,* 124–130.

Klare, G. (1984). Readability. In P. D. Pearson (Ed.), *Handbook of reading research.* New York: Longman.

Moore, D., Moore, S., Cunningham, P., and Cunningham, J. (1986). *Developing readers and writers in the content areas: K-12.* New York: Longman.

Nichols, J. N. (1980). Using paragraph frames to help remedial high school students with written assignments. *Journal of Reading, 23,* 228–231.

Olson, M. W., and Longnion, B. (1982). Pattern guides: A workable alternative for content teachers. *Journal of Reading, 25,* 736–740.

Readence, J. E., Bean, T. W., and Baldwin, R. S. (1985). *Content area reading: An integrated approach.* Dubuque, IA: Kendall/Hunt Publishing Company.

Taylor, B. M. (1982). Text structure and children's comprehension and memory for expository material. *Journal of Educational Psychology, 74,* 323–340.

Taylor, B. M., and Beach, R. W. (1984). The effects of text structure instruction on middle-grade students' comprehension and production of expository text. *Reading Research Quarterly, 19,* 134–146.

# Chapter 6

# Vocabulary Knowledge

Educators have long recognized the strong relationship between vocabulary knowledge and the ability to read and write proficiently. In fact, most educators have intuitively known that "people who do not know the meanings of many words are probably poor readers" (Anderson and Freebody, 1981, p. 44). Dale Johnson (1986), a noted expert on vocabulary development, stated that "the decade of the 1980's could be characterized as a period of rediscovery of the importance of vocabulary instruction to reading comprehension" (p. 580). Researchers have investigated the extent to which direct vocabulary instruction affects reading comprehension and are beginning to make recommendations to instructors based on this research. This chapter examines the relationship between vocabulary knowledge and reading comprehension, and then discusses the three general types of words. Next, the nature of vocabulary instruction and guidelines for instruction are presented. Finally, numerous strategies for improving vocabulary knowledge are discussed.

## VOCABULARY KNOWLEDGE AND READING COMPREHENSION

Correlations between vocabulary knowledge and reading comprehension have been substantiated by research since 1968. Thorndike (1973) reported high correlations between these two factors for ten-, fourteen-, and eighteen-year-olds, and he stated that reading performance is "completely . . . determined by word knowledge" (p. 62).

The vocabulary of any individual can be explained as the sum total of all the words that the individual can understand and/or use while listening, speaking, reading, or writing. Young children first develop their listening vocabulary and then their speaking vocabulary. When children enter school, these vocabularies are naturally larger than their reading or writing vocabularies. It has been estimated that the average six-year-old knows and understands about 6000 words (Moe, 1974). As students get older, the match between listening/speaking and reading/writing vocabulaires becomes closer; however, as adults we know and understand more words in our receptive vocabularies (listening and reading) than we normally use in our expressive vocabularies (speaking and writing). Chall (1988) suggested that in fourth or fifth grade, most students make a shift from a recognition vocabulary to a meaning vocabulary. That is, they learn to use in their writing and speaking many of the words they formerly only recognized when listening or reading.

## THREE TYPES OF WORDS

Graves and Prenn (1986) classified words into three types, each requiring a higher investment of teacher and learner time for instruction. The first type of word is one that is already in a student's oral vocabulary. He or she merely needs to identify the written symbol for this type of word. These words are generally mastered by the fourth grade, but poor readers continue to have problems with this type of word.

The second type of word is in neither the oral nor the reading vocabulary of the student, but can be easily defined through the use of more familiar synonyms. For example, a student may not know the meaning of the word *altercation,* but this word can easily be defined by the words *argument* or *quarrel.* Another type of word that fits into this category is a multiple-meaning word such as *bank, run,* or *bay.* A student may know one meaning of such a word but need a new or second meaning explained. It is estimated that one-third of commonly used words have multiple meanings. These multiple-meaning words are called *polysemous.*

Polysemous words may be historically related. For example, students may know that the word *coach* means someone who guides a team. However, they may not know that a coach is also a vehicle. This new meaning can be traced to what people in medieval England used to call the person who drove the team of horses pulling the coach. The term was later applied to tutors in college, leaders of crew teams, and even later to anyone who guided a team of spirited horses. Polysemous words may also have a specific meaning in a content area. For example, all students know the word *table*. However, in math, *table* has a very specific meaning much different from our everyday sense of the word.

The third type of word is one for which a student has acquired no concept. This type of word is encountered frequently in the content areas. The teacher must take the time to develop the concept through instruction before the word can be understood by the student. Words such as *fission* and *valence* are difficult concepts that are more readily understood after examples are given.

Words that are already in a student's listening vocabulary may be taught through language experience activities or other writing experiences; however, multiple-meaning words and words embodying unfamiliar concepts need more direct instruction. If teachers are more sensitive to the different types of words and the cost of each in instructional time, then perhaps students would learn more words through direct instruction.

# VOCABULARY INSTRUCTION

The research of Nagy and Herman (1984) has interesting implications for vocabulary instruction. These authors have estimated that in grades 3 through 9, students may encounter 88,500 distinct word families (a root word with different affixes) with more than 100,000 meanings in their school reading. Most students learn approximately 3000 new words each year. The number of unknown words a middle grades student encounters in a representative sample of 1000 words ranges from 15 to 55 words (Nagy, Herman, and Anderson, 1985).

Middle grades students seem to learn a large number of words each year. For the most part, a large number of these words are learned by the students on their own, outside of the classroom. Basal reading series and teacher's guides have been analyzed and found to suggest the instruction of only 290 to 460 words a year. So, it seems that students learn many of the 3000 words each year without direct instruction. Conversations with other students, exposure to communications media, and independent reading make large contributions to the growth of their vocabulary.

Surveys of classroom practice (Durkin, 1978–79; Roser and Juel, 1982) reveal that very little direct vocabulary instruction occurs. "There is no doubt room for improvement in the area of vocabulary instruction; but the size of the task is such that just teaching more words cannot be seen as the answer" (Nagy and Herman, 1987, p. 23). The following guidelines for instruction suggest ways to teach vocabulary in a more meaningful manner.

## Guidelines for Instruction

Although it is clear that increased vocabulary knowledge results in increased reading comprehension, how vocabulary instruction should be organized has been the subject of much debate in recent years. The preteaching of vocabulary has been shown to increase scores on vocabulary tests, but this instruction does not seem to improve scores on measures of general reading comprehension (Jenkins, Stein, and Wysocki, 1984). Moore (1987) maintained that the relative importance of words to a passage determines their subsequent effect on comprehension. Other researchers have differentiated between the kinds of instruction given. Stahl and Fairbanks (1986) found that vocabulary instruction generally improves reading comprehension, but not all methods seem to have that effect. Vocabulary instruction that promotes student involvement improves comprehension more than passive activities with words.

What does this discussion of vocabulary instruction actually mean to the classroom teacher? Let's begin with what should *not* be done. Thelen (1986) states, "Word recognition instruction in which definitions are looked up in the dictionary or glossary and then used in a sentence is meaningless and often results in rote learning and rapid forgetting" (p. 603). This exercise is probably the most used strategy for teaching vocabulary. However, the research clearly indicates that this technique is also the least effective for understanding and retaining words.

Research suggests the following principles as guidelines toward effective vocabulary instruction. The learning strategies suggested in this chapter apply these principles to instructional practice.

1. *Help students become independent word learners.*   Teachers should focus their instruction on helping students to relate new concepts to those things they already know. Graphic organizers, analogies, the study of morphemics (structural analysis), and the use of context clues are ways that can help learners make the connection between new learning and existing learning, thus giving them more power to figure out unfamiliar words in the future.

2. *Encourage active involvement.*   What students do with newly learned words is more important than the number of words presented. Teachers can help students associate new words with what they already know through a meaningful content or known synonyms. Students can also be shown how to make associations on their own in order to relate new words to their existing knowledge. Using new associations in writing and speaking is helpful to students. Direct instruction that engages students in the construction of word meanings by using context and prior knowledge has been found to be effective for learning specific vocabulary and important for the comprehension of related material (Nelson-Herber, 1986).

3. *Provide multiple exposure to words.*   The likelihood of a middle grades student acquiring an adult understanding of a word from one exposure in a natural context is very low (Nagy, Herman, and Anderson, 1985). If words are to be retained, they must be used in further reading and writing assignments. The introduction and use of new words should occur within a content area where

reinforcement can naturally occur. An obvious cause-and-effect relationship is at work here: the more students are exposed to a word that occurs in a meaningful context, the higher the chance of students using and understanding that word.

4. *Increase opportunities to learn new vocabulary.*   Reading is the best way to insure the learning of new vocabulary. The importance of silent reading every day cannot be overstated. If students read twenty minutes a day, they could learn 500 to 2000 additional words a year. Nagy, Herman, and Anderson (1985) made the following conclusion: "Our results strongly suggest that the most effective way to produce large scale vocabulary growth is through an activity that is all too often interrupted in the process of reading instruction: Reading" (p. 252).

5. *Help students develop a good attitude about learning words outside of the classroom.*   Activities and/or gimmicks that help students identify, say, hear, or see words studied in class help students experience repeated exposures in a meaningful context. Additionally, these applicative exercises help students develop the attitude that expanding one's vocabulary is a lifelong process.

## VOCABULARY STRATEGIES

The strategies presented below were chosen because they (1) help students become independent word learners through the use of context and morphemic analyses (structural analysis): (2) encourage active involvement by having students relate new words to previously learned concepts; (3) provide multiple exposures to new words through reading, writing, speaking, and listening activities; and (4) provide middle school students with opportunities for social interaction, emotional reassurance, and experimentation with abstract thought.

### List-Group-Label-Write

Taba (1967) first developed the List-Group-Label strategy as part of her Concept Development Model. This strategy can also be used as a diagnostic instrument to determine what students know about a subject and as an organizational tool to facilitate high-level thinking. Since the strategy involves the categorization and labeling of words, List-Group-Label also makes an excellent prereading strategy as well as a vocabulary development lesson.

▶   STEP 1:   **The teacher elicits from students as many words as possible related to a particular subject.**   A variety of stimuli may be used: the teacher can show a picture, read a story, show a film, or give a lecture. Pictures that depict the historical past of a city (such as Washington, DC in the late 1800s) may evoke responses such as horses, dirt roads, umbrellas, and so on. Words may also be elicited simply by asking students to brainstorm what they know about a particular topic.

▶ STEP 2:  **The teacher helps students group related items.**  Students determine appropriate categories and group words accordingly. One type of marking system is shown in Figure 6.1.

▶ STEP 3:  **The teacher helps students give a label to each group.**  After students have grouped related items, the teacher asks them to label each group of related words. The list in Figure 6.2 shows the marking system to identify the labels or concepts identified in Figure 6.1. The list was gathered by showing students pictures of Washington, DC at the turn of the century.

Taba's model extends this initial phase of categorizing into Interpretation of Data. To encourage students to think at higher levels, they would be asked to

FIGURE 6.1
Sample Marking System

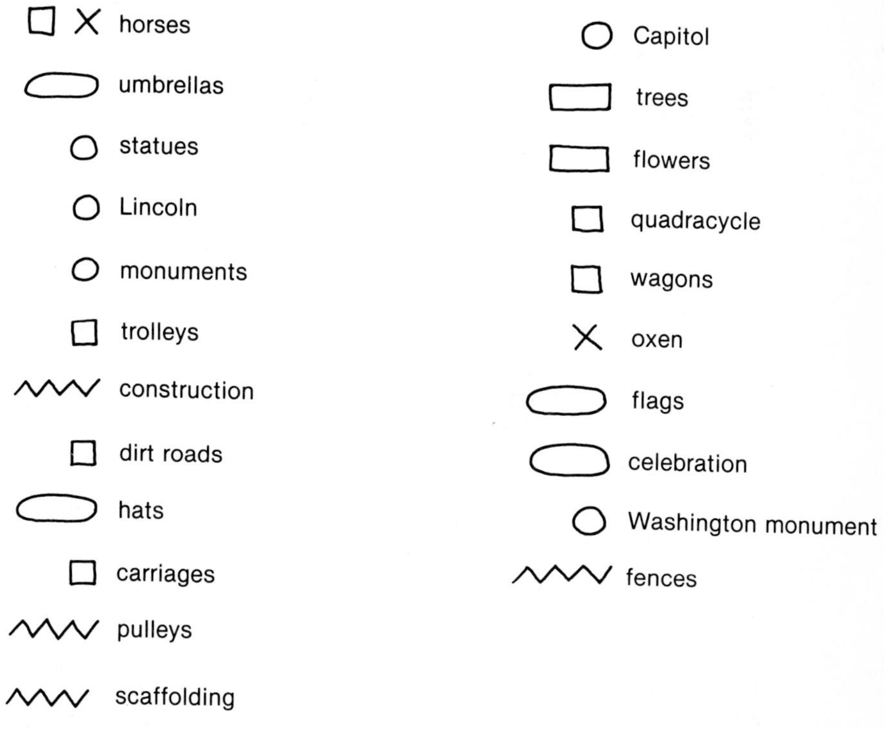

FIGURE 6.2 _____
Marking System to Identify Labels or Concepts

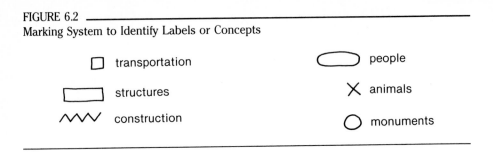

compare observations of old Washington with pictures of Washington, DC as it is today. They could then be asked to identify similarities and differences in the pictures. Further, the students would be asked to make a generalization concerning the similarities and differences noted. In the Application of Generalization phase, students would apply the generalization to a new situation and examine what would happen if the generalization were applied. To continue our example, after the List-Group-Label activity about Washington, DC, the students may form the generalization: "Transportation has changed due to advances in technology." The students then may be asked to apply this same statement to a new situation by considering the question, "How will transportation change in the next 100 years?"

Educators have used the Taba model for two decades as a means of promoting higher-level thinking and developing vocabulary knowledge. This activity provides motivation through opportunity for success. Every student can participate by sharing with the class his or her perception of a picture. Students can then develop in higher-order thinking through categorizing, interpreting, and making generalizations. In addition, students learn words by grouping them logically and in a way that makes sense to them.


## Possible Sentences

Possible Sentences is a strategy that allows students to become familiar with technical vocabulary and then to use this new vocabulary in meaningful contexts. Developed by Moore and Arthur (1981), it can be used simultaneously as a prereading lesson and a vocabulary lesson. Possible Sentences may also motivate students to read a particular passage by familiarizing them with some of the key concepts that will be encountered. This activity encourages students to use words repeatedly in speech and in writing. This strategy works best when familiar terminology is mixed with unfamiliar terminology. The Possible Sentences strategy consists of four steps. These steps will be illustrated by an example from a science lesson on volcanoes.

▶ STEP 1:  **On the board or transparency, the teacher lists key vocabulary from the chapter or reading selection.**

| | |
|---|---|
| magma | dense |
| volcano | mantle |
| molten (melted) | surface |
| lava | rock |
| eruption | earth |

▶ STEP 2:  **Individual students select two of the words and dictate a sentence using them.**  Each student writes a sentence and then some students share their sentence with the class. The teacher writes these sentences on the board exactly as they are dictated, whether or not they contain accurate information. The following sentences were dictated by eighth-grade students: "Magma is actually rock that has melted." and "Magma is formed in the mantle of the earth."

▶ STEP 3:  **Students read through the passage to verify the sentences.**   If the teacher desires, a competitive spirit can be fostered. Teams can be used to confirm the accuracy of the dictated sentences. The meanings of the sentences may be challenged by other teams. A sample reading follows:

### VOLCANOES

Did you know that some rocks can get hot enough to melt? This molten rock, deep beneath the earth's surface, is called magma. Scientists know very little about where this magma comes from but it seems to be made where layers of the earth's mantle are changing. The earth's mantle is a very thick layer of the earth reaching to a depth of about 2,900 kilometers beneath the crust of the earth. Because the magma is so hot, it is less dense than the rock around it and it tends to shoot upwards. When the magma shoots through a crack of the earth's surface, it is called lava. A volcano is then formed where the lava appears on the earth's surface.

▶ STEP 4:  **Students evaluate sentences and may generate new sentences.**   Students either verify the dictated sentences or dictate new sentences. These acceptable sentences are then entered into a notebook or incorporated into a future writing assignment.

Possible Sentences facilitates the use of language abilities other than reading. Students must use their experience to write logical sentences and share these sentences with the class. Others must listen to the associations made by their classmates. Finally, students must read to evaluate the sentences and verify that they match the meaning of the text. This strategy provides students with multiple exposures to a word by having them use and encounter the word in meaningful contexts.

## Contextual Redefinition

One of the most important aspects of assisting students in becoming independent vocabulary learners is helping them to use context effectively. The use of context allows readers to make predictions about unknown words and then to verify those predictions using syntactic and semantic clues. Contextual Redefinition (Cunningham, Cunningham, and Arthur, 1981) is a strategy that introduces new vocabulary in rich contexts. These contexts help students to define words and facilitate the retention of these words.

▶ STEP 1: **The teacher selects words that are unfamiliar to students.**   These are words that may be troublesome to students but are important to an understanding of the passage. For example, a teacher may identify such words as *lamenting, infinitesimal,* and *inexplicable.*

▶ STEP 2: **The teacher presents the words in isolation.**   The teacher asks the students to provide a definition for each unfamiliar word. Some guesses may be funny or weird, but all contributions should be accepted in the spirit of guessing. The class should then be asked to reach a consensus about the meaning of each word.

▶ STEP 3: **The teacher presents a sentence that illustrates the meaning of the unknown word.**   If such a sentence exists in the text, that sentence should be used. Different types of context clues, such as contrasts or synonyms, should be used to accustom students to making use of such clues. Following are some sentences that could be helpful to students attempting to determine the meanings of the previously mentioned words:

> Anyone could tell that Henry was deeply troubled. He always seemed to be *lamenting* his previous decisions.
>
> The animal ate almost nothing. In fact, his food requirements were *infinitesimal.*
>
> I told my teacher the problem was simply *inexplicable* because no one could help me understand it.

Using these contextually rich sentences, the teacher then asks the students to offer guesses as to the meanings of the new words. Students should be asked to provide a rationale for their guesses; this is important because it is helpful for students to hear the thought processes of others.

▶ STEP 4: **Students use the dictionary to verify guesses.** A student is asked to look the word up in the dictionary or glossary to confirm the guesses of the class.

Contextual Redefinition not only provides an opportunity for students to learn new words but it assists them in becoming independent word learners through the use of context clues. After this activity students will probably realize that trying to guess at a word's meaning in isolation is frustrating and often futile. Also, as mentioned earlier, students benefit from being actively involved in predicting and confirming word meanings. Finally, the proper role of the dictionary or glossary is emphasized throughout this activity—that of verifying guesses that have been made based on syntactic and semantic data.

## Semantic Feature Analysis

Johnson and Pearson (1978, 1984) developed Semantic Feature Analysis in order to acquaint students with the notion that synonymns are never the "same as," but rather they are "something like" another word. Through this procedure, students have the opportunity to make fine discriminations among word concepts. When using this strategy with general vocabulary, students learn the different connotations of words and better understand semantic relationships. This strategy also activates the students' prior knowledge. For example, if students in a science class are studying the effects of water temperature, the Feature Analysis shown in Figure 6.3 might be helpful. Students would first be asked to place an X on the continuum where the word would fit. Then they would list the words in order from freezing to boiling. Groups of three students could then share their lists. A lively discussion, with examples, should ensue as students attempt to agree on the order of their lists.

If Semantic Feature Analysis is used with technical vocabulary, students can discriminate between related concepts. The steps of Feature Analysis are illustrated using an example from a United States history lesson.

▶ STEP 1: **The teacher selects a category.** The category should consist of two or more items that are similar. The category selected for this example is treaties and alliances between countries.

▶ STEP 2: **The teacher lists related terms of the category.** The teacher places the related terms along the left side of the page, blackboard, or transparency, such as:

FIGURE 6.3
Semantic Feature Analysis

| | freezing ⟵————————————⟶ boiling |
|---|---|
| chill | |
| simmer | |
| cool | |
| frigid | |
| tepid | |
| cold | |
| hot | |
| frosty | |
| warm | |
| heated | |

association      alliance

coalition      treaty

confederation      affiliation

league

▶ STEP 3: **The teacher then lists features to be emphasized.** The features that will be used to describe the terms are placed across the top of the page, blackboard, or transparency, as illustrated in Figure 6.4.

▶ STEP 4: **Students complete the chart with teacher guidance.** A positive relationship is indicated by placing an "+" in the box and a negative relationship is indicated by placing an "−" in the box. "0" indicates that no relationship exists and "?" indicates that no consensus can be reached without further information. This part of the activity can be completed by small groups or the total class. A chart, as it was completed by an eighth-grade class, is shown in Figure 6.5.

▶ STEP 5: **Students and teacher explore the matrix, making observations about the chart.** The teacher may need to ask questions that elicit generalizations.

FIGURE 6.4 ─────────────────────────────────

Semantic Feature Analysis: Features Describing Terms

|  | Formal Agreement | Make Peace | More than Two Parties |
|---|---|---|---|
| alliance |  |  |  |
| treaty |  |  |  |
| affiliation |  |  |  |
| association |  |  |  |
| coalition |  |  |  |
| confederation |  |  |  |
| league |  |  |  |

After conducting numerous research studies using Semantic Feature Analysis, Anders and Bos (1986) have concluded that this strategy "enables students to learn relationships between and among the conceptual vocabulary and the major idea in the text" (p. 611).

FIGURE 6.5 ─────────────────────────────────

Semantic Feature Analysis: Indicating Relationships

|  | Formal Agreement | Make Peace | More than Two Parties |
|---|---|---|---|
| alliance | + | ? | ? |
| treaty | + | + | 0 |
| affiliation | 0 | 0 | 0 |
| association | 0 | 0 | 0 |
| coalition | ? | 0 | ? |
| confederation | + | 0 | + |
| league | + | 0 | + |

## Capsule Vocabulary

The unique feature of the Capsule Vocabulary is that it incorporates all four language areas into the process of building vocabulary. This strategy was originally developed by Crist (1975) to improve the vocabulary skills of college students in a language lab. However, it has been successfully adapted for use in middle and high school classrooms. Some teachers choose to use review words from previous units to give students an opportunity to read, write, speak, and listen to the capsule words. The steps comprising this strategy are illustrated by using a topic in which most middle school students are intensely interested: friendship.

▶ STEP 1: **The teacher prepares the capsule.** A group of words related to a particular topic is identified. These words can come from a previously studied chapter or a new topic. The list of words is handed to the students. For friendship, the following words were chosen:

| | |
|---|---|
| peer | cohort |
| ally | acquaintance |
| colleague | associate |
| companion | comrade |

▶ STEP 2: **The teacher introduces capsule words.** The teacher and students engage in a ten- to twenty-minute discussion on the topic, using as many of the capsule words as possible. The students try to identify these words. As each word is identified, it is checked off on the list of words and defined, if necessary. If students and/or the teacher are uncomfortable with the discussion format, a written format may be used, as suggested by Cunningham, Cunningham, and Arthur (1981). This format could consist of a paragraph containing the words. The students could underline the capsule words found within the paragraph.

▶ STEP 3: **Students practice using the words as part of their speaking/ listening vocabularies.** Students are placed into small groups where they have their own discussion. They are instructed to use as many of the new words in a conversation as possible.

▶ STEP 4: **Students practice using the words in writing.** The final step is to have the students write themes, dialogues, or stories about the topic, again using as many new words as possible.

Many educators agree that using all four language systems reinforces learning. This strategy provides students with an opportunity to speak the new words, read the new words, listen to others use the new words, and, finally, write those new words in a meaningful context. One young woman in Crist's original pilot group summarized the experience by saying, "It's cool—or I should say, 'gratifying'—to be verbose" (p. 149).

## Semantic Mapping

Semantic maps are diagrams that help students see the relationship among words. Semantic Mapping was first developed by Hanf (1971) and further developed by Johnson and Pearson (1978, 1984). Since that time, this strategy has been used effectively as a pre- and postreading technique, a prewriting activity, a study skill strategy, and a vocabulary development strategy, as presented here. Research supports the effectiveness of this strategy over more traditional techniques ( Johnson, Toms-Bronowski, and Pittleman, 1982; Karbon, 1984; Margosein, Pascarella, and Pflaum, 1982; Pittleman, Levin, and Johnson, 1985; Toms-Bronowski, 1983). Semantic Mapping is illustrated in the following steps.

▶ STEP 1: **The teacher selects an important word or topic.** This word should be familiar enough to students that they can readily list a group of words that relate to the word given.
▶ STEP 2: **The teacher writes the word on the chalkboard or overhead projector.** If a science class is studying clouds, for example, the teacher places the word on the board with a circle around it, as shown in Figure 6.6.
▶ STEP 3: **The teacher encourages students to think of as many related words as possible.** They can complete this step first individually and then as a group by sharing lists. The result should resemble Figure 6.7.
▶ STEP 4: **Students and the teacher then add labels to groups.** A completed map on clouds might look like Figure 6.8.
   Some teachers copy completed maps onto chart paper and keep these large-sized maps posted throughout the duration of a unit. As students learn new words or discover new relationships, those words or relationships can be added to the chart using a different colored marker. These charts give students a

FIGURE 6.6 ──────────────────────────────────
Semantic Mapping: Topic

FIGURE 6.7 ───────────────────
Semantic Mapping: Related Words

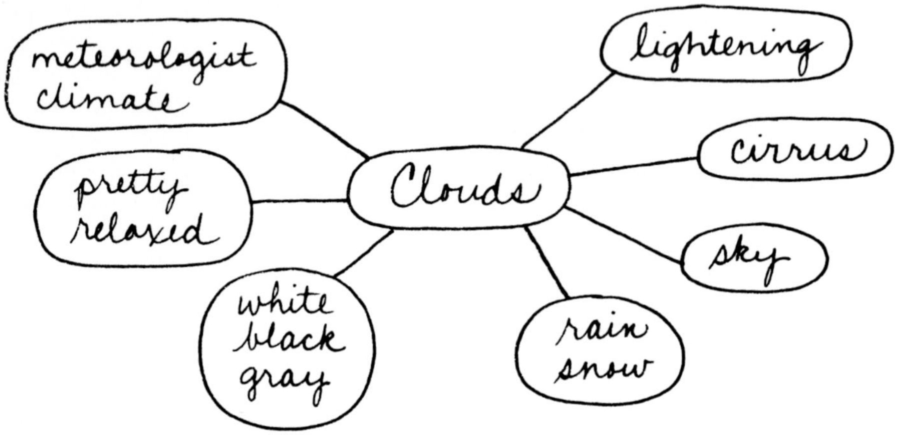

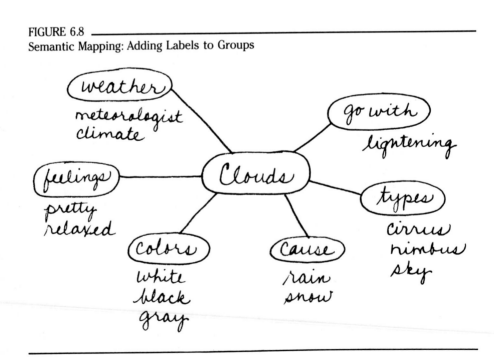

FIGURE 6.8 ───────────────────
Semantic Mapping: Adding Labels to Groups

concise overview of the key concepts within a unit and show how these concepts are related. They also enable students to relate new words to words that are already understood. One student drew the map shown in Figure 6.9 as he read an assigned chapter in physical education.

Because Semantic Mapping helps students see relationships between ideas and connect known information with new information, it is a valuable tool for developing the vocabulary and the conceptual understanding of students.

## Graphic Organizer

Originally called Structured Overviews by Ausubel (1968), Graphic Organizers have been used as pre- and postreading aids, study strategies, and vocabulary development activities. Graphic Organizers are merely a means by which relationships between words can be shown in the form of a diagram. This hierarchical order differentiates Graphic Organizers from Semantic Mapping in that semantic maps tend to group related concepts in any order. For example, a graphic organizer of the three types of words discussed previously in this chapter might look like Figure 6.10.

Moore and Readence (1984) reviewed the research on Graphic Organizers and drew four major conclusions. First, Graphic Organizers affect vocabulary test scores to a moderate degree; students who used this strategy tended to score slightly higher. Second, the maturity of the learner may influence the effectiveness of the strategy. That is, older students may benefit more from involvement with a Graphic Organizer than younger ones. Third, students who produce a Graphic Organizer after content is presented do better than those who only interact with Graphic Organizers before content is presented. The amount of involvement by the learner seems to be a significant factor in the effectiveness of this strategy. Fourth, teachers who led students through Graphic Organizers perceived themselves as better prepared and more confident than usual.

Graphic Organizers are generally thought to be an effective way to introduce new vocabulary before reading. Some teachers have found partially completed Graphic Organizers to be helpful in assisting students as they read. By having a partially completed organizer as a guide, students are better able to organize information and vocabulary hierarchically. The completed organizer may serve as a summary of the reading. Figure 6.11 shows a sample Graphic Organizer distributed to a science class before they were asked to read a selection entitled The Ocean Floor.

FIGURE 6.9
Semantic Maping: Student Example

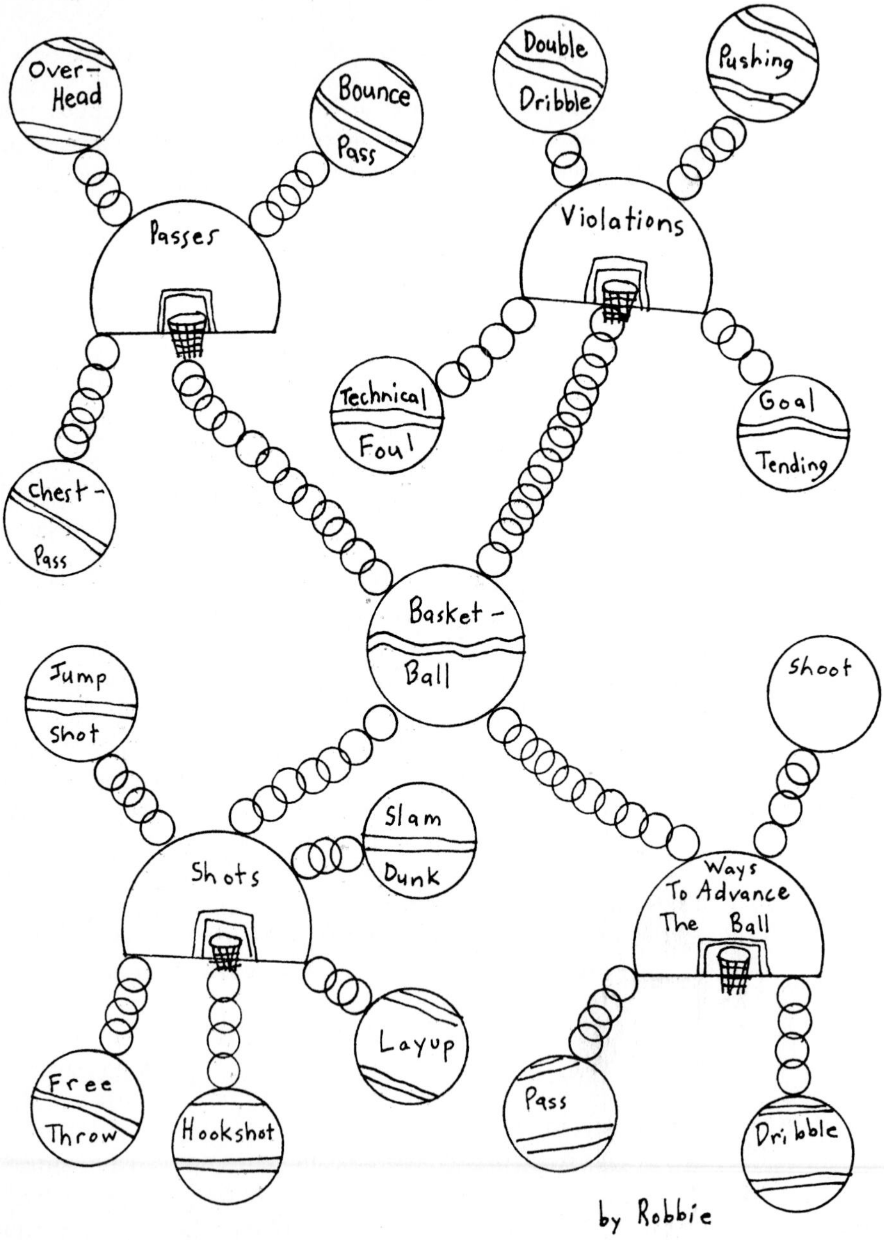

by Robbie

FIGURE 6.10
Three Types of Words

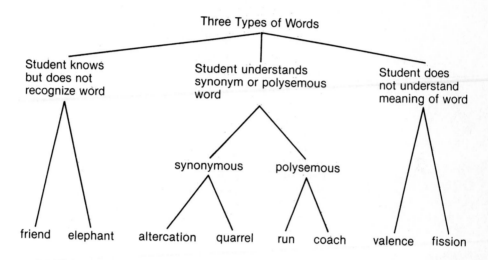

FIGURE 6.11
Cloze Graphic Organizer

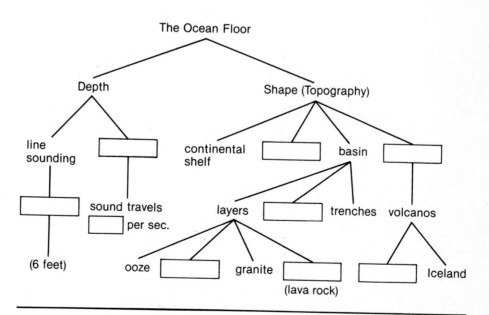

## Analogies

Analogies, especially in science, have been found to be effective in explaining difficult concepts by connecting them to concepts that are familiar (Bean, Singer, and Cowan, 1985). The key to analogies is that the teacher must base the analogy on information that is already familiar to the students. For example, after reading a selection on archaeologists and their work, students completed the following analogies.

1. Books are to students as _____ are to archaeologists.
   artifacts     bones     digs     sticks

2. Detectives search for clues to solve a crime like _____ search for artifacts to tell the history of a city.
   archaeologists     artifacts     clues     jobs

3. Voyages are to sailors as _____ are to archaeologists.
   digs     ships     artifacts     pots

Analogies are usually found on general achievement tests. It is helpful to students if they understand that there are various types of analogies. Practice with different types of analogies helps students become better at analyzing the relationships between words. To complete an analogy the students must first understand the relationship of the first set of words and then try to duplicate that relationship between the second set of words. Numerous types of analogies can be presented to students, some of which are listed below:

*Part-Whole*—arm:person :: wing:bird

*Degree*—tap:bang :: whisper:shout

*Opposite*—black:white :: night:day

*Cause-Effect*—slavery:Civil War :: oppression:Revolution

*Function*—key:ignition :: handle:drawer

Analogies can serve a "concretizing function" for students by making abstract concepts more tangible. For those who believe that many students in middle school are not ready for abstract thought, the use of analogies may be a bridge from the concrete to the abstract.

## Morphemic Analysis

In order for students to become independent word learners, they must be able to approach unfamiliar words strategically. As indicated, the use of context clues is one way to deal with unknown words; the use of Morphemic Analysis is another. Morphemes are words or parts of words that have meaning and cannot be divided into smaller meaningful parts. Breaking words into meaningful units for analysis has long been recognized as an effective way to ascertain the meaning of an unknown word. A word such as *autobiography* can be easily explained by breaking it down into its constituent parts. For example, *auto* means "self," *bio* means "life," *graph* means "write," and *y* means "an instance of an action."

The meanings of affixes, however, do not consistently apply. When learning the suffix *er* as "one who does something" (e.g., painter, writer), one student asked if a "mother was someone who moths." Moore (1987) recommended that the teacher emphasize the base words in word families and teach only the morphemes that are productive. For example, the prefix *tele* is very useful when applied to numerous words such as *telephone, telecast, telescope,* and *telegraph.* Moore, Moore, Cunningham, and Cunningham (1986, p. 70) suggested the following four steps in teaching morphemic analysis.

▶ STEP 1: **Write two familiar words containing the word part on the board and have students tell what the words mean.** Most students know that doctors are sued for *mal*practice when it is alleged they have done something wrong, and that a *mal*ignant tumor is a bad or cancerous one.

▶ STEP 2: **Underline the word part and point out to students its common meaning in the two familiar words.**

▶ STEP 3: **Write the word you wish to teach on the board in a sentence.** Ask students to use their knowledge of the word part to try to figure out the meaning of the word. For example, "If *mal* means something like 'bad,' *malnutrition* must be bad or 'not good' nutrition." Have the word read in the sentence to see if the meaning makes sense. You may want a volunteer to find the word in the dictionary and check the dictionary definition since morphemes, like context, give clues but are not always completely reliable.

▶ STEP 4: **Write at least one example of a word students know in which the word part does not have the meaning just taught.** *Mallet* and *mallard* are unrelated to the "evil" meaning of *mal.* Explain to the students, "This method won't work all the time. You shouldn't expect it to, but if your derived definition works in the context of the sentence, you have a good probability of being right."

# SUMMARY

For many years, educators have recognized the significant role that vocabulary knowledge plays in reading ability. Students learn a large number of words each year; research indicates that many of these words are learned outside the context of the classroom. However, teachers can enhance both the quality and the quantity of vocabulary learning by following a few basic guidelines. Students should be taught to learn words independently through the use of context, through morphemic analysis, and through proper use of reference materials. Students should also receive direct instruction on unfamiliar words and concepts encountered in their reading. This instruction should focus on helping students relate the unknown to the known and should give students ample opportunity to use these words and concepts in context. Students should also be exposed to a wide variety of spoken and written information. Teachers who help students build a well-organized and clearly understood vocabulary are doing much to promote those students' reading ability. The strategies suggested in this chapter provide middle school students with social interaction, emotional confirmations, and intellectual exploration associated with abstract thought.

## REFERENCES

Anders, P. L., and Bos, C. S. (1986). Semantic feature analysis: An interactive strategy for vocabulary development and text comprehension. *Journal of Reading, 29,* 610–616.

Anderson, R. C., and Freebody, P. (1981). Vocabulary knowledge. In J. T. Guthrie (Ed.), *Comprehension and teaching: Research reviews.* Newark, DE: International Reading Association.

Ausubel, D. R. (1968). *Educational psychology: A cognitive view.* New York: Holt, Rinehart and Winston.

Bean, T. W., Singer, H., and Cowan, S. (1985). Analogical study guides: Improving comprehension in science. *Journal of Reading, 29,* 246–250.

Chall, J. (1988). The beginning years. In B. L. Zakaluk and S. J. Samuels (Eds.), *Readability: It's past, present and future.* Newark, DE: International Reading Association.

Crist, B. I. (1975). One capsule a week: A painless remedy for vocabulary ills. *Journal of Reading, 19,* 147–149.

Cunningham, J. W., Cunningham, P. M., and Arthur, S. V. (1981). *Middle and secondary school reading.* New York: Longman.

Durkin, D. (1978–79). What classroom observations reveal about comprehension instruction. *Reading Research Quarterly, 14,* 481–533.

Graves, M. R., and Prenn, M. C. (1986). Costs and benefits of various methods of teaching vocabulary. *Journal of Reading, 29,* 596–602.

Hanf, M. B. (1971). Mapping: A technique for translating reading into thinking. *Journal of Reading, 14,* 225–230, 270.

Jenkins, J. R., Stein, M. L., and Wysocki, K. (1984). Learning vocabulary through reading. *American Educational Research Journal, 21,* 767–787.

Johnson, D. D. (1986). Introduction. *Journal of Reading, 29,* 580.

Johnson, D. D., and Pearson, P. D. (1978). *Teaching reading vocabulary.* New York: Holt, Rinehart and Winston.

Johnson, D. D., and Pearson, P. D. (1984). *Teaching reading vocabulary,* 2nd ed. New York: Holt, Rinehart and Winston.

Johnson, D. D., Toms-Bronowski, S., and Pittleman, S. D. (1982). An investigation of the effectiveness of semantic mapping and semantic feature analysis with intermediate grade level students. (Program Report 83-3). Madison, WI: Wisconsin Center for Education Research.

Karbon, J. C. (1984). An investigation of the relationships between prior knowledge and vocabulary development using semantic mapping with culturally diverse students. Unpublished doctoral dissertation. University of Wisconsin at Madison.

Margosein, C. M., Pascarella, E. T., and Pflaum, S. W. (1982). The effects of instruction using semantic mapping on vocabulary and comprehension. Paper presented at the Annual Meeting of the American Educational Research Association, New York (ED 217 390).

Moe, A. J. (1974). A comparative study of vocabulary diversity: The speaking vocabularies of first graders. A paper presented at the Annual Meeting of the American Educational Research Association, Chicago (ED 090 520).

Moore, D. (1987). Vocabulary. In D. Alvermann, D. Moore, and M. Conley (Eds.), *Research within reach: Secondary school reading.* Newark, DE: International Reading Association.

Moore, D., and Arthur, S. V. (1981). Possible sentences. In E. K. Dishner, T. W. Bean, and J. E. Readence (Eds.), *Reading in the content areas: Improving classroom instruction.* Dubuque, IA: Kendall/ Hunt Publishing Company.

Moore, D., Moore, S., Cunningham, P., and Cunningham, J. (1986). *Developing readers and writers in the content areas: K-12.* New York: Longman.

Moore, D. W., and Readence, J. E. (1984). A quantitative and qualitative review of graphic organizer research. *Journal of Educational Research, 78,* 11–17.

Nagy, W. E., and Herman, P. A. (1984). Limitations of vocabulary instruction. (Technical Report No. 326). Urbana, IL: Center for the Study of Reading. (ED 248 498).

Nagy, W. E., and Herman, P. A. (1987). Breadth and depth of vocabulary knowledge: Implications for acquisition and instruction. In M. G. McKeown and M. E. Curtis (Eds.), *The nature of vocabulary acquisition.* Hillsdale, NJ: Lawrence Erlbaum Associates.

Nagy, W. E., Herman, P. A., and Anderson, R. C. (1985). Learning words from context. *Reading Research Quarterly, 20,* 233–253.

Nelson-Herber, J. (1986). Expanding and refining vocabulary in content areas. *Journal of Reading, 29,* 626–633.

Pittleman, S. D., Levin, K. M., and Johnson, D. D. (1985). An investigation of two instructional settings in the use of semantic mapping with poor readers. (Program Report 85-4). Madison, WI: Wisconsin Center for Education Research.

Roser, N., and Juel, C. (1982). Effects of vocabulary instruction on reading comprehension. In J. Niles and L. A. Harris (Eds.), *New inquiries in reading: Research and instruction.* Rochester, NY: National Reading Conference.

Stahl, S. A., and Fairbanks, M. M. (1986). The effects of vocabulary instruction: A model-based meta-analysis. *Review of Educational Research, 56,* 72–110.

Taba, H. (1967). *Teacher's handbook for elementary social studies.* Reading, MA: Addison-Wesley.

Thelen, J. N. (1986). Vocabulary instruction and meaningful learning. *Journal of Reading, 29,* 603–609.

Thorndike, R. T. (1973). *Reading comprehension education in fifteen countries: An empirical study.* New York: John Wiley & Sons.

Toms-Bronowski, S. (1983). An investigation of the effectiveness of selected vocabulary teaching strategies with intermediate grade level students. Unpublished doctoral dissertation, University of Wisconsin at Madison.

# Chapter 7

# Building Background Information and Activating Prior Knowledge

Anyone who has worked extensively with computers knows that some computer manuals are written better than others. Some manuals are written in a "user friendly" fashion and some are not. Surprisingly enough, however, some people can begin to make sense out of even the worst written manuals. These people are usually already familiar with computers. That is, their prior knowledge of the subject is great, and this enables them to make up for the deficiencies of the text. Prior knowledge is one of the most important ingredients of comprehension. Johnston (1983) even went so far as to say that a test of prior knowledge may be an effective predictor of reading comprehension.

Johnston described the reading process as a "slot-filling" activity. That is, if a person already knows something about a topic, that person needs only to add more specific information—or to fill in the "slots." The more a person knows about a topic, the easier the slots can be filled; thus a smaller amount of visual information from the page is needed. On the other hand, the reader who knows little about a topic tends to rely more heavily on the text, using word recognition to build meaning, sentence by sentence.

I distinctly remember the day I took the SAT to enter college. Seated in a large auditorium on a college campus, I was asked to answer questions about passages I had read. The topic of one selection was "radar in bats." I struggled to understand the highly technical information about how bats use their radar. I pored over each word trying to make sense of my reading. I had many "slots" in my model to fill and I relied heavily on the text to make sense.

Generally, this overreliance on text inhibits efficient reading (Spiro and Taylor, 1980). On the other hand, if readers rely too heavily on what they know without attending closely enough to the text, they make reckless predictions about the meaning of what they read. A balanced interaction between the mind of the reader and the cues in the text leads to a more efficient understanding of the printed message.

## PRIOR KNOWLEDGE

Reading educators have recognized the value of background experience for many years; however, research on prior knowledge is relatively recent. As reading educators study the relationship between what readers know and how well they understand print, more precise terms have appeared. *Prior knowledge* is all the information and all the experience a reader has in memory. *Topical knowledge,* however, relates to the information a reader has on a particular topic. But readers must activate much more than what they know about a topic to have a successful reading experience. Knowledge about *social interaction* helps readers understand characters and actions. Knowledge of *text structure* helps readers predict what will happen next and confirms their understandings. The *metacognitive skill* of monitoring comprehension (discussed in Chapter 3) is another important aspect of reading to comprehend. All of these types of knowledge and skill come into play during the reading act. All learning seems to revolve around the condition that new information must be, in some way, associated with what is already known.

Not all prior knowledge is helpful, however. Sometimes misconceptions about a topic can hinder the learning of new information. Anderson and Smith (1984) found that students' "comprehension of science instruction is often affected by their prior beliefs or preconceptions" (p. 200). These researchers found that many children were strongly committed to their preconceptions and ideas about the world that were not consistent with scientific thinking.

Activating prior knowledge is one role of the teacher; another is to diagnose what students do and do not know. The prereading strategies suggested in this chapter can serve this diagnostic function. Instruction can then be adjusted accordingly. For reading to be successful, more time must be expended in the preparation to read, building the necessary background information.

The act of reading may be likened to a trip to an art museum. People with a limited appreciation for art may wander throughout the museum, glancing at paintings. For the artistically misinformed, the museum experience may serve only to reinforce misconceptions about artworks. An art student, however, may spend a good deal of time studying and analyzing a painting because prior knowledge compels the student to view the painting in more depth. The breadth and depth of prior knowledge on a particular topic partially determines how meaningful an encounter with print or any other medium will be. The extent and quality of prior knowledge will also, then, determine how new or dissimilar information is assimilated.

## Activating Prior Knowledge

Langer and Nicolich (1981) suggested that students should be helped to become aware of relevant prior knowledge and that teachers should judge whether or not that knowledge is sufficient for comprehension of the text. In some instances, teachers need to build background where little exists. The authors of *Becoming a Nation of Readers* (Anderson, Hiebert, Scott, and Wilkinson, 1985) stated:

> Systematic classroom observation reveals that preparation for reading is the phase of the . . . lesson that is most often slighted, or even skipped altogether. . . . Little focused attention is given to developing a background knowledge that will be required to understand the day's story (pp. 49–50).

Research suggests that students are not particularly good at drawing on their prior knowledge, especially in school settings (Owings and Peterson, 1980). Students may possess relevant information about the topic to be studied but not realize that what they know can be applied to what they are to learn. Therefore, it is important that teachers spend time to help students activate this prior knowledge. Vaughn and Estes (1986) argue that one-half of instructional time should be spent helping students connect new information to old. Time invested before reading will reduce the amount of time required to explain to students what they did not understand after reading.

In the past, teachers have provided students with learning activities that follow a reading assignment. Teachers have also provided certain types of study guides to aid students during reading. *Prereading strategies* include any activity that prepares the student before a passage is read. These activities help to bridge the gap between what readers already know and what they will learn while reading. In the past, the term *reading readiness* has been used to refer to the time that educators prepare children to read print. As reading theorists continue to define the acquisition of reading ability as a natural and ongoing process, readiness has come to be associated with preparing for any reading task. In this sense, prereading strategies can be considered "readiness" activities that prepare students for the reading task at hand. A good part of this preparation includes activating and building on students' prior knowledge.

## Assessing the Knowledge Base of Students

How does a teacher determine how much students know? Most of the time, this assessment takes place during instruction, often during the prereading phase. For example, the first step of the PReP prereading activity (discussed later in this chapter) is to have students brainstorm a particular topic. After the initial brainstorming session, the teacher may determine if the students lack the prior knowledge required to comprehend the text.

Another important aspect of this informal assessment is determining misconceptions about a topic. Often, students have misinformation that may interfere with their comprehension of text. Prereading activities provide teachers with the opportunity to clear up misconceptions before students begin to read about the topic of study.

Some teachers do not feel comfortable with informal assessments of prior knowledge. For those teachers who desire a more formal instrument to determine whether the level of prior knowledge is appropriate, or to determine which students may have a deficient knowledge base, the Word Association Task (Zakaluk and Samuels, 1986) may prove useful. (See Figure 7.1.) This instrument can be administered to an entire class and completed in a relatively short period of time.


# PREREADING STRATEGIES

Prereading strategies help students to activate what they know about a topic and anticipate what they will read or hear. Such strategies also direct students' attention to the major points in the reading or lecture. Teachers can also use prereading strategies to point out how a text or lecture is organized, to teach unfamiliar vocabulary or concepts, and to provide students with a purpose for reading or listening.

Knowledge of the structure of the text or lecture can help students recognize and record the most important information. For example, if students are to read a social studies text that compares two ancient civilizations, they may be directed to look for likenesses and differences with respect to certain characteristics such as religion, politics, economics, and so on. The teacher may help students further by pointing out that students may want to look for signal words such as *conversely, on the contrary,* or *like* to help them compare and contrast the two civilizations.

The prereading strategies described in the remainder of the chapter are separated into three categories: (1) building background when students know *little* about a subject, (2) anticipating information when students know *something* about a subject, and (3) organizing information when students know a *great deal* about a subject.

FIGURE 7.1 ———————————————————————

Word Association Task to Assess Students' Prior Knowledge of a Topic

*Oral Introduction*

This is a test to see how many words related to a given topic you can think of and write down in a short amount of time. You will be given a key word and you are to write down as many other words as you can that the key word brings to mind. The words that you write may be things, places, ideas, events—whatever you happen to think of when you see the word.

*Modeling and Chalkboard Demonstration*

For example, think of the word "king." (Write "king" on the chalkboard.) Some of the words or phrases that "king" brings to mind are queen/prince/palace/Charles/London/kingdom/England/ruler/kingfish/Sky King/of the road. Continue to brainstorm for other words. Add these to the chalkboard list. You may use two words, or phrases, long words or short words. Any idea is acceptable, no matter how many words.

*Practice, With Discussion*

Work on practice sheets. "Kitchen" and "transportation" are two highly familiar topics. A practice sheet for the word "kitchen" is presented below:
kitchen: ————————————————————————
kitchen: ————————————————————————
kitchen: ————————————————————————

Take the sheet with the word "kitchen" written on it. On every line, write a word or phrase that you associate with the idea of a "kitchen." Given students exactly 3 minutes. In each case, after the students are done, clarify the task by sharing ideas and discussing any questions.

*Reminders*

The following reminders are given during practice and during the actual task.
1. No one is expected to fill in all the spaces on the page, but write as many words as you can think of in association with the key word.
2. Be sure to think back to the key word or phrase after each idea you write, because the test is to see how many other ideas the key word brings to mind.
3. A good way to do this is to repeat the key word or phrase over and over to yourself as you write.

*Scoring*

Give 1 point for each reasonable association item (e.g., "coal" when the stimulus was "fossil fuels").

Give 0 points for incorrect associations (e.g., "wood" when the stimulus was "fossil fuels").

Give only 1 point for a series of sub-items (e.g., a list of various crops when the stimulus was "farming").

Give 1 more point of the category of such a series was named (e.g., for "crop" if that word appeared with a series of crop names).

———————

*Source:* Adapted from B. L. Zakaluk and S. J. Samuels, "A Simple Technique for Estimating Prior Knowledge: Word Association," *Journal of Reading, 30* (October 1986). Reprinted with permission of B. L. Zakaluk and the International Reading Association.

# BUILDING BACKGROUND INFORMATION WHEN STUDENTS KNOW LITTLE ABOUT A SUBJECT

Educators agree that background experiences and information are important in the learning process. A student raised in a rural town has a difficult time understanding the subway system in New York. Kindergarten teachers in a small rural town in northern Florida plan a trip to a mall in a nearby city so that the children can ride the elevators and escalators. Their small town has no two-story buildings. Experiences, of course, are best for facilitating learning, but reading can provide vicarious experiences for students.

Students must have some prior knowledge in order to assimilate new information, however; otherwise, the reading is meaningless. If teachers perceive that students know little or nothing about a topic to be studied, then prereading strategies become even more important in building the necessary information to relate to the unknown topic. The following three strategies can be used when students know very little about a topic: (1) Predicting and Confirming Activity, (2) ReQuest, and (3) Visual Reading Guide.

## Predicting and Confirming Activity (PACA)

Based on Beyer's (1971) inquiry model, this strategy, like most prereading strategies, uses student predictions to set a purpose for reading; this process is what most good readers do naturally. PACA allows students to make predictions about a topic, based on some initial information provided by the teacher, even if they have little prior knowledge. Given additional information, they can revise their predictions (or hypotheses) and pose them as questions for further reading.

Suppose that a teacher wishes to teach a lesson about the Hausa people of Nigeria and surmises that students will probably have little prior knowledge of the culture or geographical location of the Hausa. The teacher gives a short explanation that the Hausa people live in Nigeria and shows students where Nigeria is located within Africa.*

▶ STEP 1: **The teacher poses a general question.**  One such question may be, "What are the Hausa people like?"

▶ STEP 2: **The teacher provides initial information.**  The teacher places the students into small groups for discussion and provides them with a list of Hausa words and again poses the general question, "Based on the words

---

* This suggestion is based on Barry K. Beyer, *Inquiry in the Social Studies Classroom* (Columbus, OH: Charles E. Merrill Publishing Co., 1971), pp. 89–101.

commonly used by the Hausa, what are the Hausa people like?" Word lists, similar to the one below, can generally be found at the end of a chapter in content-area textbooks.

| | | | |
|---|---|---|---|
| cotton | goat | Sabbath | God |
| rainy season | trader | desert | yams |
| prohibition | merchant | ghost | farm |
| witchcraft | grandmother | aunt | umbrella |
| Koran | debtor | servant | slavery |
| walled town | tent | tax collector | son |
| blacksmith | camel | dry season | clay oven |
| mosque | mountain | sheep | mother |
| prophet | devil | gold | bargain |

▶ STEP 3: **Students and the teacher write predictions.** After small group discussions, the teacher again poses the question, "What are the Hausa people like?" in order to elicit predictions from the students. The teacher then writes these statements on the chalkboard and asks students to cite the word or words that caused them to make such a prediction. The teacher may also wish to record group responses using categories such as religion, politics, economics, history, and technology. Some typical responses are:

The Hausa people are Moslem.

They have a low level of technology.

The Hausa people are nomadic.

They have a structured society.

▶ STEP 4: **The teacher presents new information.** The teacher presents new information at this time. Pictures that are normally found in content textbooks are a good resource, but this additional information could be a film or story.

▶ STEP 5: **Students and teacher revise or modify statements.** Based on the visual information, students, assisted by the teacher, revise their predictions by confirming or rejecting their original hypotheses. For example, a picture of three Hausa people on motorcycles who are wearing sunglasses would help students understand the need to modify some of their original predictions. This picture might also elicit a new prediction relating to the extent to which the Hausa people engage in trade with other countries. A picture of a walled city might encourage students to reject the notion that they are a nomadic people. However, a picture of a mosque might confirm students' earlier prediction that the Hausa people are Moslem.

▶ STEP 6: **Students then read the selection in the textbook using their predictions as a purpose for reading.**    The teacher encourages students to keep their predictions in mind while reading. Writing predictions on the chalkboard for easy reference is often helpful.

▶ STEP 7:  **The teacher helps students to revise their predictions based on the reading.**    For example, suppose students made a prediction based on the word list that the Hausa people had a low level of technology, and the textbook described advanced techniques of farming used by the Hausa. The teacher would then help students revise these statements to reflect the new information. These statements, thus revised, may be used for further research or as an impetus for writing.

PACA may be used with a variety of topics for which teachers need to build background information. Teachers have found this strategy to be a good way to help students relate to the vocabulary and concepts in a text before asking them to use this information. In addition, making and revising predictions based on a limited amount of information is an excellent way to introduce students gradually to formal reasoning. Accepting the premise that knowledge is tentative and can be revised based on new information is the first step for moving students toward more abstract reasoning.

## ReQuest

ReQuest, an acronym for REciprocal QUESTioning, was developed by Manzo (1969). The purpose of this procedure is to help students develop an inquisitive attitude about what is to be read and to have students formulate questions, using them to set their own purpose for reading.

This strategy is dependent on the teacher being a model of good questioning behavior. The teacher answers the questions of students and asks thought-provoking questions in return. The students and teacher then read a predetermined section of text silently. After the reading, they take turns asking each other questions. The teacher models good questioning behavior by asking questions that promote higher-level thinking and the making of predictions.

Suppose, as part of a unit on space, a science teacher wishes to have students read about the geological features of the moon. Judging that students will have much folklore but little technical information about the moon, the teacher chooses the ReQuest procedure to stimulate thinking about the reading.

▶ STEP 1:  **Both teacher and students read the first sentence in the first paragraph of a selection.**  Let's suppose that the first sentence is, "The moon is the earth's nearest neighbor in space."

▶ STEP 2:  **The teacher closes the book; the students keep their books open. The students may ask the teacher any question they wish that relates to the first sentence.**  The teacher must answer as accurately and completely as possible. When pertinent, the teacher gives feedback to the students on the quality of the types of questions being asked. For example, questions that require analysis of synthesis can be praised. Questions such as the following may represent possible student responses: "Is the moon a planet?" "What are our other neighbors?" "How far away is the moon?"

▶ STEP 3:  **The students then close their books and the teacher asks another set of questions.**  These questions may include some that will help the students realize what knowledge they have relative to the topic, or they may be questions that students might emulate when their turn comes again. Students attempt to answer these questions as accurately as possible. For example, the following paragraph may elicit questions such as "What is the moon like?" "How do we know about the moon's surface?" and "What does it mean to have no atmosphere?"

> The moon is the earth's nearest neighbor in space. Telescopes on the earth can easily make out the main features of the moon's surface. Rugged mountain ranges, wide level plains, and hundreds of large and small craters can be clearly seen. These features stand out because there is no atmosphere to mask them. But it was not until the astronauts landed on the moon that the actual conditions on earth's closest neighbor became known.*

▶ STEP 4:  **Students and teacher begin reading paragraphs using the same reciprocal questioning technique.**  Students then read the next paragraph or two about the moon and its geological makeup, asking and answering questions as they go. Students will soon be able to project answers to such questions as "What do you think you will find out in the rest of the selection?"

Content area teachers who fear that teaching reading will take time away from their content enjoy using this strategy because it focuses on content while it facilitates effective reading abilities and questioning strategies. Eventually, students should be able to engage in self-questioning, thus improving their comprehension ability.

---

* From W. W. Ramsey, L. A. Gabriel, J. F. McGuirk, C. R. Phillips, and F. M. Watenpaugh, *General Science* (New York: Holt, Rinehart and Winston, 1979, p. 412).

## Visual Reading Guide (VRG)

Visual information, such as charts, tables, graphs, and pictures, is often ignored or used only casually by students and teachers. Students often flip through the pages of a book, randomly focusing on charts or pictures. Experienced teachers make use of this visual information by employing previewing techniques. Stein (1978) suggested that discussion and interpretation of visual information can serve as a way to build background information about a topic with which students have little prior exposure. For example, a twenty-one page social studies chapter entitled "The Roman Empire" (Cooper, 1982) contains the following visual information:

A photograph of the Coliseum today

A detailed but readable time line

A painting of Hannibal's army passing the Alps

A four-color map of the Roman Empire including roads and cities

A black and white photograph of Roman ruins in North Africa

A photograph of a statue of Julius Caesar

A black and white photograph of a model of The Forum made for a movie set

A photograph of a Roman arch found in The Forum

A photograph of Hagia Sophia or the Church of the Holy Wisdom

A photograph of the aqueduct with a caption explaining the system

A drawing of Romans building the aqueduct with cranes and pulleys

A drawing depicting everyday life in Rome

A photograph of the Appian Way

A cutaway of a cross-section of a Roman road

A photograph of the Roman baths in Bath, England

A color map of Ancient Rome including walls, bridges, and gates

A black and white photograph showing chariot races

An aerial view of the Coliseum

A painting of the Roman gladiators engaged in a contest

A drawing depicting life in Pompeii

A cutaway drawing of a typical Pompeian house

A cutaway drawing of ramps and towers built to protect cities

A photograph of the Pantheon (Rome) and the Rotunda (Virginia) showing Roman architectual influence in the United States

A teacher may wish to take a more or less structured approach to building background information using this visual data. For example, the teacher might direct students' attention to the picture of Hannibal and his army and ask students to speculate about what role elephants had in Roman history or why the Romans were clothed as they were. The answers to these questions may serve as a study guide to students while they read. Or the teacher may wish to use visual information to facilitate students' predictions about the content of the chapter. These predictions could serve to set a purpose for reading and could be checked for accuracy after the reading is completed.

Although this amount of visual information may seem lengthy, it is typical of the wealth of visual information available in content textbooks today. Visual information should be more frequently used to build students' background knowledge. Later, in reading, discussion, and assignments, students can use this acquired information to begin to formulate generalizations.

# ANTICIPATING INFORMATION WHEN STUDENTS KNOW SOMETHING ABOUT A SUBJECT

Students often know something about a topic, and reading will be more meaningful if that prior knowledge is activated before they read. Also, as mentioned earlier, misconceptions about a topic can hinder students' understanding of a selection. When teachers perceive that students know something about a topic, the following strategies can be used to help students share information and activate what they already know before reading: (1) Anticipation Guide, (2) PReP, and (3) Scavenger Hunt.

## Anticipation Guide

The purpose of the Anticipation Guide is to create a mismatch between what students may know and believe and what is presented in the text. Shablak and Castallo (1977) refer to this mismatch as "conceptual conflict" and suggest that this conflict plays a role in stimulating curiosity and motivation to learn. The Anticipation Guide was first developed by Herber (1978) who suggests that comprehension may be enhanced if students make predictions about concepts covered in the text.

The steps involved in this strategy are listed and illustrated below, using an example from a story in which a dress is stolen from a locker room during physical education.

▶ STEP 1: **The teacher identifies the major concepts and supporting details in the reading selection, lecture, or film.** In this story the major concept is "stealing."

▶ STEP 2: **The teacher elicits the students' experiences and beliefs that relate to the major concept(s) previously identified.** The teacher could ask students to write down all the words that they associate with the concept of stealing.

▶ STEP 3: **The teacher creates statements reflecting his or her own beliefs concerning a topic that may contradict or modify the beliefs of the students.** The teacher should also include some statements that are consistent with the students' experiential background and with the concepts presented in the material or lesson. Three to five statements are usually adequate. In this example, students would be asked to place a checkmark next to those statements with which they agree.

_____ a. Stealing is always wrong.

_____ b. Sometimes stealing is justified.

_____ c. Persons who steal should be punished.

_____ d. Honest people sometimes steal.

_____ e. Everyone steals sometime during their life.

▶ STEP 4: **The teacher arranges the statements on a sheet of paper, overhead transparency, or chalkboard.** The students individually respond positively or negatively to each statement. Students should then record their justification for each response in writing, so they will have a reference point for discussion.

▶ STEP 5: **The teacher engages students in a prereading discussion by asking for a hand count of responses to the five statements on stealing.** Students can then share the justifications for their responses.

▶ STEP 6: **Read the selection.** In this example, the reading would be a story about someone who had a valued object stolen.

▶ STEP 7: **The teacher engages students in a postreading discussion comparing their reactions to the statements before and after the reading.** This discussion may take place either in small groups or as a class activity.

The Anticipation Guide is an excellent method for promoting active reading. Middle school students particularly enjoy talking about value issues. As they move from the influence of their family to the influence of their peer group, it is important for students to have a forum for stating their opinions and considering the opinions of others. Additionally, when students can identify with the value issues involved in a story or passage, they tend to comprehend better on literal as well as higher levels of understanding because the information is more meaningful to them (Lunstrum and Irvin, 1979).

## A Pre-reading Plan (PReP)

Langer (1981) developed this strategy to help readers use what they know to understand new ideas. She also advocates using the technique as an assessment tool to see how much students understand the topic to be studied.

▶ STEP 1: **The teacher asks students to make a list of words they associate with a topic.** A social studies teacher may wish to discuss the topic of crime. Students would then list words such as *steal, hurt, jail,* or *murder.*

▶ STEP 2: **The teacher asks students to reflect on their reasons for making the associations.** A question such as "What made you think of that?" may help elicit responses. Through this process, teachers can help students become aware of the network of associations available to them and how to make maximum educational use of these associations. Also, by discussing reasons that one word is associated with another, a teacher can help students to cluster and categorize their responses. If students associate *jail* with *crime,* the students' rationale may be "because when people commit a crime, they are always punished." In Step 3 the teacher could explore this statement further by asking, "Are criminals always caught?" or "What is a crime?"

▶ STEP 3: **After some organizational patterns have developed, the teacher asks the students to elaborate on and clarify their initial responses.** Students, either individually or as a class, may be asked to use these patterned associations to write statements or perhaps a paragraph about the topic. The value of this activity is to encourage students to think beyond their initial response, integrate their thoughts with the thoughts of others, and organize their information before reading about the topic.

A teacher may determine through this discussion that the students' prior knowledge of a topic is insufficient and thus the reading may prove to be too difficult. In such a situation, an activity to build background information may be a more appropriate lesson at this time.

### Scavenger Hunt

Designed by Cunningham, Crawley, and Mountain (1983), the intent of this activity is to build an understanding of unfamiliar concepts before beginning a unit on a particular topic. This strategy is not only enjoyable for teachers and students, but it serves to expose students to vocabulary associated with a subject before the subject is actually studied. The steps to this strategy are as follows:

▶ STEP 1:   **A few days before a new unit of study, the teacher announces the topic for that unit and dictates to the class some of the key vocabulary words and concepts.**   Units that may lend well to such an activity are environment, democracy, and conflict.

▶ STEP 2:   **The teacher then divides the class into teams, and each team selects a captain or the teacher may select one.**

▶ STEP 3:   **Each team is given an identical list of terms for the scavenger hunt.**   Teams are allowed a limited number of days to gather all the information they can about these concepts. They may complete this assignment in or out of school (perhaps as part of a homework assignment). Information can be obtained from books, by asking others, or perhaps by sneaking a peak at the chapter. Students should be told that they need to *understand* the word and that just looking the word up in the dictionary or glossary will not be enough.

▶ STEP 4:   **On the first day of the new unit, each team shares what it found in its hunt.**   This allows every class member exposure to a wide range of sources of information. Students should be asked to use words in a sentence, explain its meaning by giving examples, and/or be able to answer questions by the teacher or other students.

▶ STEP 5:   **The teacher may wish to award points and/or credit for participation or successful completion of assigned tasks.**

Most middle school students seem to enjoy mild competition and group work if the undertaking is of interest. As discussed earlier, teachers have found that cooperative activities heighten student interest and motivation to study a topic before a unit begins and provides students with necessary prior knowledge to begin that study.

## ORGANIZING INFORMATION WHEN STUDENTS KNOW A GREAT DEAL ABOUT A SUBJECT

Teachers may wonder if precious class time is spent wisely on a prereading strategy if students already know a great deal about a topic. It is often helpful when dealing with a lot of information, such as a unit on the ocean, to organize the information for (or with) students before beginning that study. Some teachers construct a graphic organizer or semantic map with the students at the beginning of a unit, using a blue marker. As they learn new things, they fill in the new information with a red marker. Students and the teacher are always gratified to see the organizer or map become filled with more red than blue. This practice is also an excellent reminder that new information must be connected to what learners already know.

The graphic organizer and the semantic map can be used in all types of instructional settings and at all age levels. These two strategies can be used to strengthen vocabulary, as prereading or prewriting activities, to organize information during reading, or as a study guide for a test. These strategies will be discussed as prereading strategies with application, of course, during and after reading.

## Graphic Organizers

The value of graphic organizers, also known as the structured overview, has been recognized by educators ever since Ausubel (1968) first conducted his work on conceptual development. Graphic organizers introduce concepts and illustrate the nature of the relationships among these concepts. There are several benefits of employing this strategy: (1) The use of graphic organizers has a moderate positive effect on vocabulary test scores. (2) More mature learners obtain greater benefit from the use of graphic organizers. (3) Students perform better when they produce a graphic organizer after reading (instead of being presented with an organizer before reading). (4) Teachers report that they are more confident when using graphic organizers (Moore and Readence, 1984). The level of student involvement in the construction of the organizer also seems to be a significant factor.

Alvermann (1986) presented the graphic organizer as a vehicle for "improving students' main idea comprehension ability . . . as a device for cuing the reader about the relation of superordinate (more important) to subordinate (less important) textual information" (p. 211). She suggested that there are four primary types of organizational structures in textbooks. These structures include simple listing, time ordering, comparison/contrast, and cause-and-effect relationships. Graphic organizers have been used almost exclusively with expository text rather than narrative, story-type material. Aulls (1978, 1986) maintained that there are major differences in identifying the main idea in these two types of text. Therefore, the illustrations below represent only expository text.

1. *Simple Listing.*   A social studies teacher may assign a reading on the federal system of government. The graphic organizer shown in Figure 7.2, discussed

FIGURE 7.2
Simple Listing

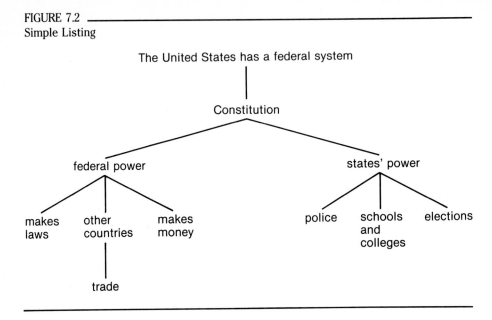

before the reading, may provide students with an overview that will help them understand their reading.

2. *Time Ordering.*   A time line often helps students understand difficult concepts such as the relationship of events in time. The time line in Figure 7.3 may help a student struggling with Russian history understand the temporal relationship of important events.

3. *Comparison/Contrast.*   A physical education teacher may wish to illustrate graphically the difference among team sports, such as that shown in Figure 7.4.

4. *Cause and Effect.*   Before asking students to read a section on the heart, a science teacher may share the graphic organizer shown in Figure 7.5 with students so that they will understand the cause-and-effect relationships before they begin reading.

*Cloze Graphic Organizer.*   As discussed earlier in this chapter, one type of prior knowledge that is helpful to readers is knowledge of text structure. Readers are more likely to comprehend new material if they know how the information will be presented. The example in Figure 7.6 is called a *cloze graphic organizer* because some of the information is intentionally left out. For example, if students were assigned a section in their science textbook about the products of the

FIGURE 7.3 ————————————————————————
Time Ordering

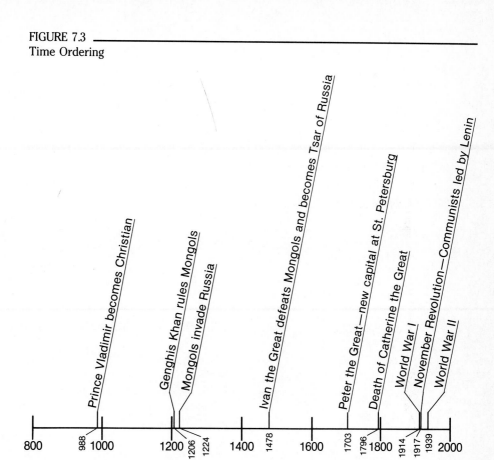

ocean, the teacher could present a cloze graphic organizer, discuss the organization of the text, and direct students to fill in the organizer either during reading or directly after reading. By using graphic organizers in this way, students become actively involved in reading as well as become more aware of the structure of text.

## Semantic Maps

Semantic maps are diagrams that help students see how words or ideas are related to one another. Circles and lines are used to show relationships between concepts. Hanf (1971) suggests mapping to help students learn how to think

FIGURE 7.4
Comparison/Contrast

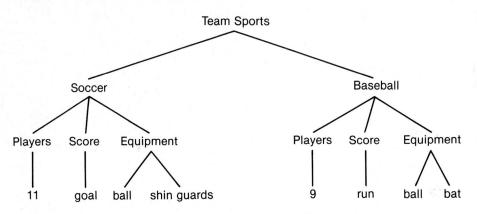

FIGURE 7.5
Cause and Effect

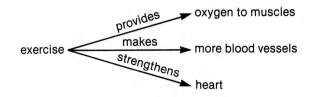

FIGURE 7.6
Cloze Graphic Organizer

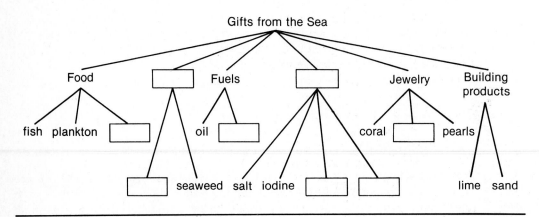

critically because in order to create a map, students must receive, organize, and evaluate information so that it makes sense to them. The map becomes a graphic display of main points, subcategories, and supporting details. *Semantic Mapping: Classroom Applications* (Heimlich and Pittleman, 1986) is an excellent publication that explains the many classroom applications of semantic mapping.

Figure 7.7 is an example of how one teacher used a map before reading to help students organize their ideas about hamburgers. Although students may not have historical information about hamburgers, the subject will certainly elicit some useful associations. Figure 7.7 shows a student-constructed semantic map.

FIGURE 7.7
Semantic Map: Hamburgers

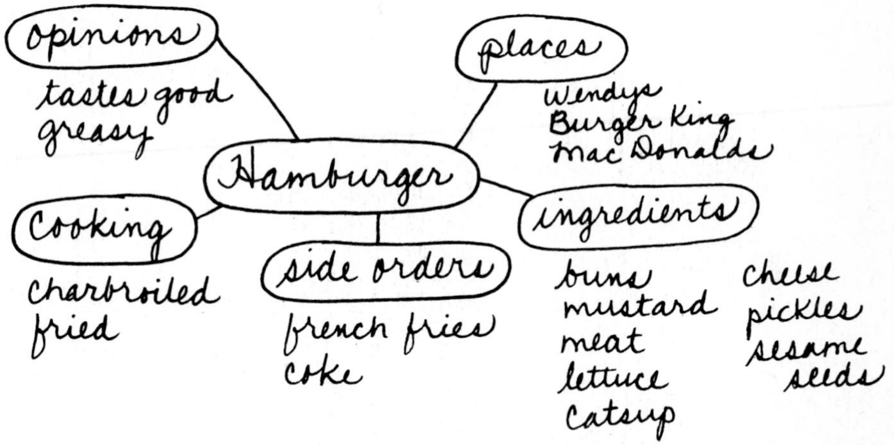

The teacher then asked students to read the following story about the history of hamburgers, using semantic mapping to summarize the information. Students were asked to compare their new map with the one they constructed before reading.

### THE HAMBURGER*

Hundreds of years ago, the Romans got the idea of eating meat and other foods between pieces of bread. They called their invention an offula. The Romans gave us the offula.

------

* From R. F. Allen and J. L. Irvin, *The Urban Reader* (St. Charles, Ill.: Educational Publishing Concepts, Inc., 1986).

Much later, around the year 1760, an Englishman named John Montague was in charge of the English Navy. He was also known as the Earl of Sandwich. The head of the Navy spent a lot of time playing cards. He did not like to stop just to eat, so he began to order meals placed between pieces of bread. That way, he could eat and play cards at the same time! Meat served between pieces of bread became known as "sandwiches!" The English gave us the sandwich.

For many years people in Northern Europe enjoyed eating raw shredded beef. The raw shredded meat was served on a plate without bread. It became especially popular in the city of Hamburg, Germany. For some reason, the dish became known as the hamburg steak. The city of Hamburg, Germany gave us the hamburg steak.

During the late 1800s, thousands of Germans came to America. They started calling their shredded meat dish a hamburger steak. Later the name was shortened to hamburger . . . and then sometimes just to burger.

As the hamburg-steak's name was changing, so was its appearance. Few Americans would be attracted to raw beef on bread. In 1904, at the St. Louis World Fair, the cooked meat hamburger got a lot of attention. Almost overnight it was a sensation. By the 1960s hamburgers were as American as apple pie and corn on the cob. Americans were eating hamburgers by the millions. McDonald's Golden Arches swept across the nation. Closely behind McDonalds were Jack in the Box, Burger King, Wendy's, Hardee's and a host of other hamburger places. Even the famous Mariott Hotel Corporation got its start selling root beer and hamburgers in Washington, DC.

The American love affair with the hamburger continues today. Every city or town in America can accommodate a visitor with a "burger all the way." The hamburger has even returned to Europe with the new, improved American hamburger sold in McDonalds restaurants and in many others. Our hamburger has gone international!

A map constructed by a student after reading "The Hamburger" is shown in Figure 7.8.

The teacher then used all three maps as a springboard for writing. Students who usually had difficulty knowing what to write used the maps to provide the information for their essay. Even students with very low writing ability produced a paragraph or two using this method. (See Figure 7.9.)

Semantic mapping has proven useful before, during, and after reading. As a prereading strategy, though, it serves to activate prior knowledge when used as a springboard for discussion or to organize a lot of information.

## SUMMARY

Prior knowledge is the sum of all experiences and information held in the mind of the reader. Reading is an interaction between the mind of the reader and the

FIGURE 7.8 ─────────────────────────────
Semantic Map: History of the Hamburger

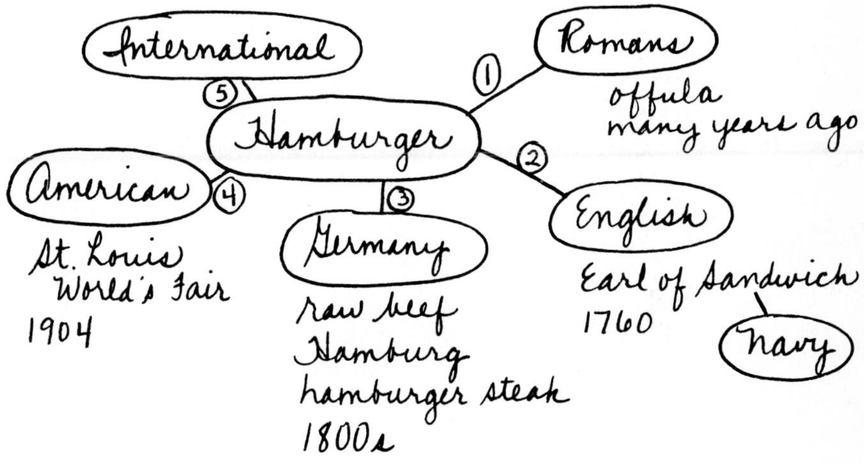

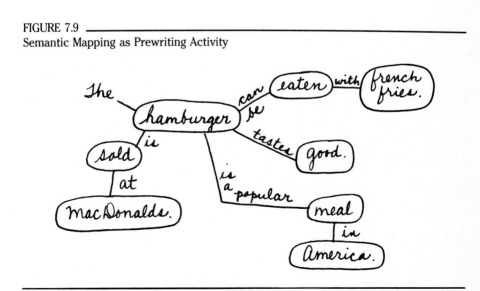

FIGURE 7.9 ─────────────────────────────
Semantic Mapping as Prewriting Activity

cues given in the text. Thus, to a large extent, the scope and depth of a reader's prior knowledge determine the quality of the reading experience. Activities involving prior knowledge can be grouped into three categories: (1) those that build knowledge related to a topic where little or none existed before, (2) those that activate and build on existing prior knowledge, and (3) those that help to organize large amounts of information. By building, activating, and organizing prior knowledge before reading, a teacher can enable students to bring the most and thus get the most from their reading experience.

# REFERENCES

Alvermann, D. E. (1986). Graphic organizers: Cuing devices for comprehending and remembering main ideas. In J. F. Bauman (Ed.), *Teaching main idea comprehension.* Newark, DE: International Reading Association.

Anderson, C. W., and Smith, E. L. (1984). Children's preconceptions and content-area textbooks. In G. G. Duffey, L. R. Roehler, and J. Mason (Eds.), *Comprehension instruction: Perspectives and suggestions.* New York: Longman.

Anderson, R. C., Hiebert, E. H., Scott, J. A., and Wilkinson, I. A. G. (1985). *Becoming a nation of readers: The report of the commission on reading.* Champaign, IL: Center for the Study of Reading.

Aulls, M. F. (1978). *Developmental and remedial reading in the middle grades.* Boston, MA: Allyn and Bacon.

Aulls, M. S. (1986). Actively teaching main idea skills. In J. F. Baumann (Ed.), *Teaching main idea comprehension.* Newark, DE: International Reading Association.

Ausubel, D. R. (1968). *Educational psychology: A cognitive view.* New York: Holt, Rinehart and Winston.

Beyer, B. K. (1971). *Inquiry in the social studies classroom.* Columbus, OH: Charles E. Merrill Publishing Company.

Cooper, K. S. (1982). *Europe, Africa, Asia, and Australia.* Atlanta, GA: Silver Burdett Company.

Cunningham, P., Crawley, S. G., and Mountain, L. (1983). Vocabulary scavenger hunts: A scheme for schema development. *Reading Horizons, 24,* 45–50.

Hanf, M. B. (1971). Mapping: A technique for translating reading into thinking. *Journal of Reading, 14,* 225–230, 270.

Heimlich, E., and Pittleman, S. D. (1986). *Semantic mapping: Classroom applications.* Newark, DE: International Reading Association.

Herber, H. L. (1978). *Teaching reading in content areas.* Englewood Cliffs, NJ: Prentice-Hall.

Johnston, P. (1983). Prior knowledge and reading comprehension test bias. (Technical Report No. 289). Champaign, IL: Center for the Study of Reading.

Langer, J. A. (1981). From theory to practice: A prereading plan. *Journal of Reading, 25,* 152–157.

Langer, J. A., and Nicolich, M. (1981). Prior knowledge and its effect on comprehension. *Journal of Reading Behavior, 13,* 375–378.

Lunstrum, J. P., and Irvin, J. L. (1979). Improving reading comprehension through value analysis. *Selected Articles on the Teaching of Reading, 30.* New York: Barnell-Loft.

Manzo, A. V. (1969). Request procedure. *Journal of Reading, 13,* 123–126.

Moore, D. W., and Readence, J. E. (1984). A quantitative and qualitative review of graphic organizer research. *Journal of Educational Research, 78,* 11–17.

Owings, R. A., and Peterson, G. A. (1980). Spontaneous monitoring and regulation of learning: A comparison of successful and less successful fifth graders. *Journal of Educational Psychology, 72,* 250–256.

Shablak, S., and Castallo, R. (1977). Curiosity arousal and motivation in the teaching/learning process. In H. L. Herber and R. T. Vacca (Eds.), *Research in reading in the content areas: The third report.* Syracuse, NY: Syracuse University, Reading and Language Arts Center.

Spiro, R. J., and Taylor, B. M. (1980). On investigating children's transition from narrative to expository discourse. (ED 199 666). Urbana, IL: Center for the Study of Reading.

Stein, H. (1978). The visual reading guide (VRG). *Social Education, 42,* 534–535.

Vaughn, J. L., and Estes, T. H. (1986). *Reading and reasoning beyond the primary grades.* Boston, MA: Allyn and Bacon.

Zakaluk, B. L., and Samuels, S. J. (1986). A simple technique for estimating prior knowledge: Word association. *Journal of Reading, 30,* 58–60.

# Chapter 8

# Comprehending Text

A recent conversation with two reading teachers—one young and only three years out of college and the other a fifteen-year veteran—delightfully illustrated old and new attitudes toward reading. The veteran reminisced how she used to teaching reading the "old fashioned way," teaching isolated skills, charting progress, and correcting workbooks. She told the younger teacher that teaching was much more fun now; the younger teacher responded that she could not imagine life any other way.

Reading comprehension has been viewed in the past as a collection of discrete subskills that could be learned and measured. Most teachers are familiar with activities that teach and assess students' ability to use such basic skills as finding the main idea, locating details, detecting sequence, and building vocabulary knowledge; comprehension was viewed as a collection of abilities that could be tested and evaluated. Numerous lists of comprehension skills, which seem to grow with each revision, can be found in state departments and school districts. These lists have served as a basis for curriculum as well as instruction.

After determining that a student lacked the ability to perform these tasks, a teacher could presumably improve comprehension by teaching the skills directly. The process of how a person went about performing these tasks (for example, finding the main idea) was given less emphasis than the final product (for example, an answer on a test).

Durkin (1978–79) examined the comprehension instruction taking place in reading and in social studies classrooms. After almost 300 hours of observation, she found that less than 1 percent of classroom time was devoted to comprehension instruction or discussion related to how one goes about comprehension tasks. Teachers spent the majority of their time giving assignments and asking questions. Additionally, she found that during social studies lessons, no time was spent on teaching reading comprehension, and only brief attention was given to vocabulary development.

This chapter presents the new view of reading comprehension and ways for changing instruction to put this theory into practice. Guidelines for instruction and strategies for teaching comprehension will also be discussed. "Changing the Face of Reading Comprehension Instruction" (Pearson, 1985, pp. 724–738) will be used as an outline for discussion of comprehension issues.

## THE NEW VIEW OF READING COMPREHENSION

These suggestions represent the new view of reading comprehension instruction based on the "research, theory, and practical wisdom" of P. David Pearson (p. 725).

*We Must Accept Comprehension for What It Is.*    The goal of reading the "old-fashioned way" was to approximate the text as closely as possible. The text was the primary stimulus. In contrast, Pearson and Johnson (1987) explain comprehension as a process of "building bridges from the new to the known" (p. 24). The way these bridges are built is by using prior knowledge, strategies, and knowledge of the task to construct the meaning. From this prospective, the act of reading is an active rather than passive task.

*We Must Change the Kinds of Questions We Ask Students About the Selections They Read.*    Teachers spend a good deal of their time asking questions (Durkin, 1978–79). These questions, however, are generally designed to check comprehension rather than teach comprehension. Teaching students to engage in self-questioning before, during, and after reading has been found to improve comprehension ability (Andre and Anderson, 1978–79).

The reasons for this improved performance may be that students are forced to pause frequently, determine whether or not they understand the text, and decide what strategic action should be taken next. Proficient readers naturally perform these tasks when they monitor their comprehension.

Self-questioning leads students to an active monitoring of the learning activity. It is critical that students be taught how to ask good questions. Teachers can model the process of asking good questions rather than simply using questions as an oral quiz. Students should be given the opportunity to practice and evaluate good questions as they read various content area paragraphs (Tei and Stewart, 1985). Self-questions can be content oriented or process oriented. Content questions focus on the content of the reading, such as "How do we get energy from fossil fuels?"; process questions encourage students to monitor and check their own comprehension, such as "Am I understanding this reading?" or "What will the author explain next?" (Davey, 1985, p. 26). Examples of content and process questions before, during, and after reading are presented below:

1. *Prior to reading,* students may ask themselves:
   a. What is my purpose for reading?
   b. What task will I be asked to perform (test, paper, speech)?
   c. What do I know about the topic?
   d. Do I know enough to skim the material or should I read slowly and carefully, perhaps taking notes?
   e. What is the organization of the text?
   f. What signal words might help me understand the text?
   g. What might I learn about from this reading?

2. *During reading,* students may ask themselves:
   a. Do I understand what I am reading? Does it make sense to me?
   b. What did I just read (summary)?
   c. How are the ideas in one paragraph (section) related to another paragraph (section)?
   d. What will I learn about next?

3. *After reading,* students might ask themselves:
   a. What were the major ideas in what I just read?
   b. What did I learn that was new to me?
   c. What will I do with this information now?

Davey (1983) suggested that students can learn self-questioning behaviors by cognitive modeling. That is, the teacher must "think aloud" and give personal responses to questions. Self-questioning charts are helpful to remind students the kinds of questions that will help them to monitor comprehension. The process may be carried out with pairs of students to help less able readers adopt a more metacognitive approach to reading. Typically, less able readers are passive, and self-questioning helps them to become more involved and active while reading.

Another activity that motivates students to ask good questions about content is to let them make up questions for the test. Teachers can share the kinds of questions they might ask and then let students share their own questions. Having these questions in mind while reading helps students focus on the major ideas in the reading and thus helps them remember the content.

*We Must Change Our Approach to Teaching Vocabulary.*    I recently asked reading teachers in a large, urban middle school to tell me how they taught vocabulary. Almost in unison, they told me that they assigned ten words from a list compiled by the state on Monday, that during the week, students were to define the words and use them in sentences, and on that Friday, students took a test. One teacher was upset because she only had time during the year to get through the R words! Unfortunately, this practice does not seem to be uncommon.

An entire chapter in this book is devoted to vocabulary instruction, not because it should be separated from comprehension instruction, but because the meaningful study of vocabulary is important to comprehension. Johnson and Pearson (1978, 1984) suggested that being able to understand and use a word is more important than merely recognizing a word and that there is a difference in these levels of understanding. Vocabulary is, of course, part of the comprehension process.

*We Must Change the Way We Teach Comprehension Skills.*    Durkin's (1978–79) observations revealed that teachers were testing *but not teaching* comprehension. Also, teacher's manuals were not very helpful in guiding teachers to provide comprehension instruction (Durkin, 1981). The teaching of comprehension must be strategic. That is, through guided instruction, teachers must show students how to become independent learners. The teaching of comprehension must also facilitate metacognition or the ability to monitor one's own comprehension. The two aspects of learning that will be discussed in this section are teaching strategic reading and developing metacognitive skill.

Much of the content that middle grades students learn in school today will be out of date by the time they are adults. Some of what we teach them will be wrong. It seems only logical, then, to focus our attention and instruction on teaching them how to learn—from reading and from listening—rather than to focus on content only. Students need "to design, monitor, evaluate, and revise their own plans for learning" (Brown, 1982, p. 26).

Students need to be taught what to do when they are reading something that does not make sense to them. Efficient readers do something about the misunderstanding. They reread the passage, they skip ahead for clues, they stop and ask themselves a question, or they review their prior knowledge to see if they can relate something known to this new information. The more that students know about the process of reading and how to cope with it, the better readers they will become. This means, of course, that teachers must understand the nature of reading and learning.

The best strategy to improve understanding is not always rereading the passage slowly and carefully. Reading to learn from text involves remembering main points, rereading important sections, slowing down or speeding up reading, and monitoring the success of various strategic reading behaviors. Most students do not naturally acquire these abilities; they must be taught how and when to use them.

Part of teaching students to become strategic learners is to help them develop metacognitive skills. Proficient readers monitor their own comprehension and are able to apply remedial strategies as needed. These strategies may include ignoring a trouble spot and reading on, rereading a part of the text, or consulting an expert source such as a dictionary (Collins and Smith, 1980). The application of these strategies depends on the purpose for reading. For example, when reading for pleasure, a reader may skip over a misunderstood passage; however, if studying for a test, the reader may consult a teacher for clarification. When students read to remember, they must have some awareness of their own understanding. They must be alert to "comprehension failure" and call upon their repertoire of strategies to fix the misunderstanding.

Younger and poorer readers are unaware that they must attempt to make sense of text. Generally, they focus on the decoding process and forget that the purpose for reading is to gain meaning and to remember the main ideas of what is read. Older and more able readers *do* notice comprehension failure and take action to improve it. Generally, more able middle school readers were found to look back, look ahead, or consult another source when they did not understand what they were reading. They monitored and corrected comprehension failures while reading text (Garner and Reis, 1981).

Metacognitive skills usually do not fully develop in students until late adolescence, but much can be done to enhance this ability during the middle level years. Before students can use metacognitive skills, they must become aware of text, their own ability, how to interpret the demands of a task, and the best ways to interact with text in order to maximize learning. Metacognitive skills include: (1) clarifying the purposes of reading, understanding both the explicit and implicit task demands; (2) identifying the important aspects of a message; (3) focusing attention on major content rather than trivia; (4) monitoring ongoing activities to determine whether comprehension is occurring; (5) engaging in self-questioning to determine whether goals are being achieved; and (6) taking corrective action when failures in comprehension are detected (Brown, 1982).

So, at the middle level, metacognitive skills can be facilitated, but not expected. One teacher asked students to write a short journal entry after each class to help them become more aware of their own learning and to give the teacher feedback on student learning. Periodically, students were asked to write journal summaries in order to draw conclusions about their learning.

*We Must Begin to Develop Curricular Materials that Capitalize on the Fact that Comprehension and Composition are Remarkably Similar in Process.*    I heard a middle school language arts teacher say that she never assigned a reading task without an accompanying writing task. Both reading and writing are acts of composition. Pearson (1985, pp. 734, 735) stated:

> The whole process of comprehension is much more active, constructive, and reader-based than our older theories suggested. No longer can we think of comprehension as passive, receptive, and text-based. . . . Suppose a group of seventh graders rewrites a part of a chapter in their science text to make it more understandable to a group of sixth graders. Is this composition or comprehension? I cannot tell.

Reading can be used to understand writing and writing can be used to understand reading. Instruction, assignments, and curricular material must change to reflect this new understanding in order to take advantage of the similarity between the process of comprehending and composition.

*We Must Change Our Conception of the Teacher's Role in the Reading Program.*    The goal of comprehension instruction is to help students become independent learners. Toward this end, teachers model, guide, and provide feedback rather than manage competencies. Teachers diagnose as they teach so they know how much responsibility students can handle. Pearson (1985) suggested that educators "replace the metaphor of teacher as manager with a metaphor of teacher as teacher" (p. 737). The following guidelines for instruction reflect this new view of the role of the teacher.

## GUIDELINES FOR INSTRUCTION

Educators have made great strides toward the development of a theory of reading in the last decade. The following guidelines for instruction may be helpful to middle level educators in designing instruction.

1. *Focus on the process of comprehension and move toward independent learning.*    The goal of instruction should be to improve the students' abilities to comprehend text, without the teacher's assistance. The emphasis during instruction should be on students acquiring the ability to use comprehension strategies on their own. All too often teachers are interested merely in the product, having students pass the test or exhibit the skill, rather than developing within students a true understanding of the process of comprehending.

This approach is often difficult for teachers because it means a transfer of control from the teacher to the student. Through guidance and discussion, teachers can help students become more metacognitively aware of the strategies they use to comprehend written text.

2. *Facilitate comprehension instruction before, during, and after reading.* The importance of building background information and activating prior knowledge *before* asking students to read was the focus of Chapter 7. Numerous ways of using prereading strategies to facilitate comprehension were presented. Equally as important as comprehension before reading is teaching students ways of being actively involved *during* reading. Students should be encouraged to monitor their own comprehension. Students should also be shown how to organize information *after* they read. This is especially necessary when students are studying or organizing information for later retrieval.

3. *Reinforce and develop reading abilities through writing.* To express one's thoughts clearly in writing, one must have the ability to organize and relate information in an understandable manner. Good reading, like effective writing, involves the creative cognitive processes by building relationships between the text and the schema of the reader. Learning to read with comprehension, then, uses the same generative skills as learning to write.

Students should be taught to "read like a writer" (Harris and Sipay, 1985). Studies (Stotsky, 1983; Squire, 1983) have shown that good writers are usually good readers, tend to read more, and produce more syntactically mature writing than poorer readers. Flood and Lapp (1986) contend that writing instruction can enhance reading development. By assigning writing tasks with reading tasks, teachers reinforce reading through writing and writing through reading.

4. *Encourage students to look back.* Teachers sometimes wonder if they should allow the students to "look back" to the reading to complete assignments or answer questions. The answer is "Yes!" In fact, referring to the text should be encouraged. Looking back allows students to revisit something encountered in the middle or beginning of the text after having completed the reading. Therefore, reference to the text facilitates comprehension and enables students to integrate ideas.

5. *Think aloud.* Many strategies can be illustrated and demonstrated by sharing your own reasoning processes with students (Davey, 1983). It is also helpful for students to share their own thought processes with teachers and other students; the students with whom they share they thought processes benefit from following another's thinking.

6. *Make questions and comprehension assessment compatible with the kinds of learning encouraged.* Students tend to understand stories better if questions focus on integrating story parts rather than on strict recall of information (Pearson, 1985). Students should be evaluated on what they understand, not what they remember.

# COMPREHENSION STRATEGIES

The strategies presented here are consistent with the guidelines for instruction just presented and have been reported to be successful with middle grades students. Strategies will be presented in three categories: (1) teacher-directed activities that facilitate comprehension before, during, and after reading; (2) comprehension-monitoring activities; and (3) study guides.

# TEACHER-GUIDED STRATEGIES

The strategies presented below provide teachers with the opportunity to model thinking processes and guide student thinking. All strategies promote comprehension before, during, and after reading.

## Reciprocal Teaching

Every teacher understands the old saying that "to teach is to learn twice." Developed and validated by Palincsar and Brown (1984), Reciprocal Teaching provides the opportunity for both teacher guidance and modeling and eventual student independence. With this strategy, the adult and the students take turns assuming the role of the teacher.

Palincsar and Brown chose the four activities of this procedure—self-questioning, summarizing, clarifying, and predicting—because they aid in *fostering* comprehension and they aid in *monitoring* comprehension.

▶ STEP 1: **Students and teacher read a short section of text together.** The reading should not be lengthy; one or two paragraphs is sufficient. Students who have difficulty reading the text alone can be paired with a more proficient reader.

▶ STEP 2: **Students are given about three minutes to summarize the content, formulate questions, and predict the next passage.** This step is not necessary in Reciprocal Teaching, but some teachers have found that by including this step, all students in the class can respond to the steps in the strategy and become actively involved in the discussion.

▶ STEP 3: **The teacher (student or adult) asks one or more "teacher-like" questions.** This activity allows students to practice self-questioning and to determine important points that may be asked on a test later.

▶ STEP 4: **The teacher (student or adult) summarizes the content.** Other students may add comments from their summaries if they choose.

▶ STEP 5: **The teacher (student or adult) asks for clarifying ques-**

**tions.**   At this point, students ask questions on parts they found difficult or needed some clarification. The teacher can ask questions and then entertain any from the class.

▶   STEP 6:   **The teacher (student or adult) makes a prediction about the future content.**   Students may add to their predictions.

▶   STEP 7:   **Another teacher is chosen and the procedure is repeated until all of the assigned content is read.**

Reciprocal Teaching generally does not run smoothly the first time it is tried. But as students become more and more proficient and comfortable in the steps, it can be a powerful tool for helping students understand and internalize the comprehension process. Over time, it is not necessary to think of Reciprocal Teaching as a series of steps, but rather as a dialogue or discussion for the purpose of understanding the text.

This strategy has been the object of much investigation (Brown and Palincsar, 1987; Palincsar, 1984; Palincsar and Brown, 1985a, 1985b). These researchers implemented the Reciprocal Teaching procedure in six middle school remedial reading classrooms. Those students learning reciprocal teaching improved their comprehension to a much larger degree than the control group. The technique was used in small and large heterogeneous groups (Palincsar and Brown, 1984). Teachers also reported that they experienced fewer behavior problems because students were actively involved in the lesson and enjoyed playing the role of the teacher.

## The K-W-L Plus

Developed by Ogle (1986), the K-W-L provides an organization for students to list (1) what they *know* (K) about a topic, (2) what they *want* (W) to learn about a topic, and (3) what they *learned* (L) about a topic. This activity can be completed individually, in small groups, or with the entire class. Group discussions can help students generate ideas and foster interest in the subject. This strategy is simple but effective. The following steps illustrate how this strategy might be used with a topic such as American Indians.

▶   STEP 1:   **The teacher provides a chart in which students fill in the K column—what they know about a topic.**   This step is designed to activate prior and topical knowledge and allow students to brainstorm ideas. After brainstorming as a class or small group, students fill in the Know column individually. (See Figure 8.1.)

▶   STEP 2:   **Students categorize the information they have generated and anticipate categories of information they may find in the reading.**   These categories serve as an impetus for further information and anticipation about the topic. Categories about the American Indians may be Location, Food, Customs, and Ways of Living.

FIGURE 8.1 ————————————————————————————————————
K-W-L: Know Column

| K (Know) | W (Want to Know) | L (Learned) |
|---|---|---|
| had ceremonies<br>ate berries<br>lived in America<br>lived in teepees<br>hunted<br>made canoes | | |

▶ STEP 3:  **The teacher leads a discussion to help students pull together information and formulate questions for reading.**  The teacher may wish to write statements on the chalkboard; in this way students' knowledge can be shared. Most students know that some American Indians lived in teepees, others may also know that other Indians lived in huts. Statements may be revised as the discussion continues.

▶ STEP 4:  **As a result of sharing and discussion, students then fill in the W column of the chart.**  This step may be completed either individually or in a group. This step is designed to help the student anticipate information. A sample chart may look like Figure 8.2.

▶ STEP 5:  **Students read the selection.**  The text should be divided into manageable units. Students should be encouraged to interrupt their reading after one or two paragraphs to check to see if any of their questions were answered. As students have additional questions, they can add them to the W column.

▶ STEP 6:  **Students fill in the L column of the chart listing the things that they learned from the reading.**  A completed chart may look like Figure 8.3. The primary value of this part of the activity is that information is shared among the students and a purpose is set for their reading. Thus this strategy activates and builds on the prior and topical knowledge of the individual but also of the class as a whole. Students learn to see each other as sources of information, an experience which seems to foster the emotional well-being of the early adolescent.

▶ STEP 7:  **Mapping: Students use the K-W-L worksheet to construct a semantic map.**  Semantic maps help students to understand relationships

FIGURE 8.2
K-W-L: Want to Know Column

| K<br>(Know) | W<br>(Want to Know) | L<br>(Learned) |
|---|---|---|
| had ceremonies<br><br>ate berries<br><br>lived in America<br><br>lived in teepees<br><br>hunted<br><br>made canoes<br>LOCATION<br>FOOD<br>CUSTOMS<br>WAYS OF LIVING | Did Indians live in one place?<br><br>Did they use stone tools?<br><br>Did they domesticate the dog?<br><br>Did they believe in spirits?<br><br>How did they make pottery? | |

between ideas. The categories established before reading may be used as the major headings of the map. The information learned during reading can serve as supporting data for the map. A sample map of American Indians is presented in Figure 8.4.

▶ STEP 8: **Summarizing: Students use the map to produce a summary.** Preparing a written summary has been shown to improve comprehension (Brown and Day, 1983). The categories on the map can be numbered and serve as topic sentences.

The K-W-L Plus strategy has been used successfully in middle school classrooms and has been found to improve comprehension and summarizing abilities as well as enhance a students' self-concepts (Carr and Ogle, 1987). It is an activity that involves students in the learning process before, during, and after reading a passage.

FIGURE 8.3 ────────────────
K-W-L: Learned Column

| K<br>(Know) | W<br>(Want to Know) | L<br>(Learned) |
|---|---|---|
| had ceremonies<br><br>ate berries<br><br>lived in America<br><br>lived in teepees<br><br>hunted<br><br>made canoes<br>LOCATION<br>FOOD<br>CUSTOMS<br>WAYS OF LIVING | Did Indians live in one place?<br><br>Did they use stone tools?<br><br>Did they domesticate the dog?<br><br>Did they believe in spirits?<br><br>How did they make pottery? | many different tribes in America<br><br>used many different kinds of tools<br><br>rode horses, had dogs, cooked many dishes<br><br>lived off the land<br><br>had sophisticated religion |

## Guided Reading Procedure

The Guided Reading Procedure (GRP) was developed by Manzo (1975). The purpose of this procedure is to (1) assist students in the recall of specific information, (2) improve the students' ability to generate their own questions as they read, (3) improve the students' ability to organize information, and (4) help students understand the process and importance of self-correction. The reading selection should be short enough to be completed in one brief sitting— approximately seven to ten minutes. The following example is used to illustrate the steps of the GRP. The example is based on "Feathered Friend" by Arthur C. Clarke (1958).

> The story is about life on a space station. Sven, the main character, smuggles a canary to the space station. Claribel soon becomes everyone's pet. One

FIGURE 8.4 ———————————————————————————
Semantic Map from K-W-L Worksheet

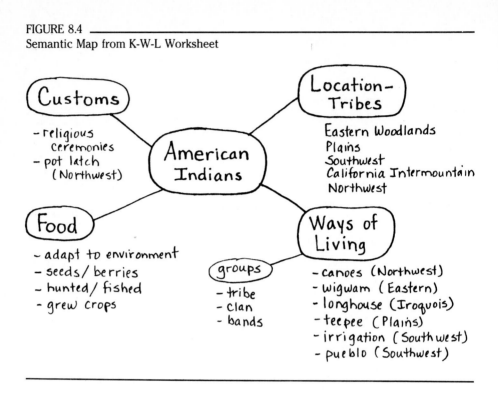

morning, Sven, feeling drowsy and heavy with sleep, finds Claribel feet up and looking rather limp. Oxygen revives Claribel. Because of this incident, the crew discoveres a leak in the oxygen system. Claribel saved the day.

▶ STEP 1: **The teacher prepares students for the reading assignment.**   The teacher should lead a discussion that motivates students to read the selection, activates prior knowledge, and helps them to identify expectations about the reading. For the story, "Feathered Friends," the teacher leads a discussion about what it would be like to live in a space station and what would be the assets and liabilities of having different animals as pets there.
▶ STEP 2: **Students read the selection silently.**
▶ STEP 3: **The teacher asks students to recall information without looking at their books.**   They may recall central ideas or details. All ideas are listed on the board or overhead. The information for this story might look like this:

Claribel needed oxygen

Sven smuggled Claribel on board the space station

The alarm did not go off

Sven was a big man

Claribel could hang in the air

Everyone wakes up drowsy

Claribel appears dead

The crew tried to hide Claribel

▶ STEP 4: **Students return to the reading for additional facts.** Students and the teacher add new information to the list.

▶ STEP 5: **The teacher helps the students organize the recalled information into an outline or semantic map.** The organization should illustrate the general idea and supporting details. A map of "Feathered Friend" was difficult to construct because students had a hard time finding the central theme of the story. Teachers should be sensitive to the fact that not all text has a main idea; therefore, students may need additional help in the construction of a map or outline. (See Figure 8.5.)

▶ STEP 6: **The teacher provides the students with a thought-provoking question.** This question may help students associate this story with something they read previously. For example, this section of the literature text dealt with plot. The teacher asked the students to compare the plot of "Feathered Friend" with the plot of two other previously read stories.

FIGURE 8.5
Semantic Map from Guided Reading Procedure

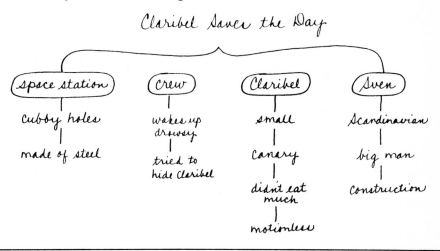

▶ STEP 7:   **Students are tested on their knowledge of the information in the text.**   It does not make any difference whether the test is essay or objective. The point is to see if students have committed the information to short-term memory.

Manzo cautions that this strategy is not one that should be used more than once every two weeks. It is a fairly intense reading activity. Also, as shown in the example, when using the GRP for narrative text, some stories do not lend themselves well to a central theme that can be easily mapped or outlined.

The GRP has been field tested in seventh-grade classes. It seemed to enhance the short- and long-term comprehension of students using content material (Bean and Pardi, 1979). The researchers found that looking over the story before reading was important in activating prior knowledge and that collaborating in the construction of the map or outline helped students organize what they had read.

## COMPREHENSION-MONITORING ACTIVITIES

In order for students to become independent learners, they must monitor their own comprehension. The strategies below are designed to help students become more proficient with metacognitive processes.

### Paired Readings

Working under the assumption that two heads are better than one, Dansereau, (1977) suggests Paired Readings as a means of helping students to learn and retain more of what they have learned.

▶ STEP 1:   **Two students silently read a short segment of an assignment (about 600 words).**   The student who finishes first can reread the material for the important points. After reading, both students put material out of sight.
▶ STEP 2:   **When both students are finished reading, the Recaller orally retells what was read without referring back to the text.**   One student recalls (the Recaller) the information in the text and the other student listens (the Listener).
▶ STEP 3:   **During the retelling, the Listener should only interrupt to obtain clarification.**
▶ STEP 4:   **After the retelling, the Listener should do two things: (a) point out and correct any ideas that were summarized incorrectly and (b) add any ideas that were not included in retelling but that the Listener thinks should have been included.**   The two students work together to note as many ideas as possible.

▶ STEP 5: **Students should alternate roles after each segment.** Students tend to recall information better than if they work alone. Students also seem to enjoy working with a partner.

Paired Readings is a particularly good strategy for middle school students because it requires them to make a social contract to work together. Students learn from each other's point of view and thinking strategies. To facilitate this learning, students should be encouraged to share their reasoning strategies with each other. Students understand material better because they have read the information in short segments and have spoken and listened to the information. One student may understand something that confuses the other. This activity strengthens students' metacognitive abilities while it provides them with an opportunity to work cooperatively with others.

## Paired Questioning

Instead of conducting the ReQuest Procedure (which is generally used with an entire class), Vaughn and Estes (1986) suggest that teachers assign *pairs* of students to proceed through the steps together in the Paired Questioning strategy. The steps in Paired Questioning are presented below.

▶ STEP 1: **Pairs of students read the title or subtitle of a manageable section of text together.**
▶ STEP 2: **Each student asks questions that come to mind about the title.** The partner answers questions if he or she can.
▶ STEP 3: **Each student reads the same section of the text silently.**
▶ STEP 4: **After completing the reading, Reader A asks a question concerning the information and ideas in the text.** Reader B answers, using the text if necessary.
▶ STEP 5: **Reader B then asks questions of Reader A.** Reader A answers the questions, again using the text if necessary.
▶ STEP 6: **Reader A identifies the important and unimportant ideas.** Reader A must explain why the ideas are important or unimportant and the process for drawing these conclusions.
▶ STEP 7: **Reader B must either agree or disagree and offer reasons for agreement or disagreement.** The following activities may be completed for extension activities.
▶ STEP 8: **Each student writes a paraphrase or summary of the reading.** Semantic mapping could also be used during this stage of the activity.
▶ STEP 9: **Students read their paraphrases to each other and come up with a synopsis upon which they both agree.** If students construct maps,

they could combine their information to form a more complete diagram. Students may want to draw pictures to enhance their summaries.

▶ STEP 10: **Students proceed to the next segment, switching roles.**

The Paired Questioning strategy serves the purpose of getting students to read thoughtfully and to ask and answer questions about their reading. The notion that "two heads are better than one" applies here.

## INSERT

Vaughn and Estes (1986) developed this simple strategy to help students become more involved in their reading; it also helps the students make decisions as they read and clarify their own reading. The strategy consists of a marking system that records the students' reaction to what is being read. If marking in a book is a problem, simply supply students with strips of paper to place along the side of the text. The marking system is shown in Figure 8.6.

One may wonder what information a sixth grader would assign a "!" to while studying ancient civilizations. Perhaps teachers need to acknowledge what may be already suspected: Students may find much of what they read boring or confusing. If teachers know which parts of the text elicit such a reaction, they can plan assignments more effectively. Students could note a "C" for confusing or a "B" for boring. Teachers can help students through such passages with added concept building. The entire INSERT marking system should be introduced gradually or simplified for some students.

FIGURE 8.6
Marking System for INSERT Strategy

    ✔  I agree

    X  I disagree/I thought differently

    +  New information

    !  Wow

    ?  I wonder

    ??  Don't understand

    *  Important

# STUDY GUIDES

The purpose of a study guide is to lead students through a reading assignment and focus their attention on main points. Study guides can motivate students by providing a structure for them, thus encouraging them to become active rather than passive readers. Group work seems to be especially effective when using study guides and is an activity early adolescents particularly enjoy.

The construction of study guides takes time and effort. Teachers should first focus on the major points to be learned and the reading abilities to be practiced. Overcrowded print may confuse students; thus the urge to overload students with information should be resisted. Teachers should try to make the study guide interesting. For example, as students identified the counties of a state, one teacher inserted riddles such as "Which counties can you eat?" Students usually need to be talked through the study guide before they begin reading. As students become more and more proficient in the use of study guides, the teacher can make them less detailed, thus releasing some of the responsibility to students as they are able to handle it. Middle grades students also enjoy making up study guides for other students. The Textbook Activity Guide provides an example of one type of study guide that middle school students enjoy.

## Textbook Activity Guides (TAG)

Textbook Activity Guides facilitate the active involvement of students using content area materials. TAGs are different from other guides in that they do not depend on hierarchical levels of comprehension and they are not dependent on clear organizational patterns in textbooks. Also, "TAGs emphasize active student involvement through cooperative learning and a self monitoring component" (Davey, 1986, p. 490).

Students are quick to understand and use coding systems designed by teachers. Again, as with the study guides, TAGs take time to construct but students seem to benefit from that time. The steps in constructing a TAG include selecting learning objectives and locating features in the text that best facilitate the mastery of those objectives. A sample TAG is presented in Figure 8.7.

Davey (1986) suggested that TAGs be used for only a limited amount of time at first (twenty minutes). She found that secondary students benefited from using the TAG because it facilitated their active involvement in textbook reading and assisted them in monitoring their comprehension of that reading. The teacher's role is to help students become independent learners. As students are more able to read expository text successfully and independently, the TAGs can be less structured. Some students have enjoyed making TAGs for other students.

FIGURE 8.7 ⎯⎯⎯⎯⎯⎯⎯⎯⎯⎯⎯⎯⎯⎯⎯⎯⎯⎯⎯⎯⎯⎯⎯⎯⎯⎯⎯⎯⎯⎯⎯⎯⎯⎯⎯
Sample TAG

### Geography Affected Indian Ways

Names: _____ Date initiated: _____

_____

Strategy codes:
      DP   = Read and discuss with your partner
      PP   = Predict with your partner
      WR   = Each partner writes response on separate paper
      Map  = Complete the semantic map
      Skim = Read quickly for the purpose stated; discuss with your partner

Self-monitoring codes:
      ___+___ I understand the information
      ___√___ I'm not sure if I fully understand this information
      ___?___ I do not understand this information. I need to restudy.

_____

1. **PP**   pp. 21–25—title and headings
   What do you think you will learn about from this section?
   List at least eight things.
2. **DP**   p. 21—headings and first three paragraphs
   Explain the second sentence in this section, beginning ''The type of shelter. . . .'' What are some examples from the passage?
   What are some examples from today?
3. **WR**   p. 21—right column, first and second paragraphs
   a. Why did the Haidas and the Iroquois need different kinds of boats?
   b. Using other resource books in the classroom, draw an Iroquois canoe and a Haida boat. Add them to your booklet on Indians.
4. **Skim**   p. 21—last two paragraphs; p. 22—first paragraph
   Purpose: Find out about the shelter and food of the Plains Indians.
5. **DP**   p. 22—second to sixth paragraphs
   How did the climate of the Southwest affect:
   _____ the materials the Pueblo Indians used for their shelters?
   _____ the way they built their shelters?
   _____ the way they grew their food?
6. **Skim**   p. 22—second to last paragraph of section
   Purpose: Find out about the features of homes of the Mayan Indians.
7. **WR**   p. 22—last paragraph of section
   Give an example from the section to prove each of the following:
   _____ Geography influenced Indian homes.
   _____ Geography influenced Indian clothing.
   _____ Geography influenced Indian food.
8. **DP**   Map pp. 24, 25
   Compare and contrast two types of Indian homes.

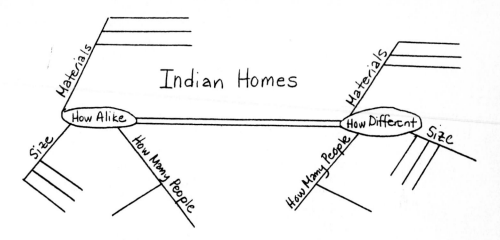

9. **WR**  Add at least three new words to your vocabulary file.
10. Get answer key 1A to check your work. Record your summary score.
    Evaluation: _____ Summary score

    _____ Written checkup

    _____ Teacher conference

## SUMMARY

Traditionally, reading has been viewed as a collection of discrete subskills, each of which could be tested and taught. Many modern educational theorists, however, have come to view reading as a whole that is greater than the sum of its parts. Reading is comprehension, and only by emphasizing the process of comprehending will we help students to acquire a knowledge of what reading means.

Students must acquire a repertoire of learning strategies to help them deal effectively with problems in comprehension. Teachers can model, guide, and provide feedback, but students must learn how to apply these strategies to their own reading.

## REFERENCES

Andre, M. D. A., and Anderson, T. H. (1978–79). The development and evaluation of a self-questioning study technique. *Reading Research Quarterly, 14,* 605–623.

Bean, T. W., and Pardi, R. (1979). A field-test of a guided reading strategy. *Journal of Reading, 23,* 144–147.

Brown, A. L. (1982). Learning how to learn from reading. In J. L. Langer and M. T. Smith-Burke (Eds.) *Reader meets author/Bridging the gap.* Newark, DE: International Reading Association.

Brown, A. L., and Day, J. D. (1983). Macrorules for summarizing texts: The development of expertise. *Journal of Verbal Learning and Verbal Behavior, 22,* 1–14.

Brown, A. L., and Palincsar, A. S. (1987). Reciprocal teaching of comprehension strategies: A natural history of one program for enhancing learning. In J. Borkowski and J. D. Day (Eds.), *Intelligence and cognition in special children: Comparative studies of giftedness, mental retardation and learning disabilities.* New York: Albex.

Carr, E., and Ogle, D. (1987). K-W-L Plus: A strategy for comprehension and summarization. *Journal of Reading, 30,* 626–631.

Clarke, A. C. (1958). Feathered friend. In *The other side of the sky.* New York: Scott Meredith Literary Agency.

Collins, A., and Smith, E. E. (1980). Teaching the process of reading comprehension. Urbana, IL: Center for the Study of Reading. (ED 193 616).

Dansereau, D. F. (1977). How to create and maintain a crummy mood. In D. F. Dansereau (Ed.), *Instructional packet: Techniques of college learning.* Ft. Worth, TX: Texas Christian University.

Davey, B. (1983). Think aloud: Modeling the cognitive processes of reading comprehension. *Journal of Reading, 27,* 44–47.

Davey, B. (1985). Helping readers think beyond print through self-questioning. *Middle School Journal, 17,* 26–27.

Davey, B. (1986). Using textbook activity guides to help students learn from textbooks. *Journal of Reading, 29,* 489–494.

Durkin, D. (1978–79). What classroom observations reveal about comprehension instruction. *Reading Research Quarterly, 14,* 481–533.

Durkin, D. (1981). Reading comprehension instruction in five basal reader series. *Reading Research Quarterly, 16,* 515–543.

Flood, J., and Lapp, D. (1986). Getting the main idea of the main idea: A writing/reading process. In J. F. Baumann (Ed.), *Teaching main idea comprehension.* Newark, DE: International Reading Association.

Garner, R., and Reis, R. (1981). Monitoring and resolving comprehension obstacles: An investigation of spontaneous text lookbacks among upper-grade good and poor comprehenders. *Reading Research Quarterly, 16,* 569–582.

Harris, A. J., and Sipay, E. R. (1985). *How to increase reading ability.* New York: Longman.

Johnson, D. D., & Pearson, D. P. (1978). *Teaching reading vocabulary.* New York: Holt, Rinehart and Winston.

Johnson, D. D., and Pearson, P. D. (1984). *Teaching reading vocabulary.* New York: Holt, Rinehart and Winston.

Manzo, A. V. (1975). Guided reading procedure. *Journal of Reading, 18,* 287–291.

Ogle, D. M. (1986). KWL: A teaching model that develops active reading of expository text. *The Reading Teacher, 39,* 64–70.

Palincsar, A. S. (1984). The quest for meaning from expository text: A teacher guided journey. In G. G. Duffy, L. R. Roehler, and J. Mason (Eds.), *Comprehension instruction: Perspectives and suggestions.* New York: Longman.

Palincsar, A. S., and Brown, A. L. (1984). Reciprocal teaching of comprehension-fostering and comprehension-monitoring activities. *Cognition and Instruction, 1,* 117–175.

Palincsar, A. S., and Brown, A. L. (1985a). A means to a meaningful end. In R. Anderson, J. Osborn, and P. Wilson (Eds.), *Research foundations for a literate America.* New York: D. C. Heath.

Palincsar, A., and Brown, A. L. (1985b). Reciprocal teaching activities to promote read(ing) with your mind. In E. J. Cooper (Ed.), *Reading, thinking, and concept development: Interactive strategies for the class.* New York: The College Board.

Pearson, P. D. (1985). Changing the face of reading comprehension instruction. *Reading Teacher, 38,* 724–738.

Pearson, P. D., and Johnson, D. D. (1987). *Teaching reading comprehension.* New York: Holt, Rinehart and Winston.

Squire, J. R. (1983). Composing and comprehending: Two sides of the same basic process. *Language Arts, 60,* 581–589.

Stotsky, S. (1983). Research on reading/writing relationships: A synthesis and suggested directions. *Language Arts, 60,* 627–642.

Tei, E., and Stewart, O. (1985). Effective studying from text: Applying metacognitive strategies. *Forum for Reading, 16,* 46–55.

Vaughn, J. L., and Estes, T. H. (1986). *Reading and reasoning beyond the primary grades.* Boston, MA: Allyn and Bacon.

# Chapter 9

# Learning and Remembering

Most students read not only for their own pleasure, but also to acquire information relevant to a test, report, project, or some other assignment. Reading for remembering—studying—involves reading for meaning and much more. Readers who have in mind a specific academic goal must be able to choose among important ideas and organize these ideas so as to remember them clearly. That is, they must know how to remember information and what information to remember.

Study skills such as outlining, summarizing, underlining, and note taking have been taught in middle schools for many years. Sometimes these skills are taught in a way that isolates the skills from the content, and sometimes this instruction takes place along with instruction of content. Research has not endorsed any one of these strategies over another, but a strategy is effective when (1) the readers are involved in a level of processing while using the strategy (being actively involved in the learning) and (2) the readers are aware of the criterion task or the task upon which they will be asked to perform, such as a test or a report (Anderson and Armbruster, 1984). In this chapter, the importance of depth of processing and knowledge of the criterion task is discussed. Next, factors in successful study skills instruction and programs are presented. Finally, strategies for teaching study skills before, during, and after reading will be discussed.

## DEPTH OF PROCESSING

When a student takes notes he or she may merely copy the author's words or synthesize and summarize the author's ideas. The former is a fairly passive task whereas the latter indicates deep processing—an understanding of the major concepts presented in the text. Deep processing is facilitated by strategies, such as chapter mapping, that allow the reader to connect ideas in the text. Whether the student is taking notes or underlining the text is not as significant as how well she or he understands the relationship between ideas presented in the text.

## KNOWLEDGE OF THE CRITERION TASK

The tasks for which students read to remember are familiar to students and teachers alike. These goals, such as multiple-choice or essay exams, research papers, book reports, or speeches, might be called *criterion tasks.* The degree of knowledge students have about the criterion task is an important variable in the effectiveness of time spent studying. "When the criterion task is made explicit to the students before they read the text, students will learn more from studying than when the criterion task remains vague" (Anderson and Armbruster, 1984, p. 658). Students who are to study effectively and efficiently must have enough information about the task at hand so that they can adjust their studying accordingly.

Meyer (1934, 1935, 1936) found that when students anticipated essay and completion exams rather than multiple-choice and true-false tests, they performed better on all types of tests. When studying for objective tests (multiple-choice and true-false), students engaged in "random" note taking and underlining. Meyer suggested that studying for an essay exam prompts students to focus on understanding the author's major points. Understanding the major concepts in a text and their relationship to each other seemed to aid students in their overall recall of the text.

## FACTORS IN SUCCESSFUL STUDY STRATEGY INSTRUCTION

The purpose of teaching study strategies to students is to foster independent learning. Content area teachers are the most capable of teaching study strategies since they can best explain the criterion task and help students adjust their studying accordingly. Content area teachers are also best able to identify important concepts to be learned and can develop the necessary background information to help students see the relationship between concepts. Additionally, such teachers are most familiar with the text and its organization and can most effectively guide students through it.

Many factors, of course, affect learning and remembering and some of them are beyond the scope of the teacher's influence. Heredity and environment play important roles, as well as the student's self-concept, management of time, and particular style of learning. A deficit in many of these areas, however, can often be overcome by hard work, determination, and motivation to learn. *What Works: Research About Teaching and Learning* (USDOE, 1986) states that "many highly successful individuals have above-average but not extraordinary intelligence. Accomplishment in a particular activity is often more dependent upon hard work and self-discipline than on innate ability" (p. 16). Beyond all this, however, Brown (1980) suggested that there are two general classes of problems that can impede effective study: impoverished background knowledge and inefficient application of rules and strategies.

Chapter 7 described the importance of activating prior knowledge before reading. Learning becomes an impossible task if the new information cannot be related in some way to what is already known. Good teachers tailor instruction to the students' level of understanding and continually help to focus students' attention on the main points. They also monitor students' degree of understanding during reading or during a lecture, and supply students with the knowledge they need to facilitate understanding. In sum, good teachers help students relate new knowledge to what they already know.

Effective teachers also help their students realize that reading is an active process and that it is important to employ "problem-solving . . . routines to enhance understanding" (Baker and Brown, 1984, p. 376). However, having knowledge of strategic routines does not seem to be adequate for effective study behavior (Brown, 1980). Students must be able to apply these strategies at the appropriate time.

## A Successful Study Skills Program

Successful study skills training programs have three main components: (1) training and practice in the use of task-specific strategies (knowing *what* to apply); (2) instruction in the monitoring of these skills (knowing *when and how* to apply strategies); and (3) information concerning the significance and outcome of these activities and their range of utility (knowing *why* we apply strategies) (Paris, Newman, and McVey, 1983). "Students who receive only instruction in the skills often fail to use them intelligently and on their own volition because they do not appreciate the reasons why such activities are useful, nor do they grasp where and when to use them" (Baker and Brown, 1984).

In summary, a middle school study skills program should include instruction in strategies as well as instruction in the metacognitive skills that help students know when and how to apply these strategies. Middle school educators should help students develop these metacognitive abilities but cannot expect that students will make rapid progress—these abilities are late-developing in most students. Middle school is a time of transition for students in their capacity for metacognitive thought; the development of such thought, however, is necessary for the effective use of study strategies.

# STRATEGIES THAT FACILITATE LEARNING AND REMEMBERING

Studying is not an act that occurs only before a test. Studying takes place as students survey a chapter before reading, take notes from a chapter, or write a summary. The strategies presented here facilitate learning and remembering *before, during,* and *after* reading.

## Before Reading

*Survey Techniques.* Survey techniques serve the purpose of helping the reader to establish expectations about the content and meaning of the text. SQ3R (Survey, Question, Read, Recite, Review) (Robinson, 1970) has been a popular survey technique for many years. Although there is nothing wrong with methods such as this, training in "cookbook methods often results in 'blind rule following' rather than self-awareness and learning to learn" (Brown, 1982, p. 48). Although such a formula may be appropriate for the reading of one text, it may be inappropriate for the reading of another. Tierney and Pearson (1981) state that "teaching prescriptions for how to process a text that disregard the ever changing interplay of text, purpose, and reader should be disregarded" (p. 1).

Generally, formula techniques have two major shortcomings: (1) they do not train the student to learn how to learn and how to evaluate the success of the strategy used and (2) they require the learning of activities that are difficult for many students (Andre and Anderson, 1978–79; Brown, Campione, and Day, 1981; Brown and Smiley, 1977; Baker, 1979). The reasons for this difficulty may be that students are often told to "just do it" rather than taught how to formulate good questions, summarize a text, and select topic sentences.

Any study technique, including SQ3R, can be effective when it helps students to focus attention on understanding important ideas in a text (Anderson and Armbruster, 1984). Anderson (1979) maintained that students are rarely given instructions on what to look for as they preview a text. Many students preview material in a haphazard way, giving little attention to titles, charts, or pictures.

Dansereau (1977) suggests the following guidelines for previewing a book before reading:

1. Think about the title of the selection, asking yourself what you already know about this concept.

2. Read any questions or summaries that may appear at the end of the sections or chapters.

3. Notice how the chapter is divided into sections.

4. Take a good look at all the pictures and graphs in the chapter so they will be easy to refer to when they are mentioned in the text.

5. Make a few preliminary notes about what you expect to learn from the reading.

6. Think about the reading you are about to do in relation to the goals it will serve.

7. Place this reading in a specific schedule of work, established on the basis of the relative importance of all you have to do.

8. Put yourself in a proper mood for study.

9. It is sometimes helpful to turn subheadings into questions that you try to answer as you read.

10. If there are things about the topic of the selection that you are curious about, try to keep those curiosities in mind as you read.

11. Think about the kinds of questions you usually see on tests of related subjects.

12. If your teacher provides study questions for you to use in the reading assignment, be sure you understand the questions before you begin reading.

Many students have found that survey techniques help them anticipate what they will study. Thus, study is made more meaningful because new information is connected to what is known (or anticipated).

## During Reading

Active reading facilitates better understanding of text. It involves self-questioning, prediction, and understanding the main points. Efficient readers make adjustments in their reading rate; therefore, a discussion of flexible reading will precede the presentation of strategies that facilitate active reading.

*Flexible Reading.* Speakers at conventions where reading educators gather occasionally relate the following anecdote: "I took a course in speed reading then read *War and Peace*. It was about Russia."

"Reading" text quickly without understanding is a waste of time. On the other hand, reading slowly and carefully is often inefficient as well. So how fast should a person read? The answer depends on the purpose for reading (including knowledge of the criterion task), the reader's prior knowledge, and the nature of the material. Reading speed also fluctuates with grade level (ability), although the relationship between reading speed and comprehension changes dramatically as children's reading abilities develop.

With primary students who struggle with word recognition, the correlation between their reading rate and their comprehension is quite high. As students progress in reading and become more proficient with word recognition, however, the correlation between reading rate and comprehension lowers. That is, the faster students at this level read, the lower their comprehension of the material. This relationship typifies the "normal" progression of reading ability. However, it is also normal for students to display a wide variety of abilities in reading rate. Table 9.1 shows average reading rates of students in grades 4 through 8. The data are taken from several standardized test scores and represent the median number of words read per minute at each grade level (Harris and Sipay, 1985, p. 533).

Note that a difference of 50 to 79 words per minute is reported between the highest and lowest test at each grade level. Although reading scores on a standardized test may not reflect reading rates in the classroom, such scores do indicate the wide variety in reading rates that one may expect to find in grades 4 through 8. The reading rate of the average U.S. high school student is 200 to 250

TABLE 9.1

Median Rates of Reading for Different Grades as Determined by Several Standardized Reading Tests

|  | 4 | 5 | Grade 6 | 7 | 8 |
|---|---|---|---|---|---|
| Highest test | 170 | 195 | 230 | 246 | 267 |
| Median test | 155 | 177 | 206 | 215 | 237 |
| Lowest test | 120 | 145 | 171 | 176 | 188 |

*Source: From How to Increase Your Reading Ability: A Guide to Developmental and Remedial Methods* by Albert J. Harris and Edward R. Sipay. Copyright © 1940, 1947, 1956, 1961, 1970, 1975, 1980, and 1985 by Longman Inc. All rights reserved.

TABLE 9.2 ————————————————
Reading Rates for Different Purposes
———————————————————————————

| | |
|---|---|
| Slow/study rate | 50–250 |
| Average/normal rate | 200–300 |
| Rapid reading | 300–800 |
| Skimming | 800–up |
| Scanning | 1000–up |

*Source:* From Marian J. Tonjes and Miles V. Zintz, *Teaching Reading/Thinking/Study Skills in Content Classrooms.* Copyright © 1981 Wm. C. Brown Publishers, Dubuque, Iowa. All rights reserved. Reprinted by permission.

———————————————————————————

words per minute. The average eighth grader is close to that rate when entering high school.

The various rates of reading can be broken down into five types, as indicated in Table 9.2. The actual rates are only approximate (Tonjes and Zintz, 1981, p. 111).

Efficient reading is "flexible." Students should be able to adjust their rate according to their purpose for reading, their prior knowledge, and the nature of the material. For example, consider two students: Alesha and Emmelyn. The physical education teacher gave them a small book on soccer and told them that they will have a test on Friday that covers soccer rules. Alesha has been playing soccer on city teams since she was six years old and her father is a soccer coach. Therefore, the game is dinner-time conversation. Emmelyn, on the other hand, has taken violin lesson since age six, her father is a chemist, and she has never played a game of soccer. Alesha needs only to skim the material, stopping periodically and checking to make sure her prior knowledge of the rules matches the text. She reads the book rapidly and hurries off to a match. Emmelyn spends hours with the book, writing down the rules so that she can study them later, and asks Alesha the meaning of such terms as *offsides* and *heading.* Good readers decide how fast to read before beginning and adjust their rate while reading according to their comprehension.

*A Self-Monitoring Approach to Reading and Thinking (SMART).*   SMART is a strategy that helps students identify what they do and do not understand in their reading. Vaughn and Estes (1986) describe the steps that comprise SMART. There are many steps but they are simple and easy to use.

▶ STEP 1:  **Instruct students to place a "$\sqrt{}$" in the margin if they**

understand what they are reading or place a "?" if they don't understand
what they are reading.

▶ STEP 2: **After each section of the assignment, have students explain
to themselves (in their own words) the facts and ideas they have
understood.** Students may look back at the text while they do this.

▶ STEP 3: **Next, after each section, tell students to examine those ideas
that they did not understand and then do these things:**

a. Read again the parts that were not understood. If you now understand
   something that was previously unclear, change your "?" to a "√".
b. If the idea remains unclear, try to specify what is causing the problem. Is it a
   word? A phrase? A relationship?
c. Try to think of something you might do to help yourself understand, and if
   you can think of something (like using the glossary, examining pictures or
   diagrams in the text, reviewing another part of the text), try it out. Again, if
   your strategy works, change your "?" to a "√".
d. Finally, try to explain to yourself those ideas that you still do not understand.

▶ STEP 4: **Have students study the entire assignment using these three
steps.** Students might find it useful to divide the assignment into sections.
After studying the entire assignment, students should be instructed to do the
following things:

a. Close the book and review the ideas that you do understand. Some people do
   this by talking out loud to themselves.
b. Look back at the book and refresh your memory for anything you left out.
c. Now, reexamine those ideas you still do not understand. Think about those
   ideas. What could they possibly mean? Is there anything else you could do to
   help you understand? Don't worry about what you don't understand. You can
   ask someone later.
d. Close the book one last time and review what you do understand.

Students should be encouraged to think about rather than to memorize
information. Students often ask for help without seeking a solution for themselves. By requiring them to specify what they do not understand (word, phrase,
relationship) and to be able to explain what they did to try to understand it, this
strategy encourages students to solve problems independently whenever possible. Thus, SMART enables students to develop their metacognitive abilities and
to become more in control of their learning.

*Underlining.* Underlining, or highlighting, is the most popular aide used to
study text. This study strategy requires that students know what is worth
underlining or remembering. Underlining has not been shown to be any more
effective than any other study technique. The major benefit of this study strategy
comes not from merely marking information but from rereading and deciding
what to underline. This decision takes a certain amount of "deep processing."

Have you ever seen a college textbook that was inundated with yellow highlighting? The reader apparently could not discriminate between important and unimportant information. Harris and Sipay (1985) suggest that students should be told not to underline until they have finished reading a headed section because waiting may reveal a summary statement. These authors also suggest at least a two-tiered system of underlining or highlighting in order to differentiate between important ideas. My two-tiered system of underlining consists of the full line side of the marker for major points and the half line side of the marker for less major points.

Devine (1987) stated that "underlining is only one step from passivity" (p. 168). He suggests that making marginal comments and using personal coding systems (such as the INSERT method described in Chaper 8) facilitate the remembering of important points better than just underlining.

*Taking Notes from Text.*   Taking notes from text has been shown to facilitate the memory of the most important ideas if it entails processing in a way that is compatible with the task students will eventually perform (Anderson and Armbruster, 1984). Some teachers instruct their students to take good notes while first reading the text and then, when studying for the test, to refer only to the notes.

In order to take good notes, one must separate the major points from the minor ones and consider the relationship between ideas (Harris and Sipay, 1985). Students can, and often times do, merely copy the author's words, but in order to take good notes, one must be an active reader.

Many middle school students have never been taught to take notes from a chapter. The best way to begin teaching note-taking skills is to start simply. Some teachers insist that students take notes in a notebook reserved just for that class. Some teachers have found it helpful to give out partial notes that require students to fill in the blanks. Over time, students are given more and more responsibility. Keep these guidelines in mind when teaching note taking.

1. Tell the students to look over the chapter first to get an idea of the overall structure.

2. Use a textbook with good subheadings.

3. Review notes from short sections before going on to longer ones.

4. Give students plenty of feedback and examples.

5. After taking notes from a textbook, students should be instructed to summarize the information using a summary, an outline, or a chapter map.

6. Most importantly, students should use the notes to study for a test.

Some schools have found it helpful to adopt a note-taking system that can be taught and reinforced in each class. One system that is the result of decades of research and is widely used is the Cornell Notetaking Method (Pauk, 1974). In this method, the paper is divided as shown in Figure 9.1. The important information is listed on the right side. In the left column a few key words are written that help students remember what is written on the right side. This example of notes was taken for a lecture on how the Cornell Notetaking Method works.

## After Reading

After students have surveyed the chapter, asked questions, and read actively, it is time for them to organize what they have read. Chapter mapping, outlining, and summarizing are discussed as methods for organizing information effectively.

*Chapter Mapping.*    This strategy comes up often because it is a powerful tool to help students comprehend and remember the important ideas in a text or lecture (Armbruster and Anderson, 1980). Mapping assists students in understanding the important relationships in the text by providing them with a visual outline of the logical connections between key ideas. This strategy helps students be more active readers or listeners, thus facilitating the all-important "deep processing." Mapping can also help students organize texts that are difficult to understand or poorly written. A sample chapter map is presented in Figure 9.2.

Mapping adds a visual dimension to the concepts presented in a text, and thus may enhance comprehension and recall of information. Two or three students can work together to produce a more complete map. Discussion about what should and should not be included helps students understand the process of distinguishing between important and unimportant information.

*Outlining.*    Outlining is probably one of the most popular methods of study. However, the process of outlining is difficult for students because they must think through the logical relationships in the text before beginning the outline. This task requires analysis and synthesis, and some students simply may not be ready to perform these cognitive operations.

Presuming the text is well organized, an outline can be a skeleton of a chapter, showing the main parts. If outlining is to be taught to middle grades students, the following steps are recommended by Devine (1987):

1. Discuss the plan of a formal outline.

FIGURE 9.1 ———————————————————————————
The Cornell Notetaking System

| Key Words | Notes |
|---|---|
| Preparing the system | 1. Take a few minutes to review notes from previous lecture or text.<br>2. Use loose-leaf paper.<br>3. Use one side of paper only.<br>4. Draw a line 1/3 from the left side of the paper.<br>5. Write ideas and facts on the right side of the line.<br>6. Skip lines between major ideas. |
| Using the System | 1. Record notes simply.<br>2. Don't make an outline.<br>3. Use abbreviation system.<br>4. Write neatly.<br>5. Leave space when day dreaming.<br>6. Strive for capturing the main ideas rather than details.<br>7. Record the lecturer's or text's examples that may clarify an abstract idea. |
| After the lecture or reading | 1. Consolidate your notes.<br>2. Read through the notes.<br>3. Neaten the scribbles.<br>4. Reduce notes to concise topics.<br>5. Check or rethink key words.<br>6. Mark important ideas.<br>7. Box or underline assignments.<br>8. Reflect on your notes. |
| Review | 1. Before class.<br>2. After class.<br>3. After study time.<br>4. On the run. |
| Review method | 1. Cover right side of notes.<br>2. Using the key words in the column, recite aloud the facts and ideas of the lecture or reading in your own words. |
| Payoff | 1. The procedure of reciting is the most powerful learning tool you can use.<br>2. Improved test scores.<br>3. Less time spent on study, better results. |

*Source:* Walter Pauk, *How to Study in College,* 3rd ed. Copyright © 1984 by Hougton Mifflin Company. Adapted with permission.

FIGURE 9.2 ──────────────────────────────
Sample of Chapter Map

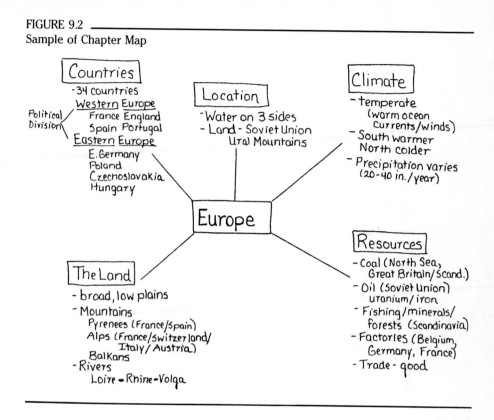

2. Give the students an already completed outline in which the details are printed but the major headings are omitted. Students then fill in these major headings as they read.

3. Give the students an outline in which more slots are to be filled.

4. Give the students the outline skeleton and tell them to fill in the information.

5. Tell the students the number of main headings in the chapter.

6. Finally, have students produce a complete outline without assistance.

*Summarizing.*  Producing a succinct but comprehensive summary after reading or listening to a lecture is a good way of estimating one's preparedness for a test. Also, as with other such strategies, summaries force learners to use in-depth processing on the more important ideas in the text (Tei and Stewart, 1985). However, composing a summary is a complex task that requires consider-able skill (Baker and Brown, 1984). This study strategy needs careful, even sequential, instruction (Devine, 1987). Apparently, the ability to formulate main ideas is a skill that develops late in students. High school students are more able than middle grades students to produce summaries that contain main ideas.

Brown, Campione, and Day (1981) identified five rules for putting ideas into a summary. They include: (1) delete irrelevant or trivial information, (2) delete redundant information, (3) select topic sentences, (4) substitute a superordinate term or event for a list of terms or actions, and (5) invent topic sentences when none is provided by the author. Research indicates that there is a developmental trend in awareness and use of these rules. Young children cannot select topic sentences or invent topic sentences. Middle school students seem to have difficulty substituting superordinate terms or inventing topics. Most middle grades students will not be able to produce summaries that clearly reflect the most important points if highly abstract thinking is required. However, students at this age are ready to learn to identify the most important ideas from a reading or a lecture. In order to accomplish this goal, direct instruction and a clear indication of the criterion task are essential.

*Hierarchical Summaries.*   Taylor (1986) also found that middle grades students typically have difficulty in writing summaries. Summaries seem to present such difficulties because students must include only main ideas and exclude many details. Perhaps details are easier for middle grades students to grasp because they are more concrete than main ideas.

Taylor suggests the use of Hierarchical Summaries for middle school students. She contends that this summary-writing instruction is most successful when it is used with textbook material that is organized into headings. An example, using social studies content, follows.

▶   STEP 1:   **Students skim three to four pages, reading headings only.**
▶   STEP 2:   **Students make a skeleton outline using a capital letter for every subsection designated by a heading.**   After reading three pages on the War of 1812, an eighth grader's summary looked like this:

### THE WAR OF 1812

A. Causes of the War

B. War in the Northwest

C. The British Strike Back

▶   STEP 3:   **Students read material in full.**
▶   STEP 4:   **For each section, students use the pertinent words from the heading that reflect the main idea of the section.**   Students should underline the main idea.

FIGURE 9.3 ———————————————————————————————————
Hierarchical Summary

## The War of 1812

A. *A major cause of the war was that neither Great Britain nor France wanted the United States to deliver supplies to the other.*
   1. The United States tried to remain neutral.
   2. Great Britain and France both attacked American ships.
B. *Settlers in the Northwest Territory hoped war with Great Britain would give them a chance to claim land in Canada for themselves.*
   1. Land fighting was not successful.
   2. Captain Oliver Perry defeated the British fleet on Lake Erie.
C. *The British attacked Washington, D.C.*
   1. Dolly Madison saved the famous portrait of George Washington.
   2. The President's home was painted white to cover burned places—The White House.

---

▶ STEP 5: **Students write one to three detail sentences under each main idea.** A full hierarchical summary is shown in Figure 9.3.

Students should formulate sentences in their own words and not copy from text. Teachers should show students how to generate both main idea and detail sentences used in these summaries. Taylor found that five or six sessions with Hierarchical Summaries was necessary before middle school students felt confident in making their own summaries.

Taylor also found that using cooperative learning (see Chapter 4) techniques could be effectively used when writing summaries. For this strategy, students are divided into groups of three and they take turns reading short segments from their content textbook. They also take turns generating main idea sentences for each topic and then together come up with the best main idea sentence in their own words. Students then suggest two details from the subsection that they feel are important to remember. Everyone writes the skeleton outline. The same procedure is repeated for every subsection in the selection. When this process is finished, the group comes up with one or two sentences that best reflect the main idea of the entire section.

# SUMMARY

Students read to pass tests, write reports, and complete assignments. That is, students are reading for a purpose, often a purpose defined by someone else. Study skills are strategies that enable students to meet these purposes. Study skills enable students to learn and remember the material that they read.

In order to study effectively, of course, students must know *what* to study. The teacher must carefully define the criterion task that students will be expected to perform after studying. Beyond this, students must learn *how* to study effectively and efficiently. Students must learn how to grasp a main idea, how to summarize information, and how to interrelate or synthesize information. They must learn how to check their comprehension and how to adjust their reading rate to the demands of the task. Students must also learn how to take effective notes from text. In short, they must learn how to achieve a deep understanding of the material they are to study. Study skills are the strategies that serve as a means to this end.

# REFERENCES

Anderson, T. H. (1979). Study stills and learning strategies. In H. F. O'Neil, Jr. and C. D. Speilberger (Eds.), *Cognitive and affective learning strategies.* New York: Academic Press.

Anderson, T. H., and Armbruster, B. B. (1984). Studying. In P. D. Pearson (Ed.), *Handbook of reading research.* New York: Longman.

Andre, M. D. A., and Anderson, T. H. (1978–79). The develoment and evaluation of a self-questioning study technique. *Reading Research Quarterly, 14,* 605–623.

Armbruster, B. B., and Anderson, T. H. (1980). The effect of mapping on the free recall of expository text. Urbana, IL: Center for the Study of Reading. (ED 182 735).

Baker, L. (1979). Do I understand or do I not understand: That is the question. Urbana IL: Center for the Study of Reading. (ED 174 948).

Baker, L., and Brown, A. L. (1984). Metacognitive skills and reading. In P. D. Pearson (Ed.), *Handbook of reading research.* New York: Longman.

Brown, A. L. (1980). Learning and development: The problems of compatibility, access, and induction. (Technical Report No. 165). Urbana, IL: Center for the Study of Reading. (ED 221 823).

Brown, A. L. (1982). Learning to learn how to read. In J. Langer and T. Smith-Burke (Eds.), *Reader meets author, bridging the gap: A psycholinguistic and sociolinguistic perspective.* Newark, DE: International Reading Association.

Brown, A. L., Campione, J. C., and Day, J. (1981). Learning to learn: On training students to learn from texts. *Educational Researcher, 10,* 14–21.

Brown, A. L., and Smiley, S. S. (1977). Rating the importance of structural units of prose passages: A problem of metacognitive development. *Child Development, 48,* 1–8.

Dansereau, D. F. (1977). How to create and maintain a crummy mood. In D. F.

Dansereau (Ed.), *Instructional packet: Techniques of college learning.* Ft. Worth, TX: Texas Christian University.

Devine, T. G. (1987). *Teaching study skills.* Boston, MA: Allyn and Bacon.

Harris, A. J., and Sipay, E. R. (1985). *How to increase reading ability.* New York: Longman.

Meyer, G. (1934). An experimental study of the old and new types of examination: The effect of the examination set on memory. *Journal of Educational Psychology, 25,* 641–660.

Meyer, G. (1935). An experimental study of the old and new types of examination: II. Methods of study. *Journal of Educational Psychology, 26,* 30–40.

Meyer, G. (1936). The effects on recall and recognition of the examination set in classroom situations. *Journal of Educational Psychology, 27,* 81–99.

Paris, S. G., Newman, R. S., and McVey, K. A. (1983). Learning the functional significance of mnemonic actions: A microgenetic study of strategy acquisition. *Journal of Experimental Child Psychology, 34,* 490–509.

Pauk, W. (1974). *How to study in college.* Boston, MA: Houghton Mifflin.

Robinson, F. P. (1970). *Effective study.* New York: Harper and Brothers.

Taylor, B. M. (1986). Teaching middle grade students to summarize content textbook material. In J. F. Baumann (Ed.), *Teaching main idea comprehension.* Newark, DE: International Reading Association.

Tei, E., and Stewart, O. (1985). Effective studying from text: Applying metacognitive strategies. *Forum for Reading, 16,* 46–55.

Tierney, R. J., and Pearson, P. D. (1981). Learning to learn from text: A framework for improving classroom practice. (ED 205 917).

Tonjes, M. J., and Zintz, M. V. (1981). *Teaching reading/thinking/study skills in content classrooms.* Dubuque, IA: William C. Brown Publishers.

United States Department of Education (1986). *What works: Research about teaching and learning.* Washington, DC: United States Department of Education.

Vaughn, J. L., and Estes, T. H. (1986). *Reading and reasoning beyond the primary grades.* Boston, MA: Allyn and Bacon.

# Chapter 10

# Using Literature Across the Curriculum

## by Carol Lynch-Brown
## Florida State University

Literature can be used across the curriculum to enrich the lives of students in middle grades. Knowledge of literature, a component of our cultural heritage, can lay a foundation for later experiences with literature. In addition, experiences with literature provide students with an opportunity to explore other worlds and other lives as they begin the process of deciding their own futures.

Reading literature serves other educational purposes as well: it can enhance the study of certain content areas, it can foster vocabulary development and reading comprehension, and it is inherently enjoyable. Because literature is usually written in a more interesting manner than textbooks, it can be a valuable resource for teaching content area courses. Textbooks, for the most part, contain passages of information that omit the narrative aspects of the events— that is, the stories of the people who made the events happen. Fiction can breathe life into the dates, places, and events of content area textbooks. Works of historical fiction and biography can motivate early adolescents to learn about the period of history described. For example, in studying World War II, Naziism and the attempted genocide of the Jewish people, a work of fiction, such as *Friedrich* by Richter (1970), can help early adolescents understand the anguish of a thirteen-year-old Jewish boy suffering injustice and humiliation. (Other books written by international authors on this topic can be found in Lynch-Brown and Tomlinson, 1986.)

Reading ability is also promoted through the wide reading of literature, which especially fosters vocabulary development and reading comprehension. Most reading selections assigned to students, whether drawn from content area textbooks, basal readers, or literary readers, share a common trait of relative brevity. By reading longer, more fully developed works, students will have opportunities to study a single topic in depth, to follow complex plots, to know characters fully depicted as real human beings, and to appreciate places and worlds different from their own.

Of the many reasons that literature should have a central role in the middle school curriculum, perhaps the most powerful reason is that literature is enjoyable. By discovering the joy of reading, students will develop a lifelong habit of reading. Literature offers students another form of recreation—recreation of the mind, a chance to stretch one's mind by encountering new ideas, and recreation for the heart, a chance to experience empathy for others.

In summary, literature belongs in the middle school for three main reasons: (1) the study of literature itself is an important curricular area, (2) literature can serve as a vehicle to enhance the learning of other subject areas, and (3) literature can provide enjoyment and can help develop a lifelong habit of reading.

The first reason, that literature is in itself a subject of study, falls primarily within the domain of the language arts teacher and will not be addressed in this chapter. (See Atwell, 1987 for an excellent treatment of the use of literature and reading in the language arts class.)

This chapter explores how literature can be used to encourage wide reading and to develop the habit of reading. It also discusses how to use literature to enhance the teaching of other subjects. A starter list of annotated titles and a list of book selection aids are included at the end of the chapter to help teachers locate titles. For the purposes of this chapter, literature is defined as good quality tradebooks (library-type books), prose and poetry, and fiction and nonfiction.

## LITERATURE FOR ENJOYMENT AND FOR THE DEVELOPMENT OF READING AS A HABIT

An approach to encourage wide reading that has enjoyed success in middle schools across the country is the sustained silent reading (SSR) program. SSR programs are often implemented schoolwide but can be instituted by individual teachers or teams of teachers. Sustained silent reading is a period of time, usually ten to thirty minutes daily, set aside for the purpose of free-choice reading by students, teachers, administrators, and other school personnel.

Adults who read during this time serve as positive role models of people who enjoy reading. Students are assured of an uninterrupted period of time when they may read materials of their own choosing without any requirement to report on what they have read—no homework, no book report, no "what is the name of the main character"—only reading for enjoyment.

SSR programs evolved in the 1960s. Fader and McNeil (1968) told of success with a program in a school for delinquent boys. This type of school program probably arose out of a new societal need for practice in reading. Until the 1950s, students read widely at home; the need to practice their reading skills was provided by the natural desire for recreation through books. However, after television became a readily available form of recreation, schools found that students were not reading as widely as before. Wide reading continues to be important to the development of good reading ability and, therefore, time must be provided in school for silent reading. Suggestions for beginning and maintaining a successful SSR program are outlined below.

## Starting a Sustained Silent Reading Program

In beginning a schoolwide SSR program, all staff (including teachers, librarians, administrators, office personnel, custodial and food service personnel) not only need to be informed of the philosophy and purposes of the program but also need to participate in its implementation. A schoolwide meeting might be an appropriate way to accomplish this goal. Practical issues that can be resolved in such a meeting are (1) when and how long the SSR period should be, (2) how a sufficient variety of reading materials will be acquired and displayed, (3) how each adult can become a "reader role model" and the importance of such a role, and (4) how to encourage and motivate reluctant readers. One middle school decided to motivate students by a kickoff program in which local luminaries, such as the nearby university football coach, local ministers, and business owners, came for a ceremony to honor the students for their posters advertising the new program and to select the contest winner for the best title for the program. All of these preliminary activities helped inform and motivate the students in readiness for the new program.

Generally, at the middle school level, SSR programs start out with ten minutes daily, at the same time each day. Later, as students are accustomed to reading, the time may be lengthened. In one middle school, the teachers agreed to shorten each class period by two minutes, providing fourteen minutes after third period for silent reading. School bells were rung as for any other period. Students are encouraged to select and bring their own reading materials. These materials may be books, magazines, or comics. Although many students will come prepared with reading materials, a table or shelf with other materials displayed (front cover showing) will assist students who have forgotten a book or who just finished what they were reading. Reading time is not "earned" by good behavior or by "finishing your work"; rather, the time is allocated to an important and enjoyable activity—reading.

Providing a few minutes at other times of the day for students to share reactions to their selections can aid all students in locating new materials to read. Permitting students to meet in small groups of four or five to discuss what they are reading can be an activity that motivates students to read. Some teachers do a "book talk"—show a book and briefly tell the title, author, and something about the story. For example, *while showing the book,* the teacher might say, "I just finished this book that some of you might enjoy. The title is *The Hatchet* by Gary Paulsen and it's the story of a boy who survives fifty-four days in the Canadian wilderness after the plane taking him to visit his father crashes. It has an exciting beginning and it held my interest all the way through. I read it because it was a 1988 Newbery Honor Book; I try to keep up with the new award winners."

Some students will need help locating materials of interest to them. Teachers can share some techniques, such as finding books in a series (science fiction series, modern fantasy series, Nancy Drew/Hardy Boys series), books by the same author, award-winning book lists, and books on the same topic (mystery, romance, adventure). Friends can recommend good books for reading enjoyment, too.

## Maintaining a Successful SSR Program

Evaluating a program periodically and correcting any problems is an important part of maintaining a successful SSR program. The checklist shown in Figure 10.1 has proved useful to teachers in evaluating different facets of the SSR program in the classroom.

Periodically, administrators need to consider ways to encourage the continued success of the SSR program schoolwide. A workshop in which teachers share ideas they have used to encourage attentive reading has been successful in some schools. New materials can be provided and teachers can be encouraged to trade materials a few times a year. Visiting "guest readers" can be invited to share a silent reading period and then tell students what they enjoy reading. The principal, guidance counselors, coaches, and community members might serve as "guest readers." These techniques, among others, can help insure a successful sustained silent reading program.

Wide reading can benefit students by increasing their reading pace, enhancing their reading comprehension and vocabulary, and improving their attitudes toward reading. Educators often enthusiastically attest to the fact that SSR programs have worked successfully in their middle level schools.

FIGURE 10.1 ————————————————————————————————
Evaluation of the Sustained Silent Reading Period: Teacher Checklist

1. Is SSR held at the same time each day?
2. Are students "staying put" during SSR?
3. Are you reading silently while the students are reading?
4. Are others in the room (aides, parents, volunteers) reading silently while the students are reading?
5. Is there a reading corner in your room with books displayed and available for students?
6. Do you rotate (freshen) the books periodically (once a month)?
7. Do you read aloud to your class and then place those books in the reading corner?
8. Do you do "book talks"—tell the class a little about some of the books in the reading corner to whet their interest in them?
9. Do you occasionally share with the class what you are reading?
10. Do students have the opportunity to go to the Media Center weekly to select new books?
11. Are all materials and work that may distract students put away?
12. Do you post signs of this reading time to prevent others from disrupting your class and to mark the importance of reading time to the students?
13. Are students permitted free choice of reading matter?
14. Are you consistent in *not* requiring written book reports and the like from students on their SSR?
15. Do your students know how to locate materials of interest to them?

————————————————————————————————————————

## LITERATURE TO ENHANCE THE TEACHING OF OTHER SUBJECTS

Literature can enhance instruction in science, social studies, health, home economics, and mathematics. Content area teachers, however, have been offered little advice on how to utilize literature in their instruction. Using literature in content area classrooms calls for shared literary experiences for the students. A single book or other work of literature, or a group of literary works involving a similar theme or topic will comprise a shared literary experience. These book experiences can then be drawn upon to expand and enrich concepts from textbooks.

Suggestions for integrating literature and textbook instruction are provided for teachers in this section. The four steps to shared literary experience are: (1) brainstorm ideas, topics, or themes related to a unit of study in the content area; (2) identify titles and locate books; (3) provide shared literary experiences and dwell on these experiences; and (4) consider alternative ways to share books and extend the book experience.

▶ STEP 1:  **Brainstorm ideas, topics, or themes related to a unit of study in the content area.**   Textbooks in most subject areas (science, health, social studies, home economics, and mathematics) are generally arranged by units of varying length which usually take three to nine weeks to focus on a particular topic. For example, a health education teacher might select a unit on nutrition and exercise. At first glance, such a topic may seem to require a nonfiction treatment. Information books on foods, exercising, and sports naturally come to mind. But what about incorporating fiction and other narrative texts? Brainstorming may bring to mind the idea that nutrition and exercise are studied for good mental and physical health; to avoid abuses such as anorexia, bulimia, and obesity; and to encourage balance in life through attention to and care of one's body. A biography of a sports figure or a story of a young person struggling to overcome anorexia would make these topics more relevant to students.

The *webbing technique* has been found useful by teachers for brainstorming the related concepts and for finding books on particular topics. A web is a means of generating ideas and linking them to a central focus. Webbing can center on concepts, topics, or themes; the focal point of a web can also be a book or group of books (Huck, Hepler, and Hickman, 1987, p. 652). Two webs are presented here: one presents a topic at the center and the other shows a work of literature.

The web shown in Figure 10.2 centers on the theme of survival. This theme could be slanted to lend itself to a unit in health (bodily needs, emotional consequences of loneliness), science (natural foods, plant and animal study) or social studies (survival in nature versus city survival, qualities needed to be a survivor, interdependence of human beings, effects of isolation).

The web shown in Figure 10.3 was developed after reading a modern retelling of the Pied Piper legend, *What Happened in Hamelin,* by Gloria Skurzynski (1979) who researched the historical background of this medieval legend. A traveling musician, Gast, convinces the baker's apprentice, Geist, to bake treats for the town's children. Afterward, Gast lures the children away.

▶ STEP 2:  **Identify titles and locate books.**   Once you have brainstormed the topics and themes that might be explored relative to the upcoming unit, you will need to identify actual titles and locate the books. Begin the search for books close to home; perhaps the collection of books in your classroom will have a few appropriate titles. Ask the school librarian to help locate books on the topics you have identified through brainstorming. Librarians have access to reference guides that can aid a content area teacher in this search. They also know the books in the school library so well that with a few minutes of browsing they can identify a dozen or more books.

Most communities have public libraries with literature for young people. Determine the availability of books and the type of help the library may be willing to offer. Some librarians will do a search of titles on the themes or topics; others will set the books aside on a special shelf to help your students when they

FIGURE 10.2
Brainstorming Ideas by Topic

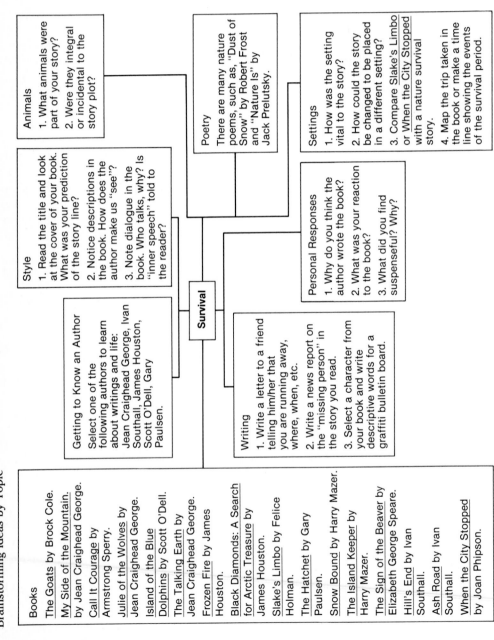

**Animals**
1. What animals were part of your story?
2. Were they integral or incidental to the story plot?

**Style**
1. Read the title and look at the cover of your book. What was your prediction of the story line?
2. Notice descriptions in the book. How does the author make us "see"?
3. Note dialogue in the book. Who talks, why? Is "inner speech" told to the reader?

**Poetry**
There are many nature poems, such as, "Dust of Snow" by Robert Frost and "Nature Is" by Jack Prelutsky.

**Settings**
1. How was the setting vital to the story?
2. How could the story be changed to be placed in a different setting?
3. Compare Slake's Limbo or When the City Stopped with a nature survival story.
4. Map the trip taken in the book or make a time line showing the events of the survival period.

**Personal Responses**
1. Why do you think the author wrote the book?
2. What was your reaction to the book?
3. What did you find suspenseful? Why?

**Getting to Know an Author**
Select one of the following authors to learn about writings and life: Jean Craighead George, Ivan Southall, James Houston, Scott O'Dell, Gary Paulsen.

**Survival**

**Writing**
1. Write a letter to a friend telling him/her that you are running away, where, when, etc.
2. Write a news report on the "missing person" in the story you read.
3. Select a character from your book and write descriptive words for a graffiti bulletin board.

**Books**
The Goats by Brock Cole.
My Side of the Mountain. by Jean Craighead George.
Call It Courage by Armstrong Sperry.
Julie of the Wolves by Jean Craighead George.
Island of the Blue Dolphins by Scott O'Dell.
The Talking Earth by Jean Craighead George.
Frozen Fire by James Houston.
Black Diamonds: A Search for Arctic Treasure by James Houston.
Slake's Limbo by Felice Holman.
The Hatchet by Gary Paulsen.
Snow Bound by Harry Mazer.
The Island Keeper by Harry Mazer.
The Sign of the Beaver by Elizabeth George Speare.
Hill's End by Ivan Southall.
Ash Road by Ivan Southall.
When the City Stopped by Joan Phipson.

FIGURE 10.3
Brainstorming Ideas by Book

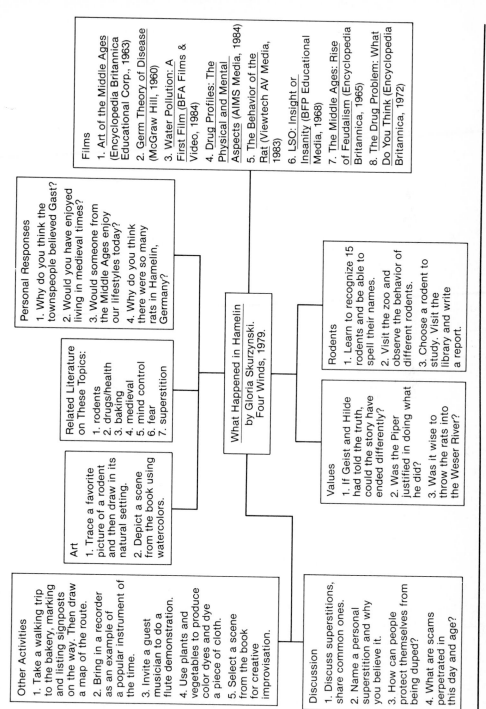

**Other Activities**

1. Take a walking trip to the bakery, marking and listing signposts on the way. Then draw a map of the route.

2. Bring in a recorder as an example of a popular instrument of the time.

3. Invite a guest musician to do a flute demonstration.

4. Use plants and vegetables to produce color dyes and dye a piece of cloth.

5. Select a scene from the book for creative improvisation.

**Art**

1. Trace a favorite picture of a rodent and then draw in its natural setting.

2. Depict a scene from the book using watercolors.

**Related Literature on These Topics:**

1. rodents
2. drugs/health
3. baking
4. medieval
5. mind control
6. fear
7. superstition

**Personal Responses**

1. Why do you think the townspeople believed Gast?

2. Would you have enjoyed living in medieval times?

3. Would someone from the Middle Ages enjoy our lifestyles today?

4. Why do you think there were so many rats in Hamelin, Germany?

**Films**

1. Art of the Middle Ages (Encyclopedia Britannica Educational Corp., 1963)

2. Germ Theory of Disease (McGraw Hill, 1960)

3. Water Pollution: A First Film (BFA Films & Video, 1984)

4. Drug Profiles: The Physical and Mental Aspects (AIMS Media, 1984)

5. The Behavior of the Rat (Viewtech AV Media, 1983)

6. LSO: Insight or Insanity (BFP Educational Media, 1968)

7. The Middle Ages: Rise of Feudalism (Encyclopedia Britannica, 1965)

8. The Drug Problem: What Do You Think (Encyclopedia Britannica, 1972)

**What Happened in Hamelin** by Gloria Skurzynski. Four Winds, 1979.

**Rodents**

1. Learn to recognize 15 rodents and be able to spell their names.

2. Visit the zoo and observe the behavior of different rodents.

3. Choose a rodent to study. Visit the library and write a report.

**Values**

1. If Geist and Hilde had told the truth, could the story have ended differently?

2. Was the Piper justified in doing what he did?

3. Was it wise to throw the rats into the Weser River?

**Discussion**

1. Discuss superstitions, share common ones.

2. Name a personal superstition and why you believe it.

3. How can people protect themselves from being duped?

4. What are scams perpetrated in this day and age?

come by. Some libraries have cooperative lending programs that permit teachers to check out a set of books for use in their classrooms.

Perusing the paperbacks in nearby bookstores may result in a discovery of some books that students could purchase. A list of these books can be provided to students for them to purchase or to check out from the library.

At the end of this chapter, reference sources for identification of related titles are provided. These sources may be particularly helpful for those seeking less common topics and themes or if library support services are limited.

Eventually, teachers who wish to utilize literature to enhance their subject matter will want to strive for the purchase of books on the themes and topics taught every year. These books can be kept in the classroom on shelves marked by topic, such as ecology, space science, animals, and earth science. The task of material selection and location becomes easier with time. Many parent-teacher organizations will provide funds for the purchase of such books. It will be incumbent upon the teacher to (1) locate the titles, authors, and ordering information; (2) write this information down; and (3) submit it with a cover letter requesting the purchase of the materials and the rationale for use of the books. This task, though time-consuming, will be well rewarded when the books arrive.

▶ STEP 3: **Provide shared literary experiences and dwell on the book experiences.**    Teachers have found many ways to provide a book experience that can be shared by all class members. Two of the most popular ways are: (1) the teacher reads aloud to the entire class and (2) the students read books selected from a list of titles on the topic or theme.

*Teachers Reading Aloud.*    The first way to provide a shared literary experience is by reading a good book to an entire class. This activity can present an experience enjoyed by both teacher and students that can be utilized for future discussion of concepts from the unit of study. A tradebook (a library-type book as opposed to a textbook) may be used as a schema and interest builder before reading the textbook or to elaborate and extend the content and concepts during and after the reading of the text (Brozo and Tomlinson, 1986). Some techniques to keep in mind for an enjoyable read-aloud experience are shown in Figure 10.4.

Drawing on the tradebook to amplify and deepen the concepts and understandings being taught in the unit of study may be accomplished by asking the students how the facts or events being studied were presented in the tradebook. For example, in studying the industries of Australia, students could be asked what types of industries were pursued in central Australia where the book, *The Fire in the Stone* by Thiele (1974), took place.

After a read-aloud session it is worthwhile to elicit students' responses to the book in order to keep them actively involved in the story. Some topics for discussion might be: What kind of story is this? What do you think of Ernie? his father? his best friend? What do you think will happen tomorrow? What does this story remind you of? Students may also record their responses in written form.

FIGURE 10.4 —————————————————————————————
Read-Aloud Techniques for Teachers

1. Select a book appropriate to the topic. Be sure the book has well-described characters that students can relate to, a fairly fast-moving plot, and strong emotional appeal. Read the book yourself before reading it aloud. You may encounter words that you need to practice for pronunciation and certain phrasings that need rehearsing. You will also want to know generally what to expect as you read the story aloud. Some books contain sensitive material that you will want to consider how to treat.
2. Minimize distractions by asking students to put papers, books, and pens aside and to remain quiet and seated. Be sure students are comfortable and relaxed. External distractions might be lowered by posting a sign on the classroom announcing reading time.
3. Give a brief introduction to the book before beginning the reading. Include the title, author, and some hint at the topic of the story in order to gain attention and build interest in the story. It often helps to permit students to see how the book may relate to their lives or connect with their prior knowledge. For example, a teacher may say, "I will be reading the book, *The Fire in the Stone,* by Colin Thiele, for the next few weeks. This story is set in Australia and is about a fourteen-year-old boy who makes friends with a boy of a different race. . . ." "What do you know about Australia? What do you think the title refers to? Now let's see what happens in this book."
4. Read fluently with lots of expression in your voice. Your voice is an effective tool for conveying the meanings, feelings, and drama of the story. You can vary your voice by using a low to high pitch, soft to loud volume, and slow to fast pace. I usually begin a story with a soft, steady voice which permits me to change volume, pace, and pitch for dramatic effects.
5. Maintain eye contact with the class while reading aloud. This provides greater closeness between the reader and the class.
6. Break at a natural stopping point, usually a chapter ending. Permit students to share their reactions to the story. It is not necessary, and often not desirable, to ask comprehension questions after reading. However, explanations of parts of the story can be made if the teacher senses that the students are having difficulty understanding.

—————————————————————————————————

Some teachers encourage students to keep a response journal in which they record their reactions to the reading.

*Students Read from a List.*    The second way to provide a shared literary experience is for individual students to read books selected from a list of related titles. When using this approach, the teacher develops a list of titles and authors with an indication of where each book can be obtained (school or class library, public library, bookstore). A brief annotation helps students to know something about each book so that they can select books of interest to them. On a designated day students may bring the books they have selected to class. A few minutes of class time may be used for each student to share first impressions of the book—gleaned from the cover, from the book jacket, or by scanning the book. The remaining twenty to twenty-five minutes of the class is best devoted to reading the books in order to help students get a good start. Students will then find it easier to continue the reading on their own outside of class. Students should be encouraged to carry the book with them so that any extra time in classes can be spent on reading.

Next, the teacher sets a date by which the books should be completely read. On this date students bring their books to class. The students will meet in book groups in order to share their reactions to the book read and to connect the book to the topic of study. These groups might be established by the type of books read; for example, all books placed in urban Australia will be discussed in one group, rural Australia in another, and stories with Aborigines separated into another group. When I have used this method, I've placed students reading the same book, or books by the same author, in the same book discussion group. The size of the groups may vary. It has been my experience that more mature and socially cooperative classes can be grouped into fewer, larger groups of as many as seven or eight. Less mature students seem to work better in groups of three or four. Also, as students become more familiar with book discussion groups, they become more adept and capable of working together.

Activities within the groups can be highly structured or open-ended. I have found a combination of both formats to be successful. I suggest that each student introduce his or her book with a standard "book talk." The student shows the book first. The book talk will include author, title, and a brief retelling of the story (six to eight sentences is a good rule of thumb for most books). Personal reactions to the book are included in the book talk. In fact, I have observed that most students start with personal reactions and follow with the story summary. After a book talk, group members are encouraged to ask questions of the reader or offer their personal thoughts on the book.

A chart that helps students identify aspects of the book that relate to the topic of study is often helpful. (See Figure 10.5.) Students may address certain points in relation to the topic of study.

Another chart compares concepts treated in the tradebooks with those presented in the textbook. An example from social studies is shown in Figure 10.6.

▶ STEP 4: **Consider alternative ways to share books and extend the book experience.**   The class discussions and book groups discussed above are two ways you can help students relate a tradebook (library-type book) to the unit of study and encourage their responses to the literary experience. Traditional book reports have often been assigned as a means to encourage response to a book. Students, however, often perceive this practice as "checking up" on them and as such, it seldom has the desired effect. In fact, many students comment that they dread reading the books because they know the inevitable

FIGURE 10.5 ────────────────────────────────────────────

Identifying Aspects of a Book

Book: <u>Fire in the Store</u>
Topic of Study: Australia
Author: Colin Thiele (1974)

|  | General Relationship to Unit of Study | Specific Incidents from Tradebook |
|---|---|---|
| <u>Setting</u><br>  Place<br>  Time | Australia— modern times | Central Australia in a mining town. Distances between places not specified. |
| <u>Characters</u><br>  Homes<br>  Families<br>  Schooling<br>  Occupations<br>  Relationships | mixed races—white and Aborigines | occupations— unskilled labor, mining of opals, no schools |
| <u>Themes</u><br>  or values | judge people by their acts, not their color or race | Ernie develops a true friendship with an Aborigine boy |

────────────────────────────────────────────

book report will follow. A list of ten book-related projects may offer additional ideas for extending the students' experiences with the book and enriching the unit of study. (See Figure 10.7.) Activities involving cooperative learning are especially appropriate with early adolescents who are naturally peer-oriented. Many of the activities presented in Figure 10.7 can be done in pairs or groups.

Providing a shared literary experience to enhance the teaching of specific content areas can (1) develop renewed interest in the content being studied, (2) deepen students' understandings of the people under study and their lives, and (3) help students develop critical thinking abilities as they weigh and compare information from different sources. In addition, using tradebooks in content area classrooms is one way to start students reading more widely. Once a student has become involved in a good book read aloud by a skilled reader or a book he or she has enjoyed reading individually, the student is ready to read other books.

FIGURE 10.6 ───────────────────────────────────
Comparing Concepts in Textbooks and Tradebooks

|  | Textbook | Tradebook |
|---|---|---|
| <u>Economy</u><br>  Natural resources<br>  Occupations<br>  Industries<br>  Transportation<br>  Money |  |  |
| <u>Political System</u><br>  Government<br>  Capitol<br>  Political divisions<br>    (states, territories) |  |  |
| <u>History</u><br>  Early<br>  Modern |  |  |
| <u>Social Institutions</u><br>  Families<br>  Schools<br>  Homes<br>  Hospitals<br>  Prisons<br>  Religion<br>  Sports<br>  Culture: art, theater,<br>    dance, music |  |  |

## SUMMARY

Literature is an important aspect of the middle level school curriculum and can readily be integrated into all content area classrooms. Sustained silent reading

FIGURE 10.7 ———————————————————————————————————
Ten Book-Related Projects

1. Prepare a brief biography of the author and present it orally or in writing.
2. Develop a TV script based on one exciting scene from the book. Groups could select, plan, write, and present different scenes to the class.
3. Describe the setting of the book and explain how the setting was important to the events.
4. Select one character from the book to discuss in detail—physical appearance; emotional, mental, and physical attributes; kinds of friends and family; and so forth.
5. Tell what kind of people would enjoy the book and why.
6. Discuss why you think the author wrote the book and what the author thought readers would get from the book.
7. Write a first-person description of an event in the story, told as though the writer was an onlooker (such as a new character, a pet, or an inanimate object).
8. As a group, plan and write a sequel to the story. Compare sequels written by different groups.
9. Develop a list of new words and their meanings. This activity can be fun when related to a book set in a foreign country. Foreign words and phrases can be explored.
10. Compare the facts found in the tradebook with those found in the textbook. Look for agreement and contradictions. Seek additional sources to determine authenticity.

programs can help early adolescent students develop the habit of wide reading. Literature can enliven and enrich the teaching of content area classes by telling the stories of the people who made the events of social studies and science happen. Strategies for using literature across the curriculum are included in this chapter.

At the end of this chapter, three lists are provided to assist teachers in their selection of books to supplement the content area curricula. Also, samples of four recent books with activities that could be used in the classrooms of different content areas are provided. Teachers who implement interdisciplinary units and want to incorporate more literature in their curricula have found these suggestions helpful.

The "Starter List of Literature for Shared Literary Experiences" suggests relatively recent titles arranged by content areas. Each title is briefly annotated to suggest the topics of the books. Many outstanding books have not been mentioned for lack of space and many fine new titles are published each year. Books on any of the lists could be considered by a language arts teacher in selecting literary texts. Various resources are available to help teachers seek out titles on specific topics. Some of these are listed in the "Book Selection Aids" section.

## REFERENCES

Atwell, N. (1987). *In the middle: Writing, reading, and learning.* Upper Montclair, NJ: Boynton/Cook Publishers.

Brozo, W. G., and Tomlinson, C. M. (1986). Literature: The key to lively content courses. *The Reading Teacher, 40,* 288–293.

Fader, D. N., and McNeil, E. B. (1968). *Hooked on books: Program and proof.* New York: Berkley.

Huck, C. S., Hepler, S., and Hickman, J. (1987). *Children's literature in the elementary school.* New York: Holt, Rinehart and Winston.

Lynch-Brown, C., and Tomlinson, C. M. (1986). Batchelder books: International read alouds. *Top of the News, 42,* 260–266.

Paulsen, G. (1987). *The hatchet.* New York: Bradbury.

Richter, H. P. (1970). *Friedrich.* New York: Holt, Rinehart and Winston.

Skurzynski, G. (1979). *What happened in Hamelin?* New York: Four Winds.

Thiele, C. (1974). *Fire in the stone.* New York: Harper.

### Samples of Books with Teaching Suggestions

Paulsen, Gary. *The Hatchet.* Bradbury, 1987. 195 pages. 1988 Newbery Honor Book.

**Summary:**  Brian Robeson spends fifty-four days in the Canadian wilderness after the plane taking him to visit his father crashes. He learns to survive with only the hatchet his mother gave him as a present, and he learns to survive his parents' divorce as well.

**Activities:**

*Language Arts:*  Compare how Karana in *The Island of the Blue Dolphins* and Brian in *The Hatchet* handle survival. In what ways did they find food and shelter? What are some of the same things they ate and did to keep alive?

*Science:*  Brian found an ingenious way to make fire without matches. How many different ways can you think of to make a fire? What elements do you need to make a fire? Is it always necessary to have a spark? What conditions must be met to maintain a fire? What benefits did fire provide Brian?

*Mathematics:*  Draw a map of New England and eastern Canada to scale or use a published map of the area. Draw a circle around Hampton, New York, indicating the distance that the plane could have traveled before it ran out of gas and crashed. Assume the plane was traveling in a northwesterly direction at 160 mph for four hours. Shade in the area in which the rescue team should concentrate its search.

*Home Economics:*  Bring in choke cherries and raspberries. Compare their taste. What are the nutritional properties of these berries? Could someone

survive on just berries and water? For how long? What other foods did Brian find and eat? What effect did his diet have on him physically and why?
*Social Science:*   Brian found porcupines, moose, and wolves during his fifty-four days alone in the Canadian wilderness. What other animals could he have encountered? During what time or year do you think the story takes place? How would the environment be different if Brian had stayed two to three months longer?

**Other books by the author:**  *Dogsong* (1986 Newbery Honor Book), *Sentries, Tracker, Dancing Carl.*

Mazer, Norma Fox. *After the Rain.* Morrow, 1987, 290 pages. 1988 Newbery Honor Book.

**Summary:**  Fifteen-year-old Rachel gets to know her grandfather well only after discovering he is dying. Her experiences in getting to know him are warm, frustrating, and bittersweet. This is the story of two individuals—one at the end of his life and the other at the beginning of womanhood.

**Activities:**
*Social Studies:*   See the movie "Cocoon" after reading this book. Discuss the different ways that the movie and this book handle their characters' responses to the elderly and the infirm. Discuss what society's responsibility is to its aging population. Who should take care of them? the family? What if the family is not able?
*Language Arts:*   Write a letter to a fictional elderly acquaintance of yours in which you describe what you did last weekend. Write a letter from the elderly acquaintance to you describing what he or she did last weekend.
*Health:*   What are mesothelioma and asbestosis? Some occupations have been associated with these diseases. What do you think they would be? Is asbestos commonly used today? Why?

**Other books by the author:**  *Taking Terri Mueller, A Figure of Speech, Saturday, the Twelfth of October, Dear Bill, Remember Me?, Downtown, Up in Seth's Room, The Solid Gold Kid.*

Voigt, Cynthia. *Homecoming.* Atheneum, 1981. 318 pages.

**Summary:**  A story of four children abandoned at a shopping mall by their confused and emotionally disturbed mother. The journey to their grandmother's house led by thirteen-year-old Dicey includes ducking authorities, sleeping in cemeteries, and doing anything to keep out of foster homes.

**Activities:**
*Home Economics:*   Plan meals for four children for two days with only $7.00. Where would you get the food? A supermarket? a 7-11? a vending machine?

Why? Where can you buy food the most economically? Find out the difference in price between the day-old and damaged goods at a grocery store and their everyday prices.

*Social Studies:* Trace the path the Tillerman children took from Provincetown, Massachusetts, to Chesapeake Bay, Maryland. How many miles did they travel?

*Language Arts:* Write a newspaper article about the missing children. Include sightings from people they met along the way. Be sure to include who, what, when, where, and why.

*Health:* What is mental illness? Is it hereditary? What are some of the symptoms of various types of mental illness? Is depression a symptom? Is it true that everyone gets depressed sometimes? What is the difference between the normal kind of depression and the kind found in mental illness?

**Other books by the author:** *Dicey's Song, Building Blocks, Solitary Blue, Tell Me If the Lovers Are Losers.*

Fox, Paula. *One-Eyed Cat.* Bradbury, 1984. 216 pages. 1985 Newbery Honor Book.

**Summary:** When Ned Wallis is given a rifle for his birthday from his uncle, his parents forbid him to use it until he is older. Ned cannot resist sneaking it out of the house and shooting it just once. He shoots at a dark shadow and later spots a wild cat with one missing eye. His guilt grows as he feels distanced from his parents and friends because he cannot bring himself to reveal his painful secret.

**Activities:**
*Science:* What is the purpose of lightning rods? How do they work? Does lightning ever strike twice? Are there areas of the country that attract lightning more than other areas? Why?

*Health:* What is rheumatoid arthritis? How does it develop and what are the symptoms and usual treatments? What is chrysotherapy?

*Home Economics:* Boil a perfect potato and prepare it like Ned's Uncle Hilary described in one of his letters. Is there a difference in the texture of a boiled and a baked potato? Take a survey of your class to find out which way is preferred.

*Social Studies:* Research the battle on South Mountain, the Antietam Campaign in the Civil War during which Mr. Scully's father was fatally wounded. Where in the country was the battle fought and who won the battle?

*Language Arts:* Write an essay on why you liked or disliked the character Ned Wallis and whether you would have handled the secret of the one-eyed cat the same as Ned.

**Other books by the author:** *Slave Dancer, Blowfish Live in the Sea, The Stone-faced Boy.*

## Starter List of Literature for
## Shared Literary Experiences

**Health:**
*After the Rain* by Norma Fox Mazer. Morrow, 1987. (aging and death)
*The Alfred Summer* by Jan Slepian. Macmillan, 1980. (cerebral palsy)
*The Contender* by Robert Lipsyte. Harper, 1967. (Harlem setting; drug abuse)
*Cracker Jackson* by Betsy Byars. Viking, 1985. (wife abuse)
*Deenie* by Judy Blume. Bradbury, 1973. (curvature of the spine)
*Dicey's Song* and *Homecoming* by Cynthia Voigt. Scribner, 1982 and Atheneum,
    1981. (mental illness)
*The Divorce Express* by Paula Danziger. Delacorte, 1982. (effects of divorce on a
    fourteen-year-old girl)
*A Hero Ain't Nothin' but a Sandwich* by Alice Childress. Putnam, 1973. (heroin
    addiction)
*I'll Get There, It Better Be Worth the Trip* by John Donovan. Harper, 1969. (brief
    homosexual encounter between two boys; alcoholism)
*The Language of Goldfish* by Zibby Oneal. Viking, 1980. (thirteen-year-old girl's
    depression, suicide attempt, and recovery)
*Summer of the Swans* by Betsy Byars. Viking, 1970. (mental retardation)
*Then Again, Maybe I Won't* by Judy Blume. Bradbury, 1971. (developing
    sexuality; thirteen-year-old-boy)

**Language Arts:**
*All Together Now* by Sue Ellen Bridgers. Knopf, 1979. (theme of love)
*Boy Alone* by Reginald Ottley. Harcourt, 1966. (Australian outback setting)
*Dear Mr. Henshaw* by Beverly Cleary. Morrow, 1983. (letter and journal writing)
*The Diary of Trilby Frost* by Diana Glaser. Holiday, 1976. (diary format)
*Fire in the Stone* by Colin Thiele. Harper, 1974. (opal mining town in Australian
    setting; exciting plot; character development)
*I, Trissy* by Norma Fox Mazer. Delacorte, 1971. (first person; letter)
*The Ice Is Coming* by Patricia Wrightson. Atheneum, 1977. (first in Australian
    trilogy; based on Aboriginal myths)
*Island of the Blue Dolphins* by Scott O'Dell. Houghton, 1960. (Indian girl survives
    on an island alone)
*The Leopard* by Cecil Bodker. Atheneum, 1975. (set in Ethiopia; exciting plot)
*The Lion, the Witch and the Wardrobe* by C. S. Lewis. Macmillan, 1961. (struggle
    between good and evil; first in a series)
*Rabble Starkey* by Lois Lowry. Houghton, 1987. (theme of home, love, and
    security)
*Sarah, Plain and Tall* by Patricia MacLachlan. Harper & Row, 1985. (descriptive
    language)
*Sweet Whispers, Brother Rush* by Virginia Hamilton. Putnam, Philomel, 1982.
    (first-person narrative)

*When Shlemiel Went to Warsaw and Other Stories* by Isaac Singer. Farrar, 1968. (folk tales)

*Where the Lilies Bloom* by Vera and Bill Cleaver. Lippincott, 1979. (integral setting; Appalachian mountain region)

*Z for Zachariah* by Robert O'Brien. Atheneum, 1975. (diary format)

**Science:**

*All Creatures Great and Small* by James Herriot. St. Martin's, 1972, Bantam, 1978. (humorous story of a country veterinarian)

*The Cry of the Crow* by Jean Craighead George. Harper, 1980. (communication between a girl and a crow)

*Dogsong* by Gary Paulsen, Bradbury. 1985. (Eskimo life; survival story)

*The Far Side of Evil* by Sylvia Engdahl. Atheneum, 1971. (misuse of nuclear power)

*Hatchet* by Gary Paulsen. Bradbury, 1987. (survival in Canadian wilderness)

*House of Stairs* by William Sleator. Dutton, 1974. (psychological experiments on humans)

*Incident at Hawk's Hill* by Allan Eckert. Little Brown, 1971. (young boy protected by a badger in Canada; based on fact)

*Julie of the Wolves* by Jean Craighead George. Harper & Row, 1972. (natural science)

*Let a River Be* by Betty Sue Cummings. Atheneum, 1978. (ecology)

*Mrs. Frisby and the Rats of NIMH* by Robert C. O'Brien. Atheneum, 1971. (animal experiments)

*Never Cry Wolf* by Farley Mowat. Brown, 1963. Bantam, 1979. (scientist's adventure in the Arctic)

*Snowbound* by Harry Mazer. Dell, 1973. (survival in nature)

*This Time of Darkness* by H. M. Hoover. Viking, 1980. (future world in which people live underground safe from outside air and sun)

*The Voyage Begun* by Nancy Bond. Atheneum, 1981. (depletion of energy supply)

*A Wizard of Earthsea* by Ursula LeGuin. Houghton, 1968. (magician and evil powers)

*A Wrinkle in Time* by Madeleine L'Engle. Farrar, 1962. (extraterrestrials in outer space)

**Social Studies:**

*Across Five Aprils* by Irene Hunt. Follett, 1964. (Civil War)

*The Battle Horse* by Harry Kullman. Bradbury, 1981. (Stockholm in 1930s by a Swedish writer)

*Beauty: A Retelling of the Story of Beauty and the Beast* by Robin McKinley. Harper, 1978. (Middle Ages based on folktale)

*The Cay* by Theodore Taylor. Doubleday, 1969. (survival in the Caribbean in 1942 by a Black man and color-conscious white boy)

*The Chocolate War* by Robert Cormier. Pantheon, 1974. (individual against the system)

*The Clan of the Cave Bear* by Jean Auel. Bantam, 1980. (fictionalized cave men)

*A Day No Pigs Would Die* by Robert Newton Peck. Knopf, 1972, Dell, 1978. (1920s in rural Vermont; a Shaker family)

*Dragonwings* by Laurence Yep. Harper & Row, 1975. (Chinese immigration to California)

*The Fire in the Stone* by Colin Thiele. Harper, 1974. (Australia; opal mines)

*Friedrich* by Hans Richter. Holt, 1970. (World War II)

*Good Night, Mr. Tom* by Michelle Magorian. Harper, 1982. (World War II)

*The Great Gilly Hopkins* by Katherine Paterson. Crowell, 1978. (girl placed in a foster family; coping with change; learning to love)

*Homesick: My Own Story* by Jean Fritz. Putnam, 1982. (Chinese communist revolution)

*The Island on Bird Street* by Uri Orlev. Houghton Mifflin, 1984. (boy struggling for survival in a Polish ghetto during World War II)

*Jacob Have I Loved* by Katherine Paterson. Harper, 1980. (isolated island setting off Maine during World War II)

*Journey to Topaz* by Yoshiko Uchida. Scribner, 1971. (internment of Japanese Americans during World War II)

*Lincoln: A Photobiography* by Russell Freedman. Houghton, 1987.

*My Brother Sam is Dead* by James and Christopher Collier. Scholastic, 1974. (Revolutionary War)

*The Outsiders* by S. E. Hinton. Viking, 1967. (gang conflict)

*The Pinballs* by Betsy Byars. Harper, 1977. (three children in a foster home)

*A Proud Taste for Scarlet and Miniver* by E. L. Konigsburg. Atheneum, 1973. (Eleanor of Aquitane)

*The Road to Camlann* by Rosemary Sutcliff. Dutton, 1982. (Middle Ages; King Arthur)

*Roll of Thunder, Hear My Cry* and sequel, *Let the Circle Be Unbroken* by Mildred Taylor. Dial, 1976 and 1981. (1930s in rural Mississippi; a Black family)

*The Sign of the Beaver* by Elizabeth George Speare. Houghton, 1983. (boy is befriended by Indians in Maine territory)

*Sing Down the Moon* by Scott O'Dell. Houghton, 1970. (story of Navaho Indians driven from their homes)

*Slake's Limbo* by Felice Holman. Scribner, 1974. (survival in New York subway system)

*The Slave Dancer* by Paula Fox. Bradbury, 1973. (pre-Civil War)

*Summer of My German Soldier* by Bette Green. Bantam, 1973. (World War II)

*What Happened in Hamelin* by Gloria Skurzynski. Four Winds, 1979. (Middle Ages)

*When the City Stopped* by Joan Phipson. Harcourt, 1978. (Sydney, Australia, closes down; havoc ensues).

*Words by Heart* by Ouida Sebestyen. Little Brown, 1979. (pioneer West; Black family)

## Book Selection Aids

### Annotated Subject Guides for Particular Topics

*Children's Catalog,* 14th ed. New York: H. W. Wilson Co., 1981, with annual supplements. Includes 5000 recent books, grade levels, summaries, and a selective list of best books in fiction and nonfiction.

*Junior High School Library Catalog.* 5th ed. New York: H. W. Wilson Co., 1985, with annual supplements. Similar to the *Children's Catalog* but includes books for early adolescents.

*Bookfinder, Volume 3: When Kids Need Books: Annotations of Books Published 1979–1982.* Circle Pines, MN: American Guidance Service, 1985. Includes cross-indexing by subject, author, and title. Books selected focus on emotions, problems, and relationships.

*Best Books for Children: Preschool Through Middle Grades.* 3rd ed. Ann Arbor, MI: R. R. Bowker, 1985. An annotated listing arranged by major curriculum areas.

*The Best of Children's Books, 1964–1978 with 1979 Addenda.* Virgina Haviland. Library of Congress. New York: University Press Books. An annotated list of 1000 titles including books for ages preschool through junior high.

*The Elementary School Library Collection.* Lois Winkel, ed. Williamsport, PA: Bro-Dart Foundation, 1984. A bibliography of print and nonprint materials for elementary school media collections. This basic list includes annotations, bibliographic information, as well as author, title, and subject indexes.

*Your Reading: A Booklist for Junior High and Middle School Students.* Urbana, IL: National Council of Teachers of English, 1983. An annotated list of books for grades 5–9, arranged in broad subject categories.

### Booklists for Separate Content Areas

*Reading Ladders for Human Relations.* 6th ed. Eileen Tway, ed. Urbana, IL: National Council of Teachers of English and American Council of Education, 1981. Annotated bibliography arranged by themes on self-concept, relationships, and cultural understandings. Includes ages preschool through high school.

*Index to Collective Biographies for Young Readers.* 3rd ed. Judith Silverman, ed. Ann Arbor, MI: R. R. Bowker, 1979. An index including over 7000 biographies by names and by subjects for students ages elementary through middle school.

*World History in Juvenile Books: A Geographical and Chronological Guide.* Seymour Metzner, ed. Bronx, NY: 1977. Includes fiction and nonfiction titles with chronological and geographical listings. Covers books for elementary and middle school students.

*Reading for Young People Series* Chicago, IL: American Library Association, 1979–1985. Eight volumes, by region, of annotated bibliographies of fiction and nonfiction for elementary through 10th grade of books on the life and history of various American regions.

*Best Science Books for Children: Selected and Annotated.* Kathryn Wolff et al., eds. Washington, DC: American Association for the Advancement of Science, 1985. An annotated bibliography of science tradebooks of good quality.

*Science Books for Children: Selections from Booklist, 1976–1983.* Selected by Denise Murcko Wilms. Chicago, IL: American Library Association, 1985. A listing of science books with author, title, and subject indexes.

*Careers in Fact and Fiction.* June Klein Bienstock and Ruth Beinstock Anolick. Chicago, IL: American Library Association, 1985. An annotated list of fiction and nonfiction, including biographies, which discuss careers.

*Children's Mathematics Books: A Critical Bibliography.* Margaret Matthias and Diane Thiessen, eds. Chicago, IL: American Library Association, 1979. Contains annotations of books in six areas of mathematics: counting, geometry, measurement, number concepts, time, and other.

*Health, Illness and Disability: A Guide to Books for Children and Young Adults.* Pat Azarnoff, ed. Ann Arbor, MI: R. R. Bowker, 1983. Reviews over 1000 books, fiction and nonfiction, about health issues and problems.

**Especially for Reading Aloud**

*The Read Aloud Handbook.* Jim Trelease. New York: Penguin Books, 1985. Lengthy annotations in which appropriateness for different age levels is included.

*For Reading Outloud! A Guide to Sharing Books with Children.* M. M. Kimmel and E. Segel. Dell, 1984. Full annotations with appropriate listening levels indicated. Also has a chapter cross-listing the books by settings—regions of the United States and other countries.

**Children's and Adolescent Literature**

The textbooks that focus on children's literature also include books for the middle school level student. The adolescent literature books focus on high schools but also provide many titles appropriate for early adolescents. There are sections in all of these textbooks in which different genres of literature and types of books within them are discussed. For example, a science teacher might read the sections on science fiction, realistic animal stories, and biographies of famous scientists in selecting related literature for the seventh-grade science curriculum.

*Children's Literature in the Elementary School.* 4th ed. Charlotte S. Huck, Susan Hepler, and Janet Hickman. New York: Holt, 1987.

*Children and Books.* 7th ed. Zena Sutherland and May Hill Arbuthnot. Glenview, IL: Scott Foresman, 1986.

*Literature for Today's Young Adults.* 2nd ed. Alleen Pace Nilsen and Kenneth L. Donelson. Glenview, IL: Scott Foresman, 1985.

*Reaching Adolescents: The Young Adult Book and the School.* Arthea J. S. Reed. New York: Holt, 1985.

# Chapter 11

# Middle Level Schools

The term *middle school* generally refers to a school for early adolescents that is seeking to follow a certain philosophical orientation called *the middle school concept*. Most of these schools consist of grades 6 through 8 but they may be organized in a variety of different ways: grades 5 through 8 or, very commonly, grades 7 and 8. In recent years *middle level* has emerged as a term that refers to the full range of grades 5 through 9. Thus, middle schools and junior high schools (usually grades 7 through 9) may both be considered middle level schools.

The name on the building and the grades included, however, are far less important than the orientation of the faculty and the way the school is organized for instruction. The central focus of any middle level school should be on the students who are served. Children of ages ten through fourteen differ significantly from those at the elementary school or those at the high school. The middle level school is just what the name implies—a school for students in the middle. The authors of *An Agenda for Excellence* (NASSP, 1984) stated:

> [Educators in a successful middle school must] be certain that everyone who
> works in the middle level schools understands how youngsters of this age

develop and how that development affects their behavior and learning. All staff members, including noncertified personnel, should receive at least minimal training in early adolescent development (p. 20).

This chapter gives a historical perspective on middle level education and presents information on the growth of the middle school movement. Next, it explores the essential elements of a "true" middle school. The chapter closes with a discussion of the implications that school organization has on the facilitation of effective reading and writing instruction.

# A HISTORICAL PERSPECTIVE ON MIDDLE LEVEL EDUCATION

After the Civil War, the number of high schools in the United States increased rapidly. The organization most school systems used was an eight-year elementary school followed by a four-year high school. In the early 1900s, however, a number of national committees issued reports that related to the 8-4 plan. A change to the 6-6 plan was often proposed, meaning that students would spend six years in elementary school and six years in high school. The plan was first advocated as a means of improving college preparation but it was soon tied to other objectives. High dropout and retention rates, the need for better transition from self-contained elementary schools to departmentalized high schools, and the newly scientifically discovered extent of individual differences all supported the need to reorganize.

Although the initial effort was a downward extension of secondary education (8-4 to 6-6), the notion of dividing the six years of secondary education into junior and senior periods appeared early in the discussions and was specifically recommended in the famous Cardinal Principles of Secondary Education (1918). The rationale for establishing separate junior high schools was rather compelling and not unlike the justification for contemporary middle schools. The considerations most frequently cited were overcrowding in the high schools, a high dropout and retention rate, the need to ease the transition into high school, the necessity for a school that meets the needs of the early adolescent, the need for improved guidance services, reducing the repetition of elementary content, and an earlier start in college preparation courses.

In 1910, the first official junior high school opened its doors in Columbus, Ohio. A surprisingly rapid growth of such schools occurred, as shown in Table 11.1.

Figure 11.1 illustrates movement in the last two decades toward more schools organized in the 6-8 configuration. Providing separate schools for early adolescents is no longer a trend in our country—it is a well-established majority practice. Until 1960, these schools were usually labeled junior high schools. The stated functions of the junior high school were to (1) integrate skills, attitudes,

TABLE 11.1 ⎯⎯⎯⎯⎯⎯⎯⎯⎯⎯⎯

| | Number of Separate Junior High Schools |
|---|---|
| 1916 | 254 |
| 1924 | 880 |
| 1934 | 1948 |
| 1945 | 2654 |
| 1960 | 4996 |
| 1963 | 7143 |

*Source:* From *Curriculum for the Middle School Years* by John H. Lounsbury and Gordon E. Vars. Copyright © 1978 by John H. Lounsbury and Gordon E. Vars. Reprinted by permission of Harper & Row.

and understandings into wholesome behavior; (2) help students explore both academic and vocational interests; (3) provide guidance for students in helping them make better decisions and to help students make satisfactory social and emotional adjustments; (4) differentiate educational opportunities in accord with varying backgrounds and personalities in order to maximize individual achievement; (5) socialize students to a complex society; and (6) articulate a smooth transition from the elementary grades to the high school (Gruhn and Douglass, 1947).

The justification for establishing junior high schools seemed clear, reasonable, and, it should be noted, quite contemporary. As junior high schools became established, they tended to be too much like the name unfortunately given them and too little in tune with the objectives set for them. The typical junior high school soon became largely indistinguishable from the high school in its organization and operation. Departmentalization, competitive athletic programs, and related activities mimicked the high school. The junior high school become big and impersonal and seemed unable to serve early adolescents as intended.

## THE MIDDLE SCHOOL MOVEMENT

The *middle school movement* initially referred to the efforts of those educators who promoted the "middle school concept," often by comparing their theory with the reality of the junior high school. In fundamental ways, the middle school concept is no different from that of the junior high school. The needs of the early adolescent must be central to the structure and content of any middle level school, so the 1970s witnessed a melding of young middle school advocates and

FIGURE 11.1
Trends in School Organization

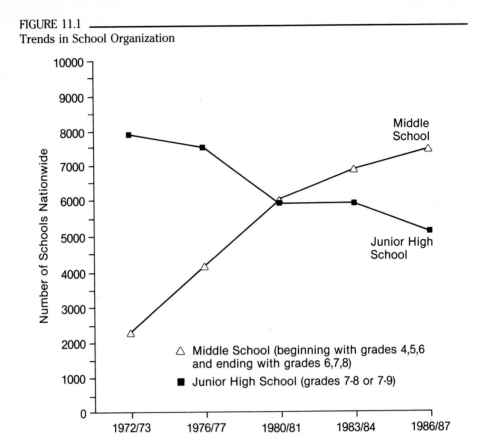

Source: U.S. Department of Education, 1988.

older junior high school educators. The term *middle level educators* encompasses both.

In the middle school, departmentalization should give way to interdisciplinary team organization, competitive sports to intramurals, and lecturing to cooperative learning. Industrial arts for boys and home economics for girls should be replaced by more broadly based exploratory programs.

The history of the middle school movement can be documented in at least two ways: by publications and by the professional organizations that support the movement.

## Publications

Donald Eichhorn (1966) published the first professional book that dealt solely with the middle school. In this book, Eichhorn not only described the unique characteristics of early adolescence, but coined the term *transescence* in order to have a specific term to label this distinctive age level. He defined the term as follows:

> The stage of development which begins prior to the onset of puberty and extends through the early stages of adolescence. Since puberty does not occur for all precisely at the same chronological time age in human development, the transescent designation is based upon the many physical, social, emotional, and intellectual changes that appear prior to the puberty cycle to the time in which the body gains a practical degree of stabilization over these complex pubescent changes (p. 3).

Eichhorn also presented a rationale for organizing a school between elementary and senior high school level which "met the physical, mental, and social needs of youngsters" (p. 2). Eichhorn advocated a school in which there was a "close relationship between the student and the adult school staff" (p. 59) and a learning environment that facilitated social involvement.

In a recently issued reprinting of *The Middle School,* Eichhorn (1987) reflected on the middle school movement. Eichhorn surmised that the middle school movement began for four reasons:

1. The recognition and reaffirmation of the belief that youngsters aged ten through fourteen are in a unique stage of development and share similar physical, mental, social, and emotional characteristics.

2. New medical evidence that youngsters attain puberty at an earlier age than ever before.

3. New technology, racial integration, and the knowledge explosion have affected society.

4. The junior high school organization was perceived and often became an institution patterned after the senior high school.

For many years, an exact definition of the middle school was not articulated. The rationale was that local initiative should be encouraged and that an articulated definition would be too limiting to developing middle schools. However, this lack of specificity seemed to result in the name *middle school* being attached to "any conceivable organizational structure and curriculum design" (National Middle School Association, 1982, p. 9). Therefore in 1982, a committee of prominent leaders of the National Middle School Association published a position paper (*This We Believe*) that articulated the essential elements of a "true" middle school. These elements will be detailed later in this chapter.

In 1984, the Middle Level Council of the National Association of Secondary School Principals issued *An Agenda for Excellence at the Middle Level.* This publication was to provide guidance for the middle school movement which was being unduly influenced by recommendations growing out of the report *A Nation at Risk* (National Commission on Excellence in Education, 1983) that really addressed the senior high school. The authors set forth twelve dimensions of schooling necessary for excellence at the middle level (p. iii). A basic theme of this document was that "we cannot teach [students] . . . all they need to know, we must teach them how to learn and how to adjust their lives to the changes that will surround them" (p. 1). Essentially, the document reaffirms generally accepted functions of a middle level school: an organization, a curriculum, and a set of instructional strategies that accommodate the needs of early adolescents and that help to prepare them for a future that we know little about.

The *Middle School Journal,* the official publication of the National Middle School Association, is the major national publication exclusively devoted to middle level education. This journal publishes reports of successful middle school programs and articles that provide insight into teaching and school organization at the middle level. The audience for this journal is primarily teachers and principals.

## Professional Organizations

When educators have common concerns, professional organizations serve the purpose of providing a vehicle for sharing ideas about those common concerns. The most prominent organizations that provide support for middle level educators are described below.

*National Middle School Association.* One of the first associations of middle school leaders, the Midwest Middle School Association decided in 1973 to go national. By 1976, the membership surpassed 1000 members and the NMSA currently has more than 5000 members, an array of publications, large annual conferences, and provides many related services. The purposes of the association are

(1) to promote the development and growth of middle level education as a distinct entity between elementary and high school in the structure of American education, (2) to promote the use of middle level education as the generic

descriptor for all school programs designed to accommodate the educational and developmental needs of youth between ages 10 and 15, (3) to promote forums which disseminate information about middle level education to educators, parents, and other lay citizens, and (4) to improve the educational experiences of youth during their middle level school years by assisting schools, the home, and other agencies as they strive to better meet the educational and developmental needs of these youngsters (NMSA brochure, n. d.).

In addition, there are thirty-two state affiliates associated with the National Middle School Association which enroll additional thousands of members. These affiliates publish a newsletter and a journal, hold annual conferences, and render other services. The New England League of Middle Schools, alone, has a membership of over 4000.

*The National Association of Secondary School Principals Council on Middle Level Education.*     This association has a membership of over 45,000 and is one of the nations strongest professional associations. Some 45 percent of its members have responsibility for the middle level grades. The association's Middle Level Council, appointed in 1981, has provided extensive services for middle level educators including special middle level publications, regular conferences, and information sharing. This group initiated the designation of National Middle Level Education Week in 1987 and is continuing to promote it each March.

*Center for Early Adolescence.*     This center "works to increase the effectiveness of agencies and individuals who have an impact upon the lives of 10 to 15 year olds. . . . The Center serves as a clearinghouse for information on the age group and trains professionals and volunteers to work with 10 to 15 year olds" (Center for Early Adolescence Publications Catalog, nd., p. 2). The fine publications from this center serve parents and educators alike. *Adolescent Literacy: What Works and Why* (Davidson and Koppenhaver, 1988) is a report of successful literacy programs across the country.

*National Resource Center for Middle Grades Education.*     The stated purpose of this relatively new resource center is to provide an "established series of activities designed to increase the effectiveness of teachers/administrators/support staff in planning, implementing, and conducting successful programs for early adolescent learners" (Schurr, personal communication, 1987). Specific functions of the resource center are to serve as a clearinghouse for materials, to provide staff development, and to make research information available to middle level educators. Each May, the resource center sponsors a research seminar in which noted leaders in middle level education speak.

## ESSENTIAL ELEMENTS OF A "TRUE" MIDDLE SCHOOL

The first statement of what a true middle school should be was set forth in *This We Believe* (National Middle School Association, 1982). Designed to provide guidance for middle level educators when making organizational, programmatic, or curricular decisions, this document identified ten elements deemed to be essential in a true middle school.

Many of these elements are conducive to the provision of effective reading and writing instruction. These elements are presented along with their implications for literacy instruction.

1. *Educators knowledgeable about and committed to transescents.*   In order to be an effective middle school educator, the unique needs and characteristics of the students must be understood and accommodated. It is important for teachers, administrators, and all support personnel, both certified and noncertified, to be knowledgeable about and committed to the middle level student.

When teachers understand the students' need to communicate, they can build instructional opportunities that facilitate communication and that improve language abilities as well. One teacher taught letter writing by providing pen pals from another city for her students. Another teacher who was sensitive to the emotional ups and downs of her students suggested books about young adults in transition. She then asked her students to write journal entries about those struggles and share them, if they wanted, in small groups. The feelings shared became topics for further study in advisor/advisee groups.

2. *A balanced curriculum based on transescent needs.*   The curriculum of a true middle school maintains a balance of academic goals and other human development needs. "The climate for learning and instructional processes used are nearly as important as the content itself" (pp. 10–22). Basic skills are usually stressed during the elementary grades as is content at the high school level. At the middle level, the learning processes should receive as much emphasis as content. That is, learning how to learn, learning to read to learn, and learning how to write to communicate and clarify thinking are all important areas for middle level instruction. But these abilities are not learned without direct instruction and opportunities for practice. The many learning strategies presented in this book will help students acquire these processes.

3. *A range of organizational arrangements.*   "A fully departmentalized, ability grouped, seven period day is incompatible with what we know about transescents and learning" (p. 11). Varied schedules and grouping patterns have a place in middle level schools. For example, when students are learning the writing process, they need a block of time to write, edit, revise, edit, and so forth. Writing instruction is more productive if students are engaged in writing everday for a month rather than one day a week for the entire year. Students need to

think, plan, read, write, revise, and rewrite. Creative scheduling can facilitate the learning of the writing process.

Some teachers combine the study of literature with writing assignments in the same genre, such as reading and writing dialogues or biographies. Such instruction takes time. An isolated language arts teacher in a tightly compartmentalized middle level school will have difficulty scheduling this full range of activities appropriately. With flexible scheduling, however, this concentrated effort can be accomplished.

4. *Varied instructional strategies.* "Transescents are curious, creative, and they like to experiment. Instructional strategies which take advantage of these desirable traits are most effective" (p. 12). Early adolescents need to move about; their attention span is only about twelve to twenty minutes. Thus, activities need to be changed regularly. Cooperative learning and discussion techniques (discussed fully in Chapter 4) are especially well suited for middle level students.

5. *A full exploratory program.* Early adolescence is a time of exploration. Middle grades students respond well to short-term, high-interest activities. Such programs offer courses to students in a variety of traditional and nontraditional areas. These courses may be in art, home economics, music, or industrial arts, supplemented by mini-courses such as photography, crocheting, or archaeology. Such courses are designed to extend beyond the basic curriculum and provide students an exposure to a variety of interests and subjects. Many schools use the expertise of parents to supplement faculty expertise in delivering these courses. Mini-courses normally are offered in shorter periods (twenty-five to thirty minutes) and for twelve to eighteen sessions, though options are innumerable and flexibility is the only rule. An exposure to a variety of subjects will help early adolescents identify or expand their interests before the specialization that characterizes high school takes over.

The role of interest and prior knowledge has long been documented as extremely important in reading and writing competence. The more that students know and have experienced, the better they will be able to read and write.

6. *Comprehensive advising and counseling.* All educators in a middle level school must, to some extent, play the role of a guidance counselor. One structured program commonly found in middle level schools is the *advisor/ advisee program.* In this program, each student is assigned to an advisor. A small group of students and that advisor meet regularly to talk about common student problems, study skills, career opportunities, and affective activities. Paul George (1983) believes that the strength of an advisor/advisee program lies in the interdisciplinary team organization, because such an organization allows topics discussed during the advisor/advisee time to be reinforced throughout the day.

Students benefit socially by the opportunity to engage discussions of value issues. Participation in an advisor/advisee program helps students see that their problems are not unique and provides them with a necessary support system.

7. *Continuous progress for students.*    Due to wide variations of physical, social, emotional, and intellectual development, the progress of early adolescents is difficult to monitor. Individual students must be helped to progress at their own rate and in accordance with their own learning styles. A single age or grade standard is indefensible given the varied rates of develoment.

8. *Evaluation procedures compatible with nature of transescents.*    "Evaluation needs to be viewed as an integral phase of the entire learning process, not just something done *to* the student *by* some outside authority" (p. 14). Self-understanding should be developed at the middle level. One way to do this is to include students actively in the evaluation process. Factors other than academic achievement need to be assessed and reported in the evaluation program.

9. *Cooperative planning.*    Schoolwide planning that involves administrators, teachers, specialists, support staff, and parents enhances the middle school program. An interdisciplinary team organization helps students feel that they belong to a group or family. A team usually consists of two to five teachers who share the same students, schedule, and area of the building. Other teachers, such as teachers of unified arts, fine arts, physical education, and reading, may be a part of the team, work with several teams, or comprise a team themselves. Many large schools have found this organization to be helpful in breaking a large faculty and student body into more manageable units, and thereby building a more familial feeling within the school.

Interdisciplinary teaming should not be confused with team teaching. In an interdisciplinary team organization, academic teachers share common students, not the same subject. Teams may occasionally plan thematic units, however. Teachers decide on a common discipline code and other management proce-dures. The key to the interdisciplinary team organization is that one group of students is directed by a group of teachers who can plan cooperatively for the students' success. George (1983) maintains that the interdisciplinary team organization is "fundamental and the fulcrum on which most of the remainder of the components are moved" (p. 6).

Without a team organization, an event such as the following can occur. After about four days into a unit on Environment in my seventh-grade social studies class, a student approached me and asked, "Is the environment we are studying in social studies the same environment we are studying in science?" Down the hall, one period earlier, and unbeknownst to me, the science teacher was teaching her own unit on environment. This was a disservice to our students. It is difficult for students to apply concepts learned in one discipline to another; team planning can make the obvious relationships easier for students to grasp.

Cooperative planning is also conducive to effective reading and writing instruction. In preparation for the Science Fair, one team finished the projects in the following way: (1) The *science* teacher helped students choose their topics. (2) The *reading* teacher helped students locate and select their references. She then taught students the Cornell Notetaking Method and guided their note taking from the references they had selected. (3) The *language arts* teacher took the notes and, through the composition process, taught students how to write a report. (4) The *math* teacher taught the students how to make tables, graphs, and charts, which all students included in their reports. (5) The *science* teacher dealt with the content of the report. Students received four grades on their reports.

What makes this type of planning especially effective is that the students learned the strategies of note taking, table/graph/chart construction, and report writing in a meaningful way, in the proper context, and from teachers competent in each area of content. In too many middle school classrooms, these processes are taught in isolation during different parts of the year and students are expected to recall the previous instruction while writing their science report. How much better to teach and apply the processes simultaneously. The necessary condition here is cooperative planning. When a school is organized for cooperative planning, many meaningful learning events can occur for students.

10. *Positive school climate.* "A good middle school is like a good family composed of persons of different ages, but all respected and all with particular roles and responsibilities" (p. 15).

A teacher I have been working with enrolled in a writing workshop. She is a wonderful language arts teacher who never considered herself to be a good writer. She wrote her first poem in that workshop, and it was published in an anthology. It was a risk for her to commit her feelings to paper, in a specific form, and make her feelings public. Her comment to me was, "Why has it taken me all of these years to write a poem?" The answer might be that she has never had a safe environment in which to try writing a poem.

All writing is a risk. Attempting to read a book with smaller print than the last one is a risk. Sharing ideas in a group discussion is a risk. But without risk taking, no learning would occur. Students, especially at the middle level, need to be encouraged to take risks. This is a time for experimentation. The environment for risk taking must be safe, however—like that found in a loving family.

# FUTURE DIRECTIONS OF MIDDLE LEVEL EDUCATION

Connors and Irvin (1989) found that many schools that were recognized as a "School for Excellence" were characterized by a high degree of "middle-schoolness"—the extent to which a school employs basic mid-

dle school concepts. That is, many more recognized schools were organized as "true" middle schools than were those from a sample chosen
randomly.

The organization of a middle school can be utilized to the benefit of reading
and writing instruction as well. The cooperative planning component of a middle
school has great potential to enhance literacy instruction in that school.
Teachers who plan instruction together for the same group of students can
provide those students with many meaningful contexts in which reading and
writing instruction can occur.

The advisor/advisee program also has potential to enhance reading and
writing instruction at the middle level. Some research indicates that talking
about the values issues in reading seems to improve comprehension (Irvin,
1980). Additionally, the wide experiences obtained through a broad-based
exploratory program help students comprehend more of what they read because
of the important role of prior knowledge in the act of reading. Effective reading
instruction does not always take place in a "true" middle school, but the
essential elements of the middle school concept lend themselves to the
successful teaching of reading and writing.

## SUMMARY

The middle school movement grew from the recognition that junior high schools
simply were not meeting the needs of early adolescents. The middle school
emerged to provide an organization, a curriculum, and an instructional approach designed specifically for the early adolescent and to ease the transition
from the elementary school to the high school.

A "true" middle school is much more a philosophy and a practice than a
name or a rigid set of grade levels. Middle level teachers must understand early
adolescent development, must teach the learning process along with content,
and must employ learning strategies that accommodate the unique characteristics of students at this age. The organization of a middle school should involve a
comprehensive advising/counseling program, cooperative planning among
teachers and administrators, an exploratory program that will help students
expand and identify their interests, and scheduling that can be adjusted to meet
specific instructional needs.

A true middle school should have all of these elements and also provide a
positive environment in which students will feel free to explore and take risks. In
short, a true middle school provides early adolescents with the physical,
emotional, social, and intellectual support they need to become active and
successful independent learners.

# REFERENCES

Center for Early Adolescence Publications Catalog (nd). Carrboro, NC: The Center for Early Adolescence.

Commission on the Reorganization of Secondary Education. (1918). *Cardinal principles of secondary education.* Bulletin No. 35. Washington, DC: United States Department of the Interior, Bureau of Education, pp. 12–13.

Connors, N. A., and Irvin, J. L. (1989). Is "middleschoolness" an indicator of excellence? *Middle School Journal, 20,* 12–14.

Davidson, J., and Koppenhaver, D. (1988). *Adolescent literacy: What works and why.* New York: Garland Publishing.

Eichhorn, D. (1966). *The middle school.* New York: The Center for Applied Research in Education.

Eichhorn, D. (1987). *The middle school.* Reston, VA: National Association for Secondary School Principals.

George, P. S. (1983). Confessions of a consultant: Middle school mistakes we made. *Middle School Journal, 14,* 3–6.

Gruhn, W. T., and Douglass, H. R. (1947). *Modern junior high school.* New York: Ronald Press Company.

Lounsbury, J. H., and Vars, G. F. (1978). *A curriculum for the middle school grades.* New York: Harper and Row Publishers.

National Association of Secondary School Principals (1984). *An agenda for excellence at the middle level.* Reston, VA: National Association of Secondary School Principals.

National Commission on Excellence in Education (1983). *A nation at risk.* Washington, DC: United States Department of Education.

National Middle School Association (1982). *This we believe.* Columbus, OH: National Middle School Association.

National Middle School Association Brochure (nd). Columbus, OH: National Middle School Association.

Schurr, S. (1988). The National Resource Center. Personal communication, May 25, 1987.

— Chapter 12 ———————

# The Reading Program

Change is an integral part of the nature of education. Successful teachers must adapt to change—change in schedules, in curriculum, and in textbooks. Students change from year to year; in fact, in a middle level school the same students often change from day to day.

Besides the changes that occur naturally in a school or within a classroom, teachers must also respond to the growing body of research on teaching and learning. How does a teacher acquire and apply all of this new knowledge so as to meet the needs of the students? The first step in understanding where we need to go is, of course, understanding where we have been. This chapter first discusses the traditional forms of reading instruction and then presents the results from a national survey of current practices in reading. Next, the components of a successful reading program and suggestions for organizing and managing a reading program are offered. Recommended ways to facilitate change in a middle level reading program are then presented.

## TRADITIONAL FORMS OF READING INSTRUCTION IN THE MIDDLE GRADES

Very little research on secondary reading practices and programs exists to guide those curriculum planners and teachers who wish to strengthen reading instruction in the middle level school. Even those who have conducted surveys in this area have not drawn conclusions specifically related to the middle level school. All surveys previously conducted relate to secondary school reading programs and practices; it is difficult to determine from these data implications for teaching at the middle level. However, the following information represents those surveys most useful to middle level educators.

Hill (1975) reported that, of the secondary schools surveyed, 81 percent have a reading program in operation. Most instruction was through a corrective or remedial reading class. Freed (1972) reported that 55 percent of junior high schools have a required reading course. Research (Early, 1973; Freed, 1972; Hill, 1971, 1975) conducted in the early 1970s indicates that most planned reading instruction is in the form of a developmental or remedial class. Most schools surveyed, however, reported not implementing a content area reading program. After reviewing reading instruction at the postelementary level, Witte and Otto (1981) concluded that "though it seems clear that both reading specialists and content area teachers want postelementary students to read effectively, they have not been particularly successful in finding ways to share their complementary expertise to build successful school-wide reading programs" (p. 157).

As a part of the Adolescents Committee of the International Reading Association, Greenlaw and Moore (1982) reported the results of a survey intended "to measure the extent of specific reading instruction in middle and secondary schools" (p. 534). They found that (1) most reading was taught through a separate course (77 percent); (2) remedial reading makes up 74 percent of the separate reading courses offered; (3) developmental and accelerated courses are offered in secondary schools; and (4) 20 percent of the schools reported that reading was a standard part of courses such as social studies, math, and science. Although it is difficult to tell which results might speak specifically to the middle level, it seems that the same patterns run consistently in grades 6 through 12. These results should be interpreted with caution, however, since the return rate for the survey was only 24 percent.

# READING INSTRUCTION IN MIDDLE LEVEL SCHOOLS: RESULTS OF A NATIONAL SURVEY

Since no clear data on the middle level were available, a colleague and I conducted a national survey (Irvin and Connors, 1989) that was designed to describe the nature and extent to which reading is taught in middle level schools.

Although it is unreasonable to expect that a student could acquire enough reading competence by the fifth grade to carry him or her through middle and high school, many middle level schools offer little or no systematic reading instruction. Table 12.1 shows the extent to which reading is taught in middle level schools.

Traditionally, reading instruction in the middle level school has taken one of four basic forms: developmental reading course, a remedial reading course, a reading lab, and/or through content classes (social studies, language arts, science). A 1988 survey conducted by Gee and Forester (1988) found that "the majority of secondary schools either had no organized reading program or offered reading instruction only in a class labeled "reading'" (p. 506). The results of the Irvin and Connors survey confirm these results. Table 12.2 shows the nature of reading instruction reported by both types of schools. In this next section, each type of reading instruction will be briefly described and the extent that it is used for instruction will be discussed.

## Developmental Reading Course

A developmental reading course is usually defined as a course that includes the development of comprehension, vocabulary, flexible reading rates, and study strategies. It is designed to be a normal part of a student's progression through the curriculum, not as a remedial course. This type of reading instruction seems to be the most popular and the most preferred. Recognized schools (those chosen by the Secondary School Recognition program in 1987) require that *all* students take a developmental reading course more frequently than randomly selected schools. Also, recognized schools seem to have a wider reading requirement earlier on in the middle school experience.

TABLE 12.1 ───────────────────────────────
Extent of Reading Instruction Offered in Middle Level Schools

|  | Percent of Recognized Schools* n = 93 | Percent of Schools Chosen Randomly n = 154 |
|---|---|---|
| No reading instruction offered | 8 | 6 |
| Reading instruction only for students reading below grade level | 35 | 28 |
| Reading instruction offered only as elective | 14 | 11 |

* Recognized schools are those chosen by the Secondary School Recognition Program in 1987. Success is measured by such factors as high expectations for students, a well-articulated curriculum, and clear educational goals. Student performance on achievement tests and attendance rates are also evaluated.

TABLE 12.2

Nature of Reading Instruction Offered in Middle Level Schools

|  | Percent of Recognized Schools* n = 93 | Percent of Schools Chosen Randomly n = 154 |
|---|---|---|
| Developmental course | 57 | 64 |
| Remedial course | 67 | 70 |
| Reading lab | 24 | 25 |
| Content reading instruction | 21 | 14 |

* Recognized schools are those chosen by the Secondary School Recognition Program in 1987. Success is measured by such factors as high expectations for students, a well-articulated curriculum, and clear educational goals. Student performance on achievement tests and attendance rates are also evaluated.

Table 12.3 supports this conclusion in that these courses are most heavily emphasized at the sixth-grade level, and the time and the requirement are reduced at the seventh- and eighth-grade levels. It appears that most schools require reading for a semester or a year in the sixth grade. For seventh and eighth grade, reading instruction is commonly offered through "the wheel," which generally refers to a slot in the school schedule when students may take exploratory courses such as typing or home economics. Students who are below grade level are sometimes counseled to take repeated reading courses on "the wheel."

Not all respondents indicated the materials they used in these courses; however, those who did respond indicated the use of basals or skill materials. Some respondents indicated the use of literature. A few said they taught learning strategies that would later be applied in content area reading instruction.

## Remedial Reading Course and Reading Lab

A remedial reading course and reading lab are usually defined as courses for students reading below grade level. They normally include instruction in vocabulary development and comprehension.

A reading lab has traditionally been the home of individualized instruction. It is usually defined as a pull-out program for students reading below grade level and offered for small groups of students. Few respondents indicated that they maintained a reading lab but some indicated that they offered the remedial course in place of the lab.

Nelson and Herber (1982) strongly recommended that a total school reading

TABLE 12.3 ————————————————————————————
Number of Schools Reporting Systematic Reading Instruction

|  | Recognized* | | | Random | | |
|---|---|---|---|---|---|---|
|  | 6th | 7th | 8th | 6th | 7th | 8th |
| **Developmental Reading Course** | | | | | | |
| Wheel** | 1 | 11 | 10 | 0 | 8 | 9 |
| Semester | 18 | 17 | 14 | 32 | 29 | 19 |
| Year | 9 | 8 | 7 | 10 | 8 | 7 |
| **Remedial Reading Course** | | | | | | |
| Wheel** | 0 | 5 | 6 | 3 | 14 | 12 |
| Semester | 17 | 27 | 30 | 21 | 33 | 30 |
| Year | 4 | 11 | 8 | 9 | 7 | 6 |
| **Reading Lab** | | | | | | |
| Wheel** | 1 | 3 | 5 | 1 | 5 | 5 |
| Semester | 7 | 8 | 8 | 8 | 14 | 11 |
| Year | 2 | 3 | 3 | 1 | 1 | 1 |

* Recognized schools are those chosen by the Secondary School Recognition Program in 1987. Success is measured by such factors as high expectations for students, a well-articulated curriculum, and clear educational goals. Student performance on achievement tests and attendance rates are also evaluated.
** The "wheel" is a slot in the school schedule where students may take exploratory courses.

program is better than a reading label. They based this recommendation on their observation that schoolwide content area reading programs "work." However, little research currently exists to suggest that one program is more effective than the other in terms of student achievement.

## Content Area Reading

Content area reading is something that educators have attempted since the early 1900s (Moore, Readence, and Rickleman, 1983). This type of instruction was more or less emphasized throughout the first half of the century and then reemerged with the publication of Herber's (1978) *Teaching Reading in the Content Area.* State Departments began to see content area reading instruction as a vehicle for improving the reading achievement of high school graduates. Despite the efforts of State Departments of Education and the International Reading Organization to promote content area reading instruction, however, this type of instruction did not seem to be widely applied in the schools of our country (Witte and Otto, 1981).

One of the reasons why content area reading instruction was so little implemented may have its foundation in the perceptions of content area teachers. Many of these teachers saw reading as teaching phonics and using workbooks, and as an activity that took valuable time from the content that they were trained and expected to teach. The notion that "every teacher was a teacher of reading" died, as it well should have, along with the notion that teaching reading was teaching skills in isolation.

The recommended approach to content area reading is one in which teachers present content and skills concurrently. Students are given direct instruction in reading skills as they learn content. This approach enhances reading and study skill ability and at the same time increases students' knowledge of content. Thus, one main reason that this method of content area reading instruction is desirable and effective is that it allows direct application of reading skills to content.

The upsurge in quality research into reading theory and practice and a new comprehension-based view of the reading process have both helped reshape many educators' ideas about reading and writing instruction in the content areas. However, the gap between current theory and practice continues to gape widely. This incongruence between knowledge and application continues to concern many educators.

In the Gee and Forester (1988) survey, 18 percent of the respondents reported having or planning a content reading program; 38 percent of these respondents were from middle level schools. The Irvin and Connors (1989) survey supported the findings of Gee and Forester: very few middle level schools have a program for content area reading instruction.

Almost half of the educators Gee and Forester surveyed believed that reading instruction was not the responsibility of content teachers. An equally high number of respondents reported that they lacked administrative support or leadership for a content reading program. Although the Irvin and Connors survey did not directly ask why a school lacked a content area reading program, informal comments indicated that the respondents felt that the developmental and remedial courses offered fulfilled the need for systematic reading instruction.

Typically, when students enter the middle level school, they meet departmentalization, content textbooks, and teachers who were trained for the secondary school. Thus, students who are accustomed to the security, the narrative-based text, and the skills-oriented teaching of elementary school must suddenly adapt to a much different set of expectations. One of the most difficult parts of adapting to this new environment is making the transition from "reading for story" to reading for content. Unfortunately, very few middle level schools have programs that help students to make this transition.

## COMPONENTS OF A SUCCESSFUL MIDDLE LEVEL READING PROGRAM

Those who agree with the tenet that learning to read is a lifelong process and that it is impossible for a student to attain reading maturity in the first six or seven years of school must endorse a secondary reading program. Students at the middle level are expected to read increasingly difficult material and increasingly more expository versus narrative material. Textbooks at the middle level often require students to understand abstract concepts for which they may not be cognitively and developmentally ready.

Middle level students are also expected to do more with what they read. Students are expected to read increasingly longer assignments, take notes, and do homework assignments based on what they read. Students at the middle level cannot be expected to accomplish all of these feats on their own. They need guidance.

What, then, are the components of a successful reading program at the middle level? The following recommendations are based on (1) the testimony of educators who have implemented successful middle level programs, (2) the knowledge of experts in the field of secondary reading, (3) an understanding of the characteristics of middle grades students, and (4) my own experience as a teacher and consultant in middle level schools.

1. *Total school/district commitment.* A commitment to improved literacy at the middle level means providing leadership and support for literacy at both school and district levels. Leadership and support at the district level means that literacy programs will be provided with an overall organization, with funding, and with careful consideration. Such leadership usually involves the appointment of a district reading coordinator who takes full or partial responsibility for the middle level/secondary reading program. Leadership at the building level means providing individual schools with reading or curriculum specialists.

2. *Content area teachers who are committed to teaching students and not just content.* In order to facilitate learning, teachers are expected to understand (1) their students; (2) their content; (3) the learning process; (4) learning strategies (when and how to use them); and (5) the materials they are using and how to adapt the text to their students. Effective teachers keep all of these things in mind as they plan for instruction.

3. *A reading program guided by learning strategies rather than by a set of materials.* In many middle level reading programs, the organization of the textbook determines the organization of the program. Such programs do little to meet the needs of individual students and specific content requirements. Reading instruction at the middle level should help students match learning strategies with the demands of content area instruction. Learning strategies

should be taught directly through the content text in coordination with a developmental reading class or by content area teachers.

Narrative reading instruction should also be continued at the middle level. Literature, not excerpts from books, should provide the reading material. The reading of literature can be successfully taught in the language arts class, and it can be meaningfully integrated with writing, speaking, listening, and thinking instruction.

4. *Instruction that integrates all of the language areas.*   Reading and writing have been taught as separate subjects in our schools for many years. Although some educators have noted the similarities between these two language processes, few have integrated them into their instruction. Reading enhances the ability to write and writing enhances the ability to read (Rubin and Hansen, 1984; Taylor and Beach, 1984; Tierney and Leys, 1984).

The benefits of integrating reading and writing instruction are that (1) students use and expand their prior knowledge through reading and writing; (2) students learn about conventions of print, increase their linguistic competence through reading, and have an opportunity to use this knowledge in writing; and (3) all of the language processes (reading, writing, speaking, listening) require and facilitate thinking, which is the common basis of language. The more language areas a teacher uses to teach content, the more likely the students will be to improve in those language areas and apply these abilities to the content under study.

5. *One or more resource teachers or curriculum facilitators in the school.*   A reading specialist or curriculum facilitator who does not have a student assignment can provide guidance to content area teachers by modeling learning strategies, by assessing text material that may be too difficult for students, or by providing diagnostic information about students. This person can also provide leadership in the recreational reading program by such activities as organizing a book fair or suggesting guidelines for a reading break time.

These support teachers must have special qualities, specifically (1) knowledge of the latest research and its classroom application, (2) excellent human relations skills and leadership qualities, (3) the ability to function as a catalyst for change, and (4) the ability to provide support at the school and district level.

6. *Evaluation that is consistent with the instruction.*   Content area teachers who have incorporated the teaching of learning strategies into their curriculum sometimes continue to evaluate (test) in a way that is not consistent with their teaching. That is, their teaching is for process and main idea; their testing is still objective and detail-oriented. Therefore, the students fail, but for good reasons; the evaluation was not consistent with their instruction. Evaluation and instruction should be tailored to the needs of the students and be consistent with each other.

7. *A reading committee.* Anders (1981) suggested that "people are the key to an effective content area reading program" (p. 316). A reading committee can serve to encourage teachers, administrators, support staff, media specialists, guidance counselors, parents, and students to more and better literacy experiences at the school level. This committee is responsible for planning and executing the reading program in a school.

8. *A recreational reading program.* Usually, a school Reading Committee provides leadership for book fairs, reading break time, book exchanges, and any special schoolwide reading activities. These activities are usually indicative of a schoolwide commitment to reading improvement and carry a strong message to the community. How to initiate and maintain a Sustained Silent Reading Program is fully described in Chapter 10.

9. *A strong staff-development program.* Once it has been determined by a school, a school district, or a classroom teacher that change is desirable, staff development generally begins. Sometimes the decision to change is made before teachers are consulted. One key element in the implementation of successful change is ownership or a feeling that everyone is a part of the change process. "Ownership must be established for any change to survive" (Gallagher, Goudvis, and Pearson, 1988, p. 36). Ownership can be facilitated by teachers setting goals, having input into the process, and mutual respect for all of the people involved in the process.

It is important in this stage, as with all stages of staff development, that those who are involved in the process consider *teacher growth* and not *teacher deficit.* All of us in our personal and professional lives cherish growth experiences. Professional growth happens in a supportive, positive environment. After ownership and a sense of respect and mutual integrity is established, growth in understanding can occur.

The second key element of change is knowledge. New knowledge can be gained through workshops, reading, discussion, observation, modeling, coaching, or attending conferences. The format is not as important as the support network that is established that will help the new ideas grow into eventual application in the classroom.

10. *Parent/community involvement.* Community leaders and parents have a difficult time resisting the opportunity to offer support to a schoolwide effort to improve reading. Parents can help collect books for classroom librarires, work in book exchanges, or talk about their reading interests to a class. Community leaders are sometimes invited to participate in Sustained Silent Reading time as "guest readers." Their job is to read with a class for a time and then chat about their reading interests and personal history. These sharing times provide positive public relations for the school and give students the opportunity to interact with positive role models.

11. *Classroom action research.* Although "teachers work hard and are constantly searching for methods and strategies that will help students achieve better, seldom do they receive proof that a different method worked effectively enough to keep at it" (Monahan, 1987, p. 678). Classroom action research consists merely of keeping track of how a particular method (e.g., graphic organizers) works with one class while continuing to teach other classes in the "old way." Pre- and posttesting is used to determine which group of students performed the best. Charts can be constructed to dramatize the results. Teachers take ownership of a strategy when they see that its use brings results in improved achievement. Classroom action research is a vehicle for facilitating ownership of new strategies and methods and professional growth.

## ORGANIZING AND MANAGING A READING PROGRAM

Experts in the field of secondary literacy instruction regard a strong content area reading program as the most effective way to teach reading at this level. Such a program helps students to use research-based strategies to learn from text. This type of program may be hard to conceptualize. An in-depth look at some exemplary programs may prove helpful in understanding how all of the necessary components work together to make an effective school reading program. The last chapter in this book describes in detail four exemplary reading programs for middle grades students.

But the traditional practices remain. What are the reasons for this discrepancy? Nelson and Herber (1982), long-standing experts in secondary reading, suggested that four assumptions keep secondary schools from implementing the kind of program recommended by the experts.

Assumption 1: *Elementary school reading instruction is adequate and sufficient to meet the more sophisticated and challenging reading tasks of the secondary school curriculum.* As discussed earlier, one of the reasons that middle level students have difficulty with reading tasks is the new form of the reading material. Their reading experiences in the elementary grades are carefully controlled by basal texts. Students are confronted with a variety of sources of text at the middle level.

In addition, the reading instruction students receive in the elementary grades is not sufficient to last a lifetime. Students must receive instruction different from that of the elementary years in order to meet the new challenges of secondary level reading. In the elementary grades, students "learn to read"; in the secondary grades, they must "learn to read to learn" (Herber, 1981).

Assumption 2: *Skills taught in reading classes transfer automatically to the reading of content area textbooks.* Most reading programs, whether they are developmental or remedial, are separate courses in which students are taught reading "skills." Since educators now recognize that reading comprehension is a constructive process whereby the reader involves all that he or she knows—conceptually, socially, and linguistically—it seems only logical that instruction in reading take place where the reading skill is to be applied. This place is in the content classroom.

Assumption 3:  *Student deficit rather than program deficit.*  Evaluations of content area reading programs show that when reading instruction is made available to all students through a meaningful context, the numbers of students needing "remedial" instruction is reduced. Perhaps the number of students with reading and writing "deficits" can be attributed to a program "deficit."

Assumption 4:  *The best use of secondary reading personnel is in organizing and managing remedial and corrective reading classes.*  When a reading specialist steps out of the clinical role and moves more toward being a facilitator and resource, he or she can improve the reading ability of many more students. Spending full time working with students in remedial classes is not an efficient nor economical use of time. A much more effective use of reading personnel is to have them model ways in which content teachers can incorporate learning strategies into the teaching of content. This key person offers "instructional leadership" (Readance, Baldwin, and Dishner, 1980) to the other teachers in the building.

## FACILITATING CHANGE

Professional growth is important for all educators but it is especially important for teachers. Ideally, change in a middle level reading program is initiated and supported by district or school personnel. But educational settings are not always ideal. Nothing prevents individual teachers or small groups of teachers from trying some of the strategies that have been supported by research and from sharing these new methods with each other.

Of course, a team of teachers who share the same students can plan more effective instruction than can teachers who do not share the same students. But if one social studies teacher and one science teacher would talk about how to integrate reading and writing instruction in one cooperatively planned unit, professional growth would occur and students would ultimately benefit.

Reading labs are generally not recommended by leaders in secondary reading. But if one reading specialist taught students a strategy for reading their health book and shared that strategy with the health teacher, professional growth would occur and students would ultimately benefit. If one language arts and one social studies teacher worked together to read and write about a piece of literature, professional growth would occur and students would ultimately benefit.

In this chapter, various components for a successful reading program have been suggested. If all the components were implemented, students could not help but improve their reading ability. "The necessary ingredients are available for improving the quality of reading programs in our schools" (Samuels, 1988, p. vii). The potential exists to improve the literacy ability in some school organizations, such as interdisciplinary team organization. But the lack of these organizations does not prohibit effective instruction and improved learning.

The possibilities for professional growth for teachers and for benefit to students are limitless. Change does not happen overnight, however. After studying schools in change, Berman and McLaughlin (1975) concluded that successful change often takes six years: two years for needs assessments, establishing priorities, altering the staff beliefs and attitudes, and improved instruction. The next two years are used to implement the plan, and the last two years are used to produce a stable effect (Samuels, 1988).

## SUMMARY

Middle level students must adjust to increasing demands on their reading abilities. They must deal with increasingly more difficult reading materials, a greater emphasis on expository text, and a growing expectation that they "read to learn." Despite these increased reading demands, however, many middle level schools still offer little or no systematic reading instruction. Of those middle level schools that do offer such instruction, fewer still offer content-based reading instruction.

An effective reading program at the middle level has several important components. First, it depends on support and commitment at both the district and school levels. It also depends on content area teachers who are willing to teach not only content but also the process of learning. It also depends on the support of specialists and on community involvement. An effective program is guided by learning strategies rather than materials and it integrates all four of the language arts during instruction. Such a program also contains a recreational reading program and is supported and encouraged through staff development. In all, an effective middle level school reading program is a schoolwide program that involves content teachers as well as specialists and aims at preparing students to meet the demands of the secondary school classroom.

## REFERENCES

Anders, P. L. (1981). Dream of a secondary reading program? People are the key. *Journal of Reading, 24,* 316–320.

Berman, P., and McLaughlin, M. W. (1975). *Federal programs supporting educational, volume 4: The findings in review.* Santa Monica, CA: Rand.

Early, M. J. (1973). Taking stock: Secondary school reading in the 70s. *Journal of Reading, 16,* 364–373.

Freed, B. F. (1972). *Teaching reading in secondary schools: Survey of state departments of education and selected school districts.* Philadelphia, PA: Research for Better Schools.

Gallagher, M. C., Goudvis, A., and Pearson, P. D. (1988). Principles of organizational change. In J. Samuels and P. D. Pearson (Eds.), *Changing school reading programs: Principles and case studies.* Newark, DE: International Reading Association.

Gee, T. C., and Forester, N. (1988). Moving reading beyond the reading classroom. *Journal of Reading, 31,* 505–511.

Greenlaw, J. M., and Moore, D. W. (1982). What kinds of reading courses are taught in junior and senior high school? *Journal of Reading,* 534–536.

Herber, H. L. (1978). *Teaching reading in content areas,* 2nd ed. Englewood Cliffs, NJ: Prentice-Hall.

Herber, H. L. (1981). An instructional model for teaching reading in content areas: Network report no. 1. Syracuse, NY: Syracuse University.

Hill, W. R. (1971). Characteristics of secondary reading: 1940–1970. In P. B. Greene (Ed.), *The right to participate* (twentieth yearbook). Milwaukee, WI: National Reading Conference.

Hill, W. R. (1975). Secondary reading activity in western New York: A Survey. *Journal of Reading, 18,* 13–19.

Irvin, J. L., and Connors, N. A. (1989). Reading instruction in middle level schools: Results from a U.S. survey. *Journal of Reading, 32,* 306–311.

Monahan, J. N. (1987). Secondary teachers do care . . . ! *Journal of Reading, 30,* 676–678.

Moore, D. W., Readence, J. E., and Rickleman, R. J. (1983). An historical explanation of content area reading instruction. *Reading Research Quarterly, 18,* 419–438.

Nelson, J., and Herber, H. (1982). Organization and management of programs. In A. Berger and A. Robinson (Eds.), *Secondary school reading: What research reveals for classroom practice.* Urbana, IL: National Council for the Teachers of English.

Readence, J. E., Baldwin, R. S., and Dishner, E. K. (1980). Establishing content reading programs in secondary schools. *Journal of Reading, 23,* 522–526.

Rubin, A., and Hansen, J. (1984). Reading and writing: How are the first two "R's" related? (Technical Report No. 51). Champaign, IL: Center for the Study of Reading.

Samuels, S. J. (1988). *Prologue.* In S. J. Samuels and P. D. Pearson (Eds.), *Changing school reading programs.* Newark, DE: International Reading Association.

Taylor, B. M., and Beach, R. W. (1984). The effects of text structure instruction on middle-grade students' comprehension and production of expository text. *Reading Research Quarterly, 19,* 134–146.

Tierney, R. J., and Leys, M. (1984). What is the value of connecting reading and writing? (Technical Report No. 55). Champaign, IL: Center for the Study of Reading.

Witte, P. L., and Otto, W. (1981). Reading instruction at the postelementary level: Review and comments. *Journal of Educational Research, 74,* 148–158.

# Chapter 13

# Exemplary Programs

The authors of *Becoming a Nation of Readers* (Anderson, Hiebert, Scott, and Wilkinson, 1985) stated that the "most logical place for instruction in most reading and thinking strategies is in social studies and science rather than in separate lessons about reading" (p. 73). Reading instruction in middle level schools, when it is offered, is generally the sole responsibility of the reading teacher (Irvin and Connors, 1989).

In the majority of middle level schools, the practice of teaching reading seems to lag far behind current reading theory. Understanding current practice might be the first step toward improving instruction. The next step is a description of exemplary models of reading organization and practice. Ideally, exemplary schools teach reading, writing, speaking, listening, and thinking as a part of an integrated curriculum in which these processes are related to content.

In this chapter, four reading programs are described. The schools/districts were chosen because they share common elements of a successful reading program at the middle level: (1) a commitment to literacy instruction for all students, (2) building- and district-level administrative support, (3) a middle school organization and orientation, (4) a commitment to teach learning strategies through content areas, and (5) success as demonstrated by formal and informal measures.

The schools/districts were identified through the national survey described in Chapter 12 (Irvin and Connors, 1989). These schools are diverse in their location, their size, and the students they serve. A brief explanation of each setting will precede the reading program descriptions.

Orange County Public Schools, Orlando, Florida, is a population center with eighteen middle schools and 20,000 students in grades 6, 7, and 8. The system has recently completed a three-year transition from junior high school to the middle schools, both in student population and in philosophy. Some of the decisions made about the reading program were a direct result of the new middle school concept orientation. This description will highlight the Orange County middle school reading program and shed light on some of the steps that were taken at the district level to begin a successful middle school reading program.

Granby Memorial Middle School is located in a small, rural town of Granby, Connecticut. It serves 1200 to 1500 students in grades 6, 7, 8 with a minority population of 7 percent. As they began to move to the middle school concept in their school, the cooperative planning of the teams naturally led to thematic teaching at each grade level. The description of their program will feature the evolution from a traditional form of reading instruction to one that is integrated throughout the curriculum with a special focus on the interdisciplinary teaching of social studies, literature, and writing at each grade level.

Parkway East Junior High School is located in Creve Coeur, Missouri, which is a suburb of St. Louis. It serves approximately 750 students in grades 7 and 8. This school has changed its racial composition in the last four years due to a new busing policy for the district; 24 percent of its students are now minorities. Parkway has many of the elements of a true middle school, such as teaming, and makes use of this organization to facilitate the interdisciplinary teaching of social studies, literature, and writing. Their Summer Essentials Program focuses on self-esteem and success and has found its way, philosophically, into the regular school year curriculum and instruction.

Ben Franklin Middle School, San Francisco, California, serves approximately 753 students in grades 6, 7, and 8. The racial composition of the school is 2 percent Caucasian, 26 percent black, 11 percent Spanish surname, 42 percent Chinese, and 19 percent of other minorities. The Ben Franklin Reading Program has received a state grant since 1969. The teams, made up of classroom teachers, reading specialists, and paraprofessionals, plan and implement reading instruction across the disciplines. Specific strategies that educators in this school have found helpful are highlighted.

# A READING PROGRAM TO DEVELOP STRATEGIC READERS
## by Joy Monahan
### Middle/Secondary Reading Program Consultant
### Orange County Public Schools
### Orlando, Florida

The Orange County School District has had established reading classes in junior high (now middle) school since the mid-1960s. Success stories abound from these reading and study skills lessons. Yet, many of these same students would fail in their other classes. The problem seemed to be that the skills taught in reading classs did not transfer to the regular subject area work.

Through a period of program evaluation (1984), the College Board's *Degrees of Reading Power* (*DRP*) was used to help determine how closely the students' comprehension ability matched the difficulty of the text they were assigned. Not surprisingly, we found that the students' comprehension ability was rarely high enough to read science, social studies, and language arts books. Although the Orange County district administration has always been supportive of the importance of reading in our secondary schools, we began to realize that a renewed effort for middle schools was imperative.

At about this same time, the district made a commitment to change its eighteen junior high schools to schools that embraced the middle school concept. Over a three-year period, a district-level coordinator provided in-service in middle school organization and orientation to all administrators and teachers. Along with inservice that stressed interdisciplinary team organization, advisor/advisee groups, and exploratory courses, middle level educators were exposed to the new views of reading and learning based on current research. Administrators and teachers were encouraged to pursue learning strategies further through the Reading in the Content Area (RICA) course or through school-based staff development sessions held during planning periods during the school day. In these sessions, strategies were demonstrated, modeled, and practiced by teachers with a peer teacher-trainer instructor.

We began to notice that when middle school teachers realize that a good student is also likely to be an interactive, constructive, strategic reader, teachers pay more attention to integrating good reading practices into their content area lessons. We also knew that content area teachers needed support and help beyond the inservice sessions provided. To this end, the district made two commitments: to provide the necessary support personnel in all middle schools and to assist with the integration of learning strategies in content area classrooms.

*Reading Resource Specialists* (RRS) were placed in every middle school. These specialists receive regular and rigorous inservice; they attend monthly day-long staff development sessions to study the research and to provide new ideas and a time for sharing. Middle school RRSs are also encouraged to become active in state and national reading associations. Twice a year, a two-day reading seminar is sponsored for all secondary reading resource teachers and content teachers in which nationally recognized reading researchers are invited to speak.

The reading resource specialist contributes expertise to guide the school's reading program. Students are not assigned to them; instead, these specialists provide training in the use of learning strategies for use by teachers and students in all content areas. In this way, *all* students can be successful in each class they attend. The RRS promotes and provides a focus on better comprehension of all content area learning through such activities as:

1. Providing *Degrees of Reading Power* ratings on students and textbooks that are used, assisting with test interpretation of DRP and other standardized tests

2. Demonstrating, modeling, and coaching in the use of learning strategies with content area teachers and students in their classroom setting

3. Conducting reading/thinking/learning inservice training sessions for school staff

4. Assisting in creating strategy materials to accompany content area texts

5. Encouraging Classroom Action Research

6. Creating a Reading/Learning Committee to communicate and carry out the schools' increased focus on comprehension and learning

7. Sharing up-to-date research findings

8. Promoting and coordinating a recreational reading program

The reading resource specialists provided the valuable service of supporting content area instruction so well that a reading teacher was added to each sixth-grade team. The reading teacher coordinates the reading program of the sixth-grade team using the assigned textbooks in content classs and help teachers incorporate learning strategies into their instruction.

*Learning strategies,* rather than the teaching of isolated skills, are beneficial in producing independent learners. Teachers in all classes are encouraged to provide direct instruction in the strategies for reading/learning through modeling and guided practice. Students need help in applying strategies to the increasingly varied and complex materials they face during school years and as adults. Some of the strategies endorsed throughout the Orange County Public Schools are listed below. The chapters in this book in which they are fully described are also indicated.

*Anticipation Guides.* This strategy challenges preconceived notions, stimulates curiosity, and helps set a purpose for reading. Anticipation guides may be used before or after reading. The teacher offers three to five general statements, individually or in small groups with discussion and justification, which is later shared by the entire group (Chapter 7).

*Cornell Notetaking Method.* This method helps students rank the importance of lecture or textbook elements and provides for effective reflection, review, and retention. The student divides a notebook paper into a 1½-inch area on the left and about 6 inches on the right. Students follow hints that help them create notes for study and review (Chapter 9).

*Framed Paragraphs.* A framed paragraph develops high-order comprehension skills including comparison/contrast analysis and cause/effect. Students are supplied with a paragraph skeleton or frame to guide them in writing well-formed paragraphs (Chapter 5).

*Graphic Organizers.* These are visual diagrams that identify and classify the major relationships of concepts, objectives, and key vocabulary of a lesson (Chapters 6 and 7).

*Guided Reading Procedure.* This is an integrated model of essential processes for understanding and remembering key information from text. After a purpose for reading has been set, students read an assignment to remember as much as possible. Next, they brainstorm everything they can remember. They then check the text for additional information and correct any inaccuracies. Finally, the class organizes the remembrances into an outline or semantic map (Chapter 8).

*List-Group-Label-Write.* This strategy helps students handle technical vocabulary by using association and categorization. Students' association to a central topic are recorded on a chalkboard. Then, working individually or in small groups, students categorize the works into groups based on common elements. Finally, students explain their categories, label them, and write about their thoughts on the topic (Chapter 6).

*Possible Sentences.* Students determine meanings and relationships of unfamiliar works by employing this strategy. After displaying and pronouncing key vocabulary for a chapter, the teacher records sentences that students think may appear in that chapter. Next, students read the passage, checking the accuracy of the "possible" sentence. The class then evaluates and revises the sentences (Chapter 6).

*PReP.* This three-step prereading assessment and instructional procedure is for teachers to use before assigning textbook reading to their classes. It helps readers activate background knowledge and provides diagnostic information to teachers. PReP links text concepts and past experiences and creates expectations in the mind of the learner (Chapter 7).

*Reciprocal Teaching.*   This system involves the teacher initially modeling a strategy and then leading students to become the "teacher." The four strategies used are (1) devising questions about the text, (2) summarizing, (3) clarifying inconsistencies, and (4) predicting what the author will say next (Chapter 8).

*ReQuest.*   Readers are helped to cope with text materials as teachers and students take turns asking each other questions about portions of an assignment they have read together. This procedure helps students develop questioning techniques and fosters an active search for meaning (Chapter 7).

*Semantic Feature Analysis.*   This strategy capitalizes on a students' prior knowledge to show how words differ and how they are unique. The teacher lists some words within a category on the left side of a matrix, in a column. Along the top border of the matrix, in a row, the teacher lists features shared by some of the words. Students put plus and minus signs on the chart to indicate which words contain the various features. Class discussion provides reinforcement and clarification (Chapter 6).

*Semantic Mapping.*   This is a visual method for extending vocabulary knowledge by displaying the relationship of words to each other. Students can work in groups, jotting down, in categories, as many words as they can think of that are related to a central concept. Next, the concept is written on the chalkboard and the categories are attached to it. The class compiles one joint semantic map on the chalkboard with full and rich discussion focusing on key categories (Chapter 6, 7, and 8).

*Story/Chapter Mapping.*   This procedure visually represents key concepts and supporting details of an assignment. Each student makes a personal map that represents his or her interpretation of the text and the main points. The process encourages critical thinking and imagination (Chapters 7, 8, and 9).

*Think Aloud.*   The teacher verbalizes thoughts created while reading aloud— modeling the kinds of strategies a skilled reader uses during reading and pointing out specifically what he or she is doing to cope with a particular comprehension problem. The teacher may verbalize (1) making predictions, (2) describing a mental picture, (3) linking new knowledge with prior knowledge, (4) a confusing point to show comprehension monitoring, and (5) "fix-up" strategies such as rereading, reading ahead for clarification, or checking the context to determine the meaning of a new word (Chapter 8).

*Think-Pair-Share.*    This is a highly effective way to organize a think time strategy in which students write or diagram their thoughts during a period of individual thinking time, addressing a higher-level question or problem. Next, the students pair to share and clarify ideas, and even later this is followed by a full class discussion. Think-Pair-Share's structure promotes the involvement of all student in active processing of ideas (Chapter 4).

## Key Factors for Success

We have found the following elements to be the key factors in the success of our middle school reading program:

1. Rather than fragmented isolated lists of skills, sixth-grade reading classes teach generic learning strategies that will help search out meaning from a variety of reading tasks. The use of these strategies are supported by the RRSs in the seventh and eighth grades.

2. Teachers have modified their testing procedures to be more consistent with the strategies taught in their classes.

3. Classroom action research helps teachers assume ownership for strategies.

4. Sixth-grade reading teachers serve as mini-reading resource specialists to the members of their team.

5. Middle school RRSs publish newsletters with information about scheduled strategy workshops, sample ideas from teachers in various content areas, recreational reading monthly themes, and other news about reading. Framed quotations that contain an abbreviated bit of research information are put in mailboxes so that teachers can read them on the way back to their classrooms.

6. Administrators are kept well informed about the newest trends in reading.

7. RRSs meet in small groups to study recent research, discuss articles in educational journals, and share experiences at state and national conferences.

8. A reading committee has been formed in each school, thereby expanding and endorsing efforts to promote reading.

9. Recreational reading activities have served to get the entire school involved in reading. A theme for the month, such as mysteries, humor, or science fiction, can focus attention on a particular topic. Paperback libraries are placed in reading nooks in hallways within the school buildings. Books are

donated, swapped, and sometimes stolen—but they are read. Guest readers are invited to join a class during sustained silent reading time.

In analyzing our middle school reading program, there is no single key to success. Action research in the classroom, teachers who publish their experiences in national magazines, reciprocal teaching, semantic mapping and other reading/thinking/learning strategies, a steady stream of reprints and bulletins and newsletters, strong and frequent inservice options, mechanisms for sharing ideas and techniques, and an openness to research and what is says to classroom teachers are all a part of the whirlwind of activity that has earned Orange County's middle school reading effort a national reputation.

---

# EVOLUTION OF A READING PROGRAM
## by Dr. Elizabeth Nero Rumohr
## Reading Consultant/Specialist
## Granby Middle School
## Granby, Connecticut

Granby Middle School was selected by the United States Department of Education to receive "Exemplary School Status" and nationwide recognition in 1987 as part of the Secondary School Recognition Program. Among the exemplary school highlights were the five-subject core program, a schoolwide writing program, integrated study skills instruction, and high student performance. Granby Middle School has also been distinguished by being ranked first in the state in 1986 based on test scores, and has maintained high rank (within the top 2 percent) in subsequent years. This commitment to excellence, however, did not happen overnight; it took years of planning, evaluation, implementation, and reevaluation. The narrative that follows contains brief historical information on the stages of development of our program along with a fuller explanation of the program in its current state.

In 1971, a middle school "component" of senior high school was drafted. Although the two schools occupied the same site, the program for grades 6, 7, and 8 was designed to meet the needs of the early adolescent. A concerted effort was made to widen the knowledge base relative to reading instruction of the existing faculty and to hire new faculty with strengths in reading and writing instruction. Reading was promoted as an activity that should pervade every discipline. During this time, seventh and eighth graders received fifteen weeks of reading instruction each year five days a week. Students in grade 6 received reading instruction all year long, five times a week.

During the next stage (1979–1981), teaming, a "Reading for Everyone" program, enrichment mini-courses, and tutorials were added to the Granby program. To facilitate these changes, we instituted a seven-period day and a rotating schedule.

Grade level teams were formed of six teachers who taught five core subjects, reading being taught as a separate class. As with any interdisciplinary team organization, we immediately began to reap the benefits of cooperative planning for a common group of students. Expanding on our original "Excellence in Reading" commitment, reading instruction was offered every day for all students. Mini-courses in Great Books, drama reading, debating, storytelling, plays, and puppetry naturally augmented the reading program. The need for coordination of the different aspects of the reading program led to giving release time to one faculty member to act as a resource to other teachers. As teachers felt more and more comfortable teaching reading through their disciplines, study skills and library skills were systematically added to the existing curriculum.

In 1979, a full-time consultant/specialist position was funded. The individual coordinated the total school reading program, provided demonstration lessons, and helped with the transition from "pull-out" programs to "into" the classroom. This coordination helped build the current program at Granby. Reading is viewed not only as important for students but integral to learning. Reading abilities are not taught in isolation but are interwoven systematically throughout the curriculum.

Currently, reading is taught in two ways: through two separate classes (English and reading) and through content classes. The English/reading program will be explained in some detail below. The basic philosophy, however, is contained in Figure 13.1.

FIGURE 13.1 ────────────────────────────────────────

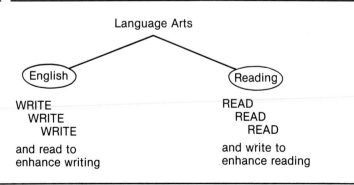

All three grades incorporate a central theme. These themes are developed through reading and English classes and further supported by math, social studies, and science classes.

The sixth grade theme is "Survival," which we thought seemed appropriate for students entering middle school. The reading curriculum includes an in-depth reinforcement of reading skills and processes, and students read such novels as *My Side of the Mountain* (George, 1959). The theme for the seventh grade is "Family." Literature anthologies are used and students are taught basic literary concepts as well as critical and analytical reading. One novel read in the seventh grade is *Edgar Allen* (Neufeld, 1968). The theme for the eighth grade is "Courage." Novels such as *Where the Red Fern Grows* (Rawls, 1974) reinforce personal courage. Study skills are taught in each content area but are especially reinforced in the eighth grade. Essays and formal research papers are also reinforced in these classes.

"Reading for Excellence" is a dominant theme at Granby Middle School. The following schoolwide activities stimulate the excitement for reading held by students, teachers, and parents alike:

1. Book Fairs

2. Book Club

3. Student-generated "Lists of Favorite Books"

4. Summer Reading List

5. Interest Inventories given to each student

6. Critical thinking and study skill instructional components at each grade level.

7. Reinforcement of reading ability in content area classrooms

8. Interdisciplinary Study Units for reading/language arts/content areas

9. Classroom libraries

10. Success Cards, Activity Cards, and Awards

11. Storytelling

12. Writing to enhance reading and reading to enhance writing

"Reading for Excellence" is pervasive at Granby Middle School. This program has been almost two decades in the making and is the result of much discussion, evaluation, and struggle. The results, though, are definitely worth the effort.

# A MIDDLE SCHOOL PROGRAM EVOLVES
## by Kay Sandweiss
### Reading Resource Specialist
### Parkway East Junior High School
### Parkway School District
### Creve Coeur, Missouri

At Parkway East Junior High School, a seventh- and eighth-grade middle school in a suburb of St. Louis, we are strongly committed to the concept of teaching reading and writing in content areas. From this broad-based philosophical orientation, content area teachers assume the responsibility of providing successful "learning to read to learn" experiences to students. We found that the change in focus to content area reading from the more traditional view of teaching reading in a reading class does not and cannot happen overnight. This change, of necessity, becomes a step-by-step growth experience for each content area teacher and for students as well.

In 1986, the school board adopted the middle school concept which, of course, meant instituting interdisciplinary teaming. In 1987, the board adopted two goals which served to provide impetus to our initial direction. These goals, in priority order, were:

1. Emphasize student growth in reading, writing, thinking, speaking, and listening throughout and across the curriculum

2. Emphasize the development of plans and projects to empower students and to maximize their educational opportunity with special focus on "at risk" students

As we began our transition to the middle school concept, staff development sessions became integral to the growth of our teachers. Along with inservice, we incorporated team planning as well as individual planning in our seven-period day. Each team was comprised of five members: three from the unified studies block (social studies, language arts, reading), one from the science department, and one from the math department.

Unified 7 (made up of the three seventh-grade teams) began to coordinate and refine their instructional strategies. For example, the reading teacher taught students how to write a term paper; science teachers then reinforced the teaching of research skills by reacting to the content of the paper. Students got two grades on one paper and soon recognized the value of putting more effort into the completed project. As another example, math students were taught mileage, metrics, and graph and chart skills. Art and writing teachers directed students to illustrate word problems using their new skill in metrics and mileage.

Helping students design their own cartouches and writing Grecian Urn cinquains was yet another way to interrelate art with reading and writing. Writing and editing their own version of a Roman newspaper from the front page headline to the editorial cartoon and subsequent news analysis further engaged students in interdisciplinary reading and writing activities.

Unified 8 (the eighth-grade teams) chose to design and write teaching guides around specific social studies, literature, and writing objectives. Each guide also contained suggestions for a variety of readings and hands-on projects to exemplify the interdisciplinary nature of learning. For example, the unit on America and Americans, typically taught in the eighth grade, now includes writing an essay after reading Steinbeck. Paper folding (origami) of frogs in art is an activity based on the reading of "Jumping Frog of Calaveras County" by Mark Twain; and measurement in math (converted to metric) is yet another component required to compete in "The Great Frog Race," which serves as a culminating activity of this unit. Writing a biographical sketch of each entrant frog further enhances the reading/writing connection. Two samples of student writing are presented in Figures 13.2 and 13.3: an essay on paradoxes of the American Experience and a poem about the American Dream.

Social studies and language arts teachers found a unit on the Westward Expansion particularly interesting to students as they reinforced their writing skill by writing an imaginary journal of a trip west. Two sample "journal entries" are presented in Figure 13.4.

As we began to reach out and widen our parameters, to experiment with change, we found that the change gathered its own momentum and generated its own excitement; this, in turn, elicited a deeper sense of commitment from all of us.

As we began to focus on the "positives," we recognized that our student council empowers students in many ways, especially in the concepts of personal development and democracy, and that our simulations in American government allow students to engage in and experience the democratic process. A twice weekly student/teacher advisory program adds yet another link in self-esteem learning process.

We then began to look at coordinating our activities throughout the building. To aid in this coordination effort, a secondary reading specialist was assigned to work with junior high schools in the district. "Learning to read to learn" across the curriculum was the primary goal for our middle school program with a special emphasis for our "at risk" students.

The Parkway District Summer Essentials Program was developed for the student who, while not achieving success during the traditional school year, showed the potential and need for such a such a program. Philosophically, we based our program on three assumptions: (1) all students can and will learn, (2) success will lead to more success and improved self-esteem, and (3) a strong foundation in the "essentials" will foster academic success and enhance self-esteem.

The Summer Essentials Program is not a make-up program; rather, its focus

FIGURE 13.2
Paradoxical Experience

## Paradoxal Experiences

When I was given this assignment I had no grasp on what a paradox was, but now, when I think about it, I can see that I am surrounded by paradoxes. A paradox is something said to be one thing, but in actuality it is something entirely different. In the following essay I will tell you about paradoxes that are around me every day.

Paradoxes are not limited to school and the outside world, they even enter into the confines of the American home. At church and around the neighborhood we are known for being peaceful, but upon arriving at home, we start to go at each others' throats. We pride ourselves in having good communication, but we fail to interact more than an half hour a day. Paradoxes live and thrive in American homes.

School can not escape paradoxes either. Parkway East Junior High School boasts excellence in education, but without any trouble at all I can see people making failing grades. At the beginning of the year all students received a book full of rules and regulations. Some of these rules are neither observed nor enforced. School is full of paradoxes.

by Ted

FIGURE 13.3
Poem

## Poem

Today in our world we have dreams
Among all;
These dreams are going to happen some day
When we start doing what we can
to make them happen.
Equal opportunity for all can be reached
If we try to accomplish it with our peers;
Peace with Russia can be declared
If we really get to it peace could be shared.
Astronauts may rise up into the sky;
No more nuclear war-heads we see in our eyes.
All these dreams can come true;
With everyone's help;
Me and You.

*by Robert*

is on academic success and self-esteem. This program has proven to be highly successful. What we learned from the Summer Essentials Program is that if instruction begins with self-concept, empowering students to engage actively in the learning process, structuring opportunities to achieve success, and building upon that success in a positive, nonthreatening manner, this instruction leads to improved academic performance. The philosophy of the Summer Essentials Program began to make its way into the regular school year's curriculum and planning.

While we, at East Junior, are a long way from reaching our goal, we are strongly committed to the concept of teaching reading and writing throughout and across the curriculum. We recognize that this designates the responsibility to each content area teacher to provide successful "learning to read to learn" experiences that promote skill application and carry over into other discipline areas. We believe that allowing students to discover and practice the interdisciplinary nature of this kind of learning validates its usefulness as a lifetime skill,

FIGURE 13.4 ————————————————————————————————————
Journal

April 4, 1834

     Today, my wife and I and the three kids set out on the Oregon Trail. Back home things were getting crowded, and in Oregon there is land all around just wating for the taking. We start in Independence, or will, with some other people. Ourselves, we'll be carrying everything on our wagon drawn by four horses. I hated to leave mama behind, but at least all of us are fit for the journey. After the trip life will be clear sailing.

April 26, 1834

     Here we are, Independence. We'll start out tomorrow with other families, about 20. I have been chosen leader but for no apparent reason. Talking to the guide I hired, the trail seems to be much harder than any of us expected. Our supplies are low, but there seems to be plenty of game, and the weather looks fine. I have no skill at handling these dealings, and I'm doing a horrible job, but I will keep on trying.

by Erik

————————————————————————————————————————————————

thereby enhancing the students' perception of the necessity to achieve competency in learning how to learn. We realize that we have only just begun to implement change at our school, but the success we have experienced has renewed our commitment and excitement to continue our momentum of change.

Parkway East Junior High School acknowledges the contribution of Mrs. Bonnie Reid, principal, who continually sets the positive tone and climate for our pursuit of excellence in education, and Ms. Jody Carter who directs the Parkway Summer Essentials Program.

# DEVELOPING LANGUAGE ACROSS THE CURRICULUM
## by Audrey Fielding
### Project Director
## The Benjamin Franklin Reading Demonstration Program
## San Francisco Unified School District
## San Francisco, California

The Benjamin Franklin Reading Program has been in existence at Benjamin Franklin Middle School since 1969. From its inception, the goals of the program focused on making the classroom the "laboratory." Students are not pulled out by specialists for work on reading skills. Instead, the reading specialists and paraprofessionals go into the classroom and join the teacher to make a reading resource "team"; the team plans the interdisciplinary curriculum, writes weekly lesson plans, monitors success, and evaluates progress.

Our program has a history of success because of the continued support of the school's administration. The program has always had a director who worked closely with the school administration to insure support for the program by assigning staff, scheduling students, and providing planning time for the teachers within the school day.

Student success in the program has been shown through consistent growth in reading test scores (California Test of Basic Skills) and by teacher reports of the improved quality of work completed by the students each week.

## Management

The management features that facilitate the program are:

1. The reading lab is a staff of people rather than a physical place.

2. All students are served by the program regardless of reading level or ability.

3. Classroom teachers and reading specialists plan together and are equally responsible for language skills and content curriculum.

4. A majority of the instruction is provided in a small group of six to twelve students.

The two aspects to the management system of the Ben Franklin Reading Program are (1) the organization of the staff and (2) the organization of the students. The program is staffed by the regular English and social science teachers, two reading specialists, and some paraprofessionals. This group of people work together as a team to plan and implement the program. Two ingredients are essential to the success of the program: the time and the willingness of the staff to work together as a team. At the end of each year the staff evaluates the year's progress and plans the curriculum calendar and its lessons and activities for the coming year. Additionally, the staff meets at least two times a week for ongoing planning, updating, and the evaluation of the program. The majority of the classroom instruction is conducted in small groups. It is essential, therefore, that all staff members serve as small group leaders. Group leaders rotate among the groups on a six-week schedule so that both students and teachers will be exposed to a variety of teaching and learning styles.

## Curriculum

The curriculum features that facilitate the program are:

1. Language skills are taught in the context of middle school curriculum.

2. The curriculum is planned and presented in an interdisciplinary manner.

3. The goal of the program is to help students acquire the learning strategies necessary to become life-long learners.

The salient features of the Ben Franklin Reading Program curriculum are twofold: (1) skills are integrated into the content areas through interdisciplinary teaching and (2) students are taught to use learning strategies that develop in reading, writing, speaking, and thinking abilities.

The interdisciplinary nature of the curriculum resulted from using the social science content as the thematic basis of the reading instruction across the disciplines. The state-adopted social science textbooks were used to develop curriculum topics. These texts are used as basic reading materials; however, they are often supplemented with primary source materials. Once those topics are established, the appropriate assignments are planned and implemented. A facsimile of part of the annual plan is presented in Figure 13.5.

Learning strategies are presented using content area material. The use of content area classes as the framework for teaching reading is based on the belief that language skills cannot be taught in isolation. Remedial and second language learners are especially dependent on the context in which language occurs in order to grasp the meaning. Therefore, the use of information as the scaffold for developing both comprehension and language makes pedagogical sense. What follows is a description of those language development strategies that are used across the curriculum to help students read and comprehend content materials.

FIGURE 13.5
Sample Plan

| 7 Oct. 24-28 | 8 Oct. 31-4 | 9 Nov. 7-11 | 10 Nov. 14-18 | 11 Nov. 21-25 | 12 Nov. 28-2 | 13 Dec. 5-9 |
|---|---|---|---|---|---|---|
| **ENGLISH** | | | | 3 DAY WEEK | 24-25 Thanks. | A resource C class / teacher teacher / B para DC para |
| A _____ class para / B Class D Recorp | | | | | | |
| Preposition Conjunction | Capitalization | punctuation | MINI-COURSE PROJECTS | | Minimums Standards Test. Prep. WRITING "I Search" re; mini course | Administer Min. Std. |
| READ | WRITE | SPEAK | 11/9 Teachers give "Commercials" in English. | | | SPEAKING |
| A, B, C, D exploration colonization | Exploration – "I Search" interview | | | | | |
| **SOCIAL STUDIES** | | | | | | |
| Tituba of Sallem Village. | AMERICAN LITERATURE OF REVOLUTIONARY TIMES | | | | | – copies of Constitution |
| ← Colonization → | | 810 MSS CONFLICTS | 1. KACHINA DOLLS 2. POP-UP BOOK OF AMERICAN HISTORY 3. SHIPS 4. POTTERY 5. TOTEMS 6. JAMESTOWN MODEL 7. QUILTING 8. COYOTE TALES | | Establishing Government → | |

*Clustering.*    This strategy is similar to the construction of an outline, but it is a visual map of ideas rather than linear in format. A student begins by scanning the social science reading for the week and then using the heading and subheadings in the text as a "skeleton" cluster. Then, as the student reads, her or his cluster becomes a place to put the notes regarding what was read; put more concretely, "to put meat on the skeleton." (See Figure 13.6.) When the student is ready to answer comprehension questions or study for a test, the information is readily available on the cluster. Often, the skeleton cluster is constructed as a group activity before reading to activate prior topical knowledge.

Another use of the cluster is as a prewriting activity. Students organize their topics for paragraphs around the central theme of the writing assignment and then fill in the supporting details prior to writing the first draft.

*Word of the Day.*    Social science and English teachers use this strategy to develop student vocabulary in the content area and to teach students helpful ways to analyze words. The process is simple and takes only a few minutes of class time. Each day a new word is placed on the board. The teacher pronounces the word, uses it in a context sentence or two, and then asks the students to decide on a meaning or synonym. When the class has come to a consensus definition, it is written on the board. Students then copy the word with its definition and write an original sentence using the word. A quiz on all the words for the week is given in English class at the end of the week.

FIGURE 13.6 ——————————————————————————————
Sample of Clustering

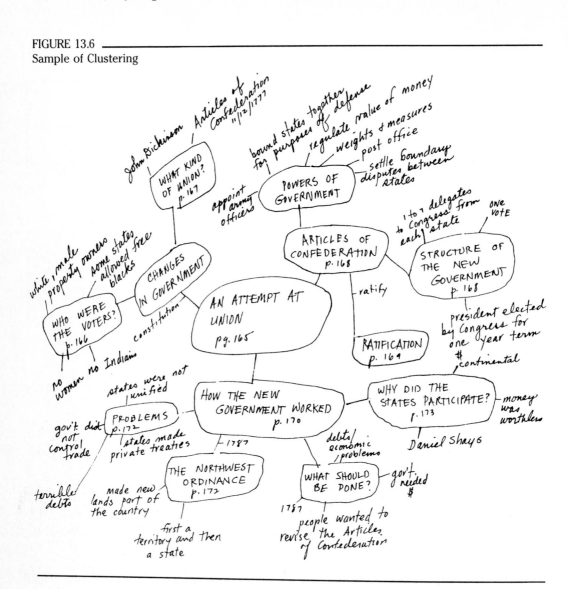

*Thinking Skills.*   Weekly lesson plans in both English and social science reflect
Bloom's model of cognitive objectives so that students learn to read at all levels
of comprehension. Comprehension of expository text along with reading from a
variety of genres and writing styles of narrative text is developed from a simple
level of recall to the more complex levels of analysis and evaluation. Sample
social science and English lessons are included in Figure 13.7.

FIGURE 13.7 —————————————————————————————————————————————
"Expanding the Frontier"

READING: *America, America*, pages 267–268
COPY THE SKELETON CLUSTER

Complete the reading and the cluster.

VOCABULARY:  pioneers      expedition      missionaries
                    headwaters      annexed        to convert

1. Draw a picture of a typical "pioneer."
2. What do "missionaries" do?
3. Use "expedition" in a sentence that shows you understand what it means.

KNOWLEDGE/COMPREHENSION:
1. Explain how the size of the U.S. was doubled in 1803.
2. What is Sacajawea famous for?
3. What ocean did Lewis and Clark finally see at the mouth of the Columbia River?
4. What did Pike accomplish on his expedition?

APPLICATION: Answer the 8 questions on page 277 "Interpreting Maps."
Answer in complete sentences, please.

ANALYSIS:
1. Draw a map of the United States.
2. Show (illustrate) Lewis and Clark's expedition.
3. Include the rivers, the kinds of mountains they crossed, what their boat looked
   like, the people who helped them and where they helped them.
   Review pages 268–269 so you will know what to put on your map and where to
   put it.

SYNTHESIS:
Pretend you are *one* of the following people and draw a picture *or* write a diary
entry of one of your most exciting experiences on the new frontier.
              • Major Bridger              • Kit Carson
              • Sacajawea                  • Stephen Bonga

EVALUATION:
Frontier families did not have many of the conveniences or sources of entertain-
ment that we have today. Can you name some of these things? Considering
these differences, do you think your life is better than a typical pioneer's life
was? Why or why not?

—————————————————————————————————————————————

*Writing.* The staff recognizes the strong connection between good writing and good reading. Students write regularly in a variety of formal and informal settings. Part of each student's weekly grade in English is a journal entry of 2½ pages. This writing is not edited, but the teacher checks to make sure the assignment was completed. Some teachers respond to student journal writing entries by writing back to students. Journal entries may be on any topic, but teachers occasionally assign topics. Sometimes students treat the journal as a "learning log" in which they share their thoughts regarding a reading assignment, a field trip experience, or a lesson. More formal writing assignments occur in English class and are implemented over a three- to four-week period so that prewriting, rough draft writing, student response groups, revision, and editing can occur. Formal writing assignments are eventually published.

*Show Paragraphs.* Students are given a simple sentence that "tells something." They may use this sentence as the topic sentence for their "showing paragraph," which should be their best effort in making the telling sentence come alive. In other words, the paragraph, when completed, should be filled with rich description illustrative of the simple "telling" sentence. This assignment is a regular homework activity two or three days a week in social science class. An example is shown in Figure 13.8.

FIGURE 13.8 ——————————————————————————————
A "Showing Paragraph"

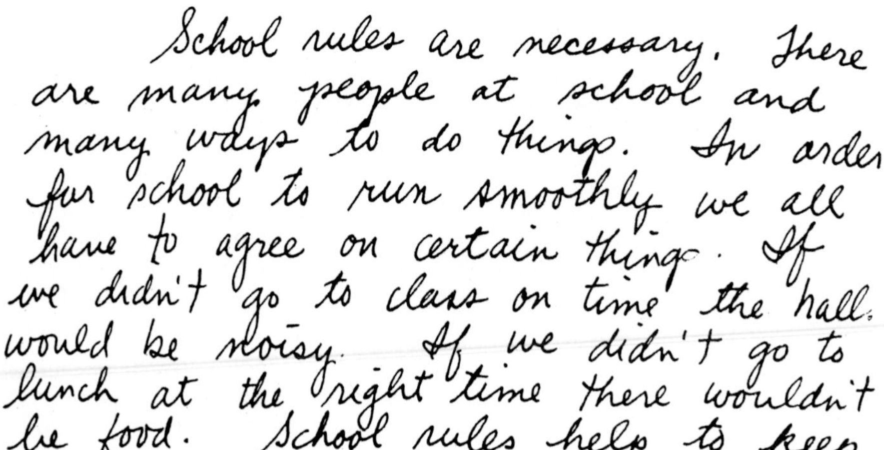

School rules are necessary. There are many people at school and many ways to do things. In order for school to run smoothly we all have to agree on certain things. If we didn't go to class on time the halls would be noisy. If we didn't go to lunch at the right time there wouldn't be food. School rules help to keep things reasonable.

*Reading Log.* This technique is a simple, effective way to increase our students' willingness to read for enjoyment on their own, outside of class. The reading log represents a part of the students' grade (see Figure 13.9).

*Math/Language Development.* As a way of integrating reading into the math curriculum, the Ben Franklin Reading Program uses the sheet illustrated in Figure 13.10 to supply students with a strategy for figuring out math word problems.

FIGURE 13.9 ——————————————————————————————————
Reading Log

### Ben Franklin Middle School
### Demonstration Reading Program

One of the requirements of our English classes is that each student will read. They will read for the first ten (10) minutes of each English class, and they will read at home. This is a chart which shows their grade for their reading time.

| GRADE | GROUP D | GROUP C | GROUP B | GROUP A |
|-------|---------|---------|---------|---------|
| A | 180 | 180 | 140 | 140 |
| B | 160 | 160 | 125 | 125 |
| C | 149 | 149 | 111 | 111 |
| D | 126 | 126 | 97 | 97 |
| F | < 126 | < 126 | < 97 | < 97 |

A Reading Log for _____

| Date | Time Began | Page Began | Time Ended | Page Ended | Time Read | Week's Total |
|------|-----------|-----------|-----------|-----------|-----------|--------------|
|  |  |  |  |  |  |  |
|  |  |  |  |  |  |  |
|  |  |  |  |  |  |  |
|  |  |  |  |  |  |  |
|  |  |  |  |  |  |  |
|  |  |  |  |  |  |  |
|  |  |  |  |  |  |  |
|  |  |  |  |  |  |  |

FIGURE 13.10
Word Problem Strategy

> *Seventy-five Red Coats marched toward Lexington Green.*
> *Twenty-nine Minutemen blocked the road. How many more*
> *Red Coats were there than Minutemen?*

TO SOLVE A MATH WORD PROBLEM YOU MUST FOLLOW THESE STEPS:

1) SCAN the math problem for any new vocabulary words.
    a) UNDERLINE the new vocabulary words.
    b) WRITE the new vocabulary word below. WRITE the word in
       syllables. WRITE the meaning of each new word.

| word | word in syllables | meaning |
|------|-------------------|---------|
| *Minutemen* | *Min ute men* | *colonial soldiers* |
| *Red Coats* | | *English soldiers* |

2) READ the whole word problem.

3) Answer the following questions about the information in the story.
   WRITE your answers in COMPLETE SENTENCES.

   a) Who or what is the problem about?
     *The problem is about Red Coats and Minutemen.*

   b) What information is given?
     *The information given is that there are seventy-five Red Coats and*

   c) What information are we to find?       *twenty-nine Minutemen.*
     *We are to find how many more Red Coats than Minutemen.*

   d) What words tell us the math OPERATION to use?
     *The words HOW MANY MORE tell us what math operation to use.*

   e) What math operation do we use?
     *We use subtraction.*

4) a) Use NUMBERS and mathematical SIGNS to write a number sentence.
     $75 - 29 = N$

   b) Use WORDS to rewrite your number sentence.
     *Seventy-five minus twenty-nine equals N.*

5) Write down the problem in the form you need to solve the math.
   SOLVE the math problem. Use the back of this paper if you need
   more room.

$$\begin{array}{r} {}^{6}\!\!\not{7}{}^{15}\!\!\not{5} \\ -\,29 \\ \hline 46 \end{array}$$

6) In a complete sentence, answer question #3c.
    *There were forty-six more Red Coats than Minutemen.*

### Evaluation

In addition to formal test evaluation data, such as the CTBS (California Test of Basic Skills) and CAP (California Assessment Program), the Ben Franklin Reading Program employs an outside evaluator to conduct ongoing classroom observations and student and staff interviews to determine the areas of success and to make suggestions for improvement. The data are used in the year-end planning sessions.

## SUMMARY

Exciting things for kids are happening in these schools, and these schools represent only a sample of exemplary schools across our country. As middle level schools begin to understand the implications that the middle school concept has for improved reading and writing instruction, more schools will improve their programs.

The cooperative planning of interdisciplinary team organization naturally leads to thematic units and the integration of social studies and science content with literature and writing. Exploratory courses naturally support the recreational reading activities of a school. Advisor/advisee groups are a logical extension of discussions that began with value issues first encountered in literature.

Change is difficult and challenging. But change can also be fun and invigorating, and when teachers feel revitalized they cannot help but pass this enthusiasm for learning on to their students.

## REFERENCES

Anderson, R. C., Hiebert, E. H., Scott, J. A., and Wilkinson, I. A. G. (1985). *Becoming a nation of readers: The report of the commission on reading.* Champaign, IL: Center for the Seudy of Reading.

College Board (1979). *Degrees of reading power.* New York: author.

George, J. C. (1959). *My side of the mountain.* New York: Dutton.

Irvin, J. L., and Connors, N. A. (1989). Reading instruction in middle level schools: Results of a U.S. survey. *Journal of Reading, 32,* 306–311.

Neufeld, J. (1968). *Edgar Allen.* Norwalk, CT: Phillips.

Rawls, W. (1974). *Where the red fern grows.* New York: Bantam.

# Index